Nelly Erichsen
A Hidden Life

Sarah Harkness

Sally / thank you! Sarah

ENCANTA PUBLISHING

Published in 2018 by Encanta Publishing
Windrush Farm, Bourton on the Water, Cheltenham,
Gloucestershire, GL54 3BY, United Kingdom.

www.encantapublishing.com

Distributed by Encanta Publishing.

ISBN: 978-1-9996078-0-7

Designed, typeset and printed by
Nikki Coffey Design
nikkicoffeydesign@gmail.com

Contents

List of Images

Cover illustration: Golden Hair by Nelly Erichsen

Inside Front Cover illustration: Castle of Trebbio by Nelly Erichsen

Nelly Erichsen's drawing of Fiorence from the Boboli Gardens

Prologue

'Someone, I say, will remember us in the future.' **Sappho**

Bagni di Lucca is not the most glamorous town in Tuscany. For a start, it is well off the beaten track, nearly an hour's drive north of Lucca. In this part of the region, there are no traces of the familiar sun-baked sienna-brown hills, nor of the vineyards and olive groves of the Tuscany so loved by tourists. All the famous Renaissance artists gave it a miss, preferring to decorate sandgold churches in sunlit piazzas. It is a damp, forgotten corner, surrounded by dark, forbidding beech forest. Its river, often swollen by rain, gushes between crumbling houses, and a grey mist covers the looming mountains.

For Tuscany's Victorian visitors, drawn initially to the romance and history of Florence, Bagni was nevertheless a picturesque destination for picnic outings a well-known spot for literary pilgrims wishing to follow in the footsteps of the Brownings and their set. The cooler climate was a welcome relief from the heat of the valleys. Yet, as the nineteenth century drew to a close, the elegance it once had was already fading.

With none of the glamour of fin-de-siecle Biarritz or Baden-Baden, as a resort it only survived because of its spa waters, which drew the more impoverished northern European travellers with weak chests and feeble constitutions. Perhaps it was also a refuge from the hurly burly, gossipy life of the Anglo-American community that dominated Florence. It is hard to imagine that the climate of these dank, misty valleys actually did the visitors any good at all, and many now lie in the well-stocked English graveyard, across the river on the edge of the town.

One very wet Saturday morning in October 2003, three damp, disheartened but otherwise healthy English travellers peered wistfully through the rusty iron gate of that same graveyard. In a plastic envelope we carried a rather damp map of the town, a tourist leaflet in laughably poor translation and some scribbled notes: all clues to three forgotten lives. The quest had started a couple of years earlier, with the chance find in a London auction house of a dusty brown paper wallet containing a portfolio of original book illustrations dating from the 19th century extraordinarily detailed and rather beautiful line drawings of stunning Florentine villas. After months of sporadic research, the trail to find the artist had led to Bagni - it seemed so unfair that having come this far, the cemetery gates should be locked. No-one in the town seemed to know who had the key. In no time at all we would have to leave to catch our plane home. In so many ways, this frustration was a metaphor for our entire project we could catch a glimpse of our woman through the railings, but we just could not reach her.

My husband, my eldest daughter and I had arrived late the evening before, after a much longer drive than expected, along roads which had looked temptingly picturesque and straightforward on the map, but were actually hair-raising. An hour or so was spent poking around the town in miserable, drizzly conditions. Most of the houses were only accessible on foot, and the higgledy-piggledy layout of the streets winding up the hill, and lack of nameplates combined with the mist and rain were not conducive to systematic exploration. There was no-one to ask. We found a few traces of our quarry a street named Via Evangeline Whipple; a house that may once have been our artist's last known address, Casa Bernardini; and a small Anglican church now only used to store a dusty collection of books left behind by long dead or departed English residents. It was too dark and miserable to do more. We consoled ourselves with spaghetti and hot chocolate, the best comfort food. We asked the hotel manager how to get access to the English graveyard and he shrugged apologetically. He would try to find out. He did not look hopeful. Overnight, as we struggled to sleep in the scruffy pensione, the autumn rain began in earnest. The next morning, when we stood on the old footbridge that crossed the Lima, on our way towards the cemetery, the river had doubled in size, changed colour to a murky threatening brown, and bore in its wake the debris of a terrible night on the mountainside. This felt like a hopeless waste of time.

We parked a little way down the road and walked back to the cemetery gate. It was firmly bolted and the rust on the padlock suggested that visitors were an unusual event. Determined to teach my eleven-year-old daughter a lesson in resilience, I scrambled over the wall at the back where the ground sloped upwards, at least one of us should try to complete the quest. Hattie, appalled by my willingness to make an unnecessary exhibition of myself, retreated to hide in the car. But Italy being Italy, just as I was fighting my way through the sodden nettles, help did arrive, in the shape of a fussing, elderly woman in a headscarf waving a huge iron key, talking nineteen to the dozen under her breath in Italian, and hurrying Peter and Hattie through the gates. I tried to look nonchalant, avoiding the woman's eye, avoiding the question of why I was already inside.

The graveyard had been laid out nearly two hundred years earlier, with two paths in the shape of a cross, and a small chapel at the back. It was now truly dilapidated a muddle of overgrown, broken and almost illegible tombstones the lichen-encrusted inscriptions telling tales of military men, sons lost at sea, faithful wives and lonely spinsters. Colonel Henry Stisted of the Royal Dragoons seemed to be particularly well-regarded and celebrated at the time of his death in 1859, in fact the cemetery was his idea, his wife Elizabeth had entertained Byron, Shelley, Sir Walter Scott and the Brownings at their villa in Bagni, but now no-one remembers him. Wordsworth's daughter-in-law Isabella was buried here in 1848, a long way from her Lake District home. To one side loomed a truly bleak memorial to a very wretched woman, the English writer known as Ouida, once the toast of literary London and Florence. Her tomb, decorated, if that was the word, with an effigy of the writer at rest, had been funded by an anonymous donor. It seems that by the time she died in 1908, quite possibly of malnutrition, certainly lonely and impoverished, no-one even wanted to admit to being her admirer or friend, except perhaps the little dog now carved in stone at her feet. And then, right at the back of the graveyard, in an untended private plot surrounded by a low stone wall, we finally spotted the resting place of the women whose story we had come to pursue. Two tall crosses standing to attention, one horizontal stone with a solid cross lying on it.

In sacred and loving memory of
ROSE ELIZABETH CLEVELAND
Born in New York, USA. Author and philanthropist, a loyal lover of her country and a true friend of Italy. She died 22 November 1918 at Bagni di Lucca, stricken by the epidemic, Spanish fever, which with her band of nurses she was nobly combating among the refugees of the Great War
John XV:13 (Greater love hath no man than this, that a man lay down his life for his friends)

In loving remembrance of
EVANGELINE WHIPPLE
Born in CANTON, MASSACHUSETTS USA
Wife of the Rt Rev Henry B Whipple, Bishop of Minnesota

An honorary citizen of Bagni di Lucca devoted to all good works, beloved by all her friends, loyal and unfaltering in her religious faith. She died 1 September 1930 in London England.
Blessed are the dead which die in the Lord from henceforth. Yea saith the spirit that they may rest from their labors and their works do follow them. Rev XIV.13

[Prologue]

And finally:

To the loved and honoured memory of Nelly Ericksen, who died at Bagni di Lucca of the epidemic Spanish Fever 15 November 1918 while working for the relief of the refugees in the Great War. Born Newcastle-upon-Tyne England

Usque ad mortem fidelis

'Faithful unto death'. Her surname was misspelt, an issue with which we had often struggled when trying to track her down, but it seemed particularly depressing to find it preserved like that on her gravestone.

Three remarkable lives. One very neglected burial plot. These women made up a formidable trio; each had been a pioneer in her own way. Evangeline ('Eve') was an attractive and wealthy widow when she married an elderly bishop renowned for his missionary work with the Sioux in the era of the Native American Wars. Rose had served as First Lady of America when her bachelor brother was elected 22nd President of the USA, an unwanted but brief interruption to her career as a writer and educationalist. Rose and Evangeline first met in the winter of 1889-90, but separated when Eve married her bishop. After his death, they were reunited and finally left America to live together in 1910 theirs was a passionate and loving relationship, which had to be lived well beyond the glare of public curiosity.

And Nelly, who had led us to the place of their self-imposed exile, was one of the first women to challenge the male dominance of both fine art and commercial art in Britain, and to make a living from it. The youngest of the three, with the simplest gravestone, she was born in Newcastle-upon-Tyne, the daughter of a wealthy professional Danish family. After studying at London's Royal Academy in the 1880s, she had carved out a moderately successful career for herself as a painter, book-illustrator, translator and writer. She worked with the giants of the Victorian publishing world, Alexander Macmillan and JM Dent, and jointly published travel and architectural guides with better-known authors such as Janet Ross and Edward Hutton. She was the one that we had primarily come to find, driven by extraordinary curiosity about the life of an artist whose work we had come to love. But she, like her gravestone, had almost disappeared.

I have a photograph that I took that day, the first of our visits to Bagni, of Peter leaning with his foot on the low wall around the burial plot, lost in contemplation of Nelly's tombstone. To be honest, he looks a little tearful. When we had planned our trip, we had expected it to be the end of the quest, but in fact seeing her lonely grave, being forced to confront how and why she died, so far from her home and her family, filled us both with a determination to tell her story. But what story was there to tell? We knew so little about her at that stage, just the bare facts of her birth and death. And, of course, we knew her glorious art.

Peter at Nelly's Grave 2003

In The Orchard

Chapter One: Introduction

There is one painting by Nelly that many people will have seen, even if they have no idea who created it. Put her name into Google Images and up will pop 'In The Orchard'. It is a pretty pastel picture of a young couple courting beneath apple trees at harvest time, with piles of rosy apples all around. The lad in the hat is asking or imploring, the blushing redhead with an apron has her eyes cast down. If it is a scene of biblical temptation, then for once it does not seem to be Eve doing the tempting. The image was acquired at some stage in the 1980s by a flamboyant London art dealer and now it can be seen on posters, book covers, even cushions and bath towels. I have it as a jigsaw puzzle. It is unlikely that Nelly ever made as much from all of her artwork put together as this image may now be worth in a month. The image survives, but what of the artist?

There are two photographs which purport to show Nelly in adult life but confusingly they do not seem to feature the same woman. The first we ever saw was shown to us by Dan, the great grandson of Nelly's sister Alice, clearly labelled in handwriting on the back *'Nelly and The Cotterills, Russian Easter 1918.'* It is one of those black and white photographs which merit close study: the more I look, the more I see.

The photo shows seven mostly elderly men and women grouped around a small table with a white cloth set for tea, all smiling politely at the camera. So far, so unremarkable. In the foreground, in front of the table, is a rough wooden four-legged stool, on which is perched a tortoise. Next to it sits a black and white cat, his back, in typical cat fashion, turned on the proceedings. There are four women seated at the table, beautifully dressed in high necked blouses, elaborate necklaces, long skirts and lace, one sporting a marvellous straw hat with a wide, elegant brim. At least three of the seated women seem to be related, they share similar round baggy eyes and snub noses. The woman with the hat, on the

Nelly and the Cotterills, Russian Easter 1918

other hand, seems more elegant, more knowing, and has an angular face with a pronounced nose, but a kind and intelligent smile. There are two men in the photo with heavy dark suits, bald heads and white beards, one beard neatly trimmed, one significantly more substantial. They look like brothers. Maybe I can see a dog collar under the trimmed beard?

At the back of the table, looking directly into the camera but with a hand on one of the seated women's shoulders, stands a small figure with a frightful black hat, a dark jacket, cream shirt, pale skirt, sunken eyes and gaunt cheeks. She does not look like the other women, she looks as if she has been ill, she looks like she needs a good meal and something to make her laugh. She seems to be the outsider at the event, so perhaps she is the reason for the photograph. With no other evidence to go on, we looked at the photo and assumed it was Nelly. The outsider, also the invalid. Our hearts sank. She did not look fun, she looked like the maiden aunt whose visit you dreaded. This photo has attached itself to Nelly's name on the web, when you type Nelly Erichsen into a search engine, up pops this photo, and it makes you decide to look for someone else instead.

There are many mysteries that bother me now about this photo. Why the cat and the tortoise? Who is taking the photograph? The Cotterills are old family friends of the extended Erichsen clan. Henry Cotterill went to school in Brighton with Edgar Lucas, Nelly's brother-in-law. They are somewhere warm, not in England. The table is laid in an open verandah, with bright sun streaming through bougainvillea from the left, and the chairs are actually garden benches with embroidered cushions. The walls are rough plaster with a frieze at waist height. In the top right-hand corner above their heads stands a sculpted bust on a small shelf. Are they in an Italian villa? Maybe in Florence, or even in Eve's house in Bagni di Lucca? But this is labeled 1918, Italy is suffering appalling military defeats, hardly the time for a jolly foreign holiday. And why are the Cotterills, a staunch Anglican family, celebrating Russian Easter? In 1918, it would have fallen in early May - just a few months before Nelly died, when she was up to her elbows looking after the refugees in Bagna. And are we even right to think that the fright in the black bonnet is Nelly? How much nicer if she were the distinguished lady with the straw hat. Or perhaps she is the younger, dark haired, artistic looking woman with the flowing gown on the right of the photograph. Wouldn't she have looked attractive, inviting, on the cover of this book? None of the ages seem to fit. Nelly would only have been 55 when this photo was taken, these women all look older, apart from one who looks younger.

Nelly Erichsen and Ida Suhrw

The second surviving photograph was taken maybe thirty years earlier. I have never seen the original, but I found it on a website set up by The Suhr Foundation in Denmark, to commemorate a once-famous Danish family which counts Nelly as a descendant. It shows two young women, one sitting at a table, one standing behind, and is labelled 'Ida Suhr and Nelly Erichsen, 1889'. Further research on the same website makes it clear that of the two, Ida is the older, thinner woman, and Nelly is seated. In 1889 she would have been 27, but she looks even younger. She is plump, certainly in comparison to her more severe older cousin, and swathed in tight fitting light-coloured silk with her hair piled rather elaborately and unflatteringly on top of her head. But her features are soft, her nose small and snub, her face quite pretty. She is doing her best to smile at the camera. It seems extremely unlikely that this plump round-faced girl could have developed the black-hatted sunken features staring from the back of the later photograph. But she does not seem to be any of the other women round that tea table either.

Then there is a drawing. A pencil drawing, shown to me by Nicholas, another of Nelly's relations, and the work of Frank Lucas, Nelly's nephew, when he was in Venice in 1902 with his fiancée Helen. Nelly, who certainly knew her way around Italy by then, was their chaperone. The drawing is quite a simple sketch, not of professional standard, but it shows a prim woman sitting in the prow of a gondola, with a kettle whistling, presumably on a primus stove, a tiny cup and saucer, a bottle of milk and a tiny teapot, all out of proportion to the kettle and the woman. The gondola is travelling back to St Mark's Square from the Lido. The woman has her hands on her knees but seems unconscious that she is being drawn. Maybe she has offered to sit sideways because profiles are so much easier for the amateur artist. She wears a hat and a high collared jacket. Her face is only half visible, but it has a definite resemblance to the earliest photograph, a small upturned nose, a pretty face.

It seems important, to me at least, to know what Nelly looked like: so many famous biographies have been written with photographs of the subject pinned above the author's desk. Was she pretty, was she plain? Does it matter? It would matter less, surely, if she were male. There is no surviving evidence of actual romance in her life, was she too plain to catch a husband? She lived at a time when unmarried middle-class women began to outnumber their male counterparts, so her single life was not that unusual, does not necessarily imply lack of physical charm. There are three surviving records of male responses to meeting her: the playwright George Bernard Shaw; the academic Thomas Lindsay; and the art expert Bernard Berenson, and all wrote kind things about her, seemed pleased to have met her and known her, found her to be an interesting companion. Shaw says he found her attractive. Lindsay describes her as a 'tall and stately daughter of Denmark' and 'a Norse-woman'. Evangeline Whipple called Nelly 'our beautiful friend'. None of this seems to describe the small, sad

Drawing by Frank Lucas

woman in the first photograph. What Nelly looked like is just the first of the assumptions I am going to make arbitrarily, and as two of the three pictures show a pretty, soft-featured woman with a snub nose, I have decided that is my Nelly, and the Russian Easter photograph is just an unexplained mystery, perhaps even a red herring. There is never any dispute about Nelly's art: every piece of art that I have seen attributed to Nelly also bears her signature, or at least her initials, in a very distinctive handwriting, usually in the bottom right hand corner. I can read what Nelly wrote, I can see what Nelly drew or painted, how she signed her name, and that matters more than disputed photographs, indistinct likenesses.

Nelly Erichsen was born exactly 100 years before I was, in the first half of the reign of Queen Victoria, when women's rights were few and far between. She lived through an explosion of change for women across the western world sweeping across the spectrum of education, politics, property rights and sexual behaviour. By the time she died, women had even won the right to vote in British parliamentary elections. In her own quiet way, Nelly's story illustrates a new way of living for independent middle-class females: she was single, self-financing (though not without worry, ill-health and struggle), and found fulfillment in her work. Ultimately, as her tombstone notes, she died helping others, one of the many millions who succumbed to the Spanish influenza epidemic which wreaked such havoc worldwide in the aftermath of the Great War. Her death resulted from her courageous decision to devote herself, in her late 50s, to the refugees displaced by an undistinguished military campaign in Italy, the country she so loved and where she had chosen to live. Working with refugees seems worthy and brave even today in the twenty-first century, but a hundred years ago, to a quiet spinster from Tooting, it must have been daunting in the extreme.

For those of us women who take a career and financial independence for granted, she deserves our admiration and respect, for she pioneered the path we now all follow not by protesting, fighting or shouting, but by quiet professional determination. Her life deserves notice for that alone. I certainly feel I owe her that. But there is more: the communities in which Nelly lived, and the circles in which she moved, were fascinating. Something about her her talent with a brush and pencil, her knowledge and love of European and classical literature and languages, her capacity for hard work and her will to succeed, marked her out for notice by better known members of late Victorian intellectual society. As a girl of 18, she was enrolled into the Royal Academy Schools on the recommendation of her art teacher John Sparkes, later headmaster of The National Art Training School in South Kensington. She developed close friendships, which seem to have gone beyond family acquaintance, with the Macmillan publishing dynasty. In the 1890s she spent time with George Bernard Shaw and his circle of Fabian thinkers and writers; in Italy she often stayed and collaborated with Janet Ross, doyenne of Anglo-Florence society, and through her she met the famous art historian and dealer Bernard Berenson who enjoyed her company. Shortly before she went to live in Italy for good, she spent time in the heart of the Cotswolds, at Chipping Campden, as an associate of Charles Ashbee's Arts and Handicrafts Guild, and for the last six years of her life she lived and worked with two other women, born on a different continent but living similarly independent, bluestocking lives.

The people she knew, where she travelled and what she achieved as a self-supporting professional woman in the dying years of the nineteenth century, make her life a window through which one can glimpse more than three decades of English Victorian and Edwardian intellectual and artistic life. More importantly, the route she took and the struggles she faced to support herself, make her an unsung pioneer for women's experience during the nineteenth and twentieth century. This is what caught our imagination, and led Peter and me on a journey we never expected to take, actually or metaphorically. And that is why this book will seek to tell her story.

During the final months of the preparation of this book for publication, we came across a poor quality photograph of a drawing, which we believe to be a self-portrait by Nelly. The original seems to have been lost.

Nelly Erichsen's drawing of the gardens of Villa La Petraia, Tuscany

Chapter Two: Beginnings

The quest for Nelly Erichsen started nearly twenty years ago, when Peter, bored and with time on his hands between meetings, wandered into a London auction house and found himself flicking through a cardboard folder of line drawings. The upcoming sale was concerned with Victorian artwork, and Peter, an amateur artist himself, was captivated by this portfolio of original book illustrations dating from the 19th century - extraordinarily detailed and rather beautiful sketches of stunning Florentine villas. At that point in his life, Peter had never been to Tuscany, and knew little of the architecture or history of the area, so it was something about the quality of the work alone which captured his attention. There was no information about the artist or the provenance of the drawings, and without thinking too much about it, he placed a commission bid and left the gallery. Within an hour he was back in the world of meetings and deals and had probably forgotten all about this little interlude. But just a couple of days later he discovered that he was now indeed the proud owner of the portfolio in its entirety.

When, two or three years later, and remarkably soon after I had first met Peter, he showed me the collection of line drawings that he had acquired and cherished, I did not really understand what I was looking at. But Peter's earliest professional training had been in the world of newspapers, and he understood that these were illustrations that had been created to be scaled down and reproduced onto printers' plates to illustrate a book. The drawings are large, usually around 12 by 18 inches, and on a thick white card called Bristol board. They are done in black ink, but sometimes you can see the pencil marks of the first sketches underneath, or little errors that have been covered over with tiny dabs of china white. One or two suggest that Nelly had started drawing with the wrong scale, in one case she had to attach another piece of board to the end of her drawing to fit in the whole balustrade wall of a particular palazzo. The various combinations of outline, cross-hatching, stippling and shading produce a three-dimensional illusion with its own beauty and clarity. The lines that create the palace walls are precise and solid, but the leaves and grass are various combinations of what I, the complete amateur, would call scribble. Most of the drawings are at first sight architectural, placing the villas and palaces of Tuscany solidly within their gardens and terraces. But some of them are more ambitious views of far horizons, such as a view of Florence from the terraces of Fiesole, and some of them are enlivened and given scale by the introduction of a figure, perhaps a gardener, or a woman carrying a basket, two hurrying nuns, some pigeons, even a small dog standing by his kennel.

Many of the drawings contain reproductions of garden statuary, and I particularly love these ones, as Nelly has drawn the statues in a way that almost suggests the figures are alive lions are laughing, naked women holding garlands of flowers appear to be swinging their hips, posing for the artist. She drew what she saw: in the sketch of a little hill town called Montelupo you can see the sign for the Trattoria and the washing hanging from a window. Nelly created these works for others to engrave, and there are instructions to the printer scribbled on the reverse 'Please reproduce as large as the appearance of the book will allow. The reliefs are so delicate and detailed that fine work was necessary to reproduce the character.' In turning from painting, her original training, to illustration, Nelly did not turn down the dial of her artistic endeavor, in fact she brought all her natural talent and the skills she had learnt to the new field, and the results leap from the pages of her work.

The first thing Peter did after discovering that he had indeed acquired this mysterious portfolio of drawings was to look for Nelly's name in the reference books. Today one would start on Google, but at that time there were very few online resources. She was by no means famous - like many female artists she barely merits a mention even in the Dictionary of 19th Century British Illustrators. But she was there, with the briefest of details, including reference to exhibitions at the Royal Academy. This led him to the wonderful archives of the RA, on the topmost floor of the Academy building in Piccadilly, who provided him with the date of her admission to the Schools, and an address in Tooting. So then Peter turned to the UK census records and found an Erichsen family living in Tooting in 1881, which told him that Nelly's parents were Danish and the children had been born in Newcastle. And then he really got hooked: why had these people come to England, and what had led them from the North East to London.

Nelly Erichsen was born in Jesmond, one of the smarter suburbs of Victorian Newcastle upon Tyne, in December 1862. She was the fourth child, and third daughter, of Danish immigrants, so some of her lifelong determination to be independent can be attributed to having parents who were prepared to take risks, but were amply rewarded for being in the right place at the right time by making a small fortune. Her father, Hermann Erichsen, was born in Copenhagen in 1828, the son of a merchant trader. A crucial element in his success was the business connection, cemented through his marriage, to one of the wealthiest industrial and banking families in Denmark: the House of JP Suhr. His involvement, through these wealthy family connections, first in shipping and later in the rapidly expanding international telegraph industry, was eventually to bring him to London and make him rich.

Nelly's parents, Hermann and his wife Anna, are prime examples of the emerging Victorian middle class: enterprising, industrious, ambitious for their children, proud of their culture and heritage, and philanthropic in outlook. There is a fuzzy photograph floating in the ether of the worldwide web, its original perhaps mislaid, taken in the late 1860s, which demonstrates their pride in their achievement. It shows a family - mother, father and five young children, all staring solidly at the camera. These are the Erichsens, in their Jesmond garden, arranged around a bench. Behind the bench stands the proud father and his eldest son, also called Herman, (but with only one 'n', did that seem more English?) both wearing derby hats. Young Herman is only nine or ten, but his hat is clearly chosen to match his father's. The oldest daughter Alice sits at one end of the bench, a large bow in her long dark hair, with the younger Dora leaning against her. At the other end of the bench sits the mother, Anna, face partially obscured by a large hat. Between them are two very small children: one little boy, Charles, still in petticoats; and a small girl with blond curls, in a short skirt, legs dangling. This is Nelly. The final addition to the family, Frederick, is not even in the picture, not yet born, so this was taken when Nelly was five or six, and they are still living in Newcastle. Formally posed, this was a professional photograph taken to be sent back to relatives in Denmark, to demonstrate achievement, a healthy growing family that looks typically Victorian, even English. The Erichsens were putting down firm roots in foreign soil.

The decisions Hermann and Anna made - to leave Denmark in early adulthood, to make a new home in England, to take citizenship, build a prosperous life in Newcastle, then uproot again and move their young family to London, and to educate their children as English gentlemen and women - were brave, and crucial for the family's success. In the photograph they appear highly conventional, but their lives exhibit a willingness to challenge conventions, in particular by allowing an unchaperoned seventeen-year-old Nelly to attend art school in central London at a time when middle-class girls were usually tied to

The Erichsen Family

the home. Thinking about her parents' lives, and about the energetic, entrepreneurial family they left behind in Denmark, Nelly had evidence of the rewards that can come from striking out on an independent course. The family was not afraid to seize opportunities that came their way, and neither was Nelly.

Nelly's grandfather, Johann Fredrick Erichsen, was a Copenhagen merchant with five children. His oldest son would take over the family firm, and it just so happened that in 1848, as his second son turned 20, universal male military conscription was introduced in Denmark as part of a new political settlement. Apparently draft-dodging, the young Hermann set off to make his fortune. He eventually settled in Newcastle upon Tyne, after what was described in his obituary as 'a thorough commercial education…, completed by visits to several of the more important places on the Continent.' According to his naturalisation papers, filed in 1852, Hermann arrived in England on 3 July 1848, and for the first year or so found work as a managing clerk and foreign correspondent for a Mr Edward Bilton, who had offices right on the quayside in Newcastle, and who, as well as being a merchant, was vice consul for Portugal, Sardinia, Sicily, Tuscany and the Brazils. In January 1850, Hermann moved to work for John Joseph Hunter in the same capacity, but within eighteen months had been taken into partnership, as Hunter testified: *"from his steady industry and regular habits of business and from the trust and confidence I was thereby led to repose in him I admitted the said Hermann Gustav Erichsen to a share of my business as a partner."* The new firm was to be named Hunter and Erichsen and their trade was general export and import, primarily bringing in Scandinavian tar and exporting British coal.

It is no surprise that Hermann first made a home in Newcastle. The town was long established as the key English seaport for trade with Scandinavia; it was said that Tyneside had more in common with Scandinavia than with southern England and there are traces of the Norse language in Tyneside dialects. The city was growing rapidly when Hermann arrived in 1848 - this was the year that the railway line from London finally made it across the Tyne, and the following year saw great excitement when Queen Victoria travelled through Newcastle by train on her way to Balmoral, the first time an English Queen had visited the city since 1461. In 1846, the repeal of the British Corn Laws removed a long- standing ban on Danish corn imports to the United Kingdom and led to some 30 years of prosperous grain trading between the two nations. By 1850, Britain was taking more than 50 per cent of Denmark's total grain exports and the ships returned to Denmark carrying heavier goods such as coal, iron and salt.

The expansion of the railways led to major growth in the local coal industry - however the state of the Tyne was a major constraint on the export trade. In 1849 the average depth of the harbour bar was only six feet. Dredging began in 1859 and from 1860 onwards the clearing of the harbour and construction of proper piers greatly improved the economic viability of the port, leading to rapid development of the shipbuilding industry. In 1852 Charles Palmer built the first steam-propelled iron ship to meet the competition from the rail industry and by 1862 there were ten shipyards in Newcastle building iron ships.

The city was developing a reputation as a mecca for entrepreneurs and inventors - it was after all the home town of George Stephenson - railway engineering; of Armstrong and Palmer - shipbuilding; in the 1870's, of Joseph Swan - electrical engineering; and in the 1880's of Parsons marine and turbine engineering. Continued technological advances attracted many immigrants hoping to ride the wave of successful industrial development and prosperity. The population grew dramatically - in 1801, Newcastle had less than 30,000 inhabitants (although that still made it the fourth biggest town in England behind London, Bristol and Norwich). By the 1890's, the population had reached 200,000.

It was not just a town of engineers and industrialists - the increasingly affluent Victorian middle classes were as keen to build a cultural life here as they were elsewhere in the country. Tyneside was the home of a number of painters of distinction, architects and designers. Nearby Durham University was founded in 1832, and from the late 1830s the centre of Newcastle was completely redeveloped in grand classical style, reinforcing the town's position as the centre of the region. The city centre was being remodeled under the guidance of builder Richard Grainger, architect John Dobson and Town Clerk John Clayton - it is said that when the city's Common Council gave its assent to their plans in 1834, the church bells rang out across the town. *'Grey Street, [the main thoroughfare] was described by Gladstone as the best modern street in Britain, and the Central Exchange, with its domes and three angles was as fine an edifice as any town hall.'* [1]

Partnership with a local businessman was the obvious way forward for an ambitious immigrant - Erichsen provided the crucial overseas contacts and Baltic language skills, and Hunter the local presence. Their business was based at 43 Sandhill, right on the quayside. On 28 November 1851 the firm announced in the Newcastle Courant, where traders, importers and merchants regularly advertised their wares, the arrival from Copenhagen of '770 barrels and 50 half-barrels of tar, one box contents unknown, and two casks of white paint'. Later announcements listed fire bricks, 'Venetian red', Stockholm tar, 20,000 pieces of earthenware, and the export of coal and grindstones. In September 1853 the partnership was importing wheat and barley, and household items such as floormats and a box of busts. They were truly entrepreneurial.

Hermann's naturalisation papers, submitted in November 1852, were supported by a number of highly respectable character references including two local traders, a clergyman and a lawyer. The ten pages of perfect copper-plate handwriting, with Hermann's signature appended, attest to his 'highly respectable standing and undoubted loyalty to Her Most Gracious Majesty the Queen and Her Government'. By 1854 Hermann was approaching 26, no great age for an immigrant who had started from scratch, but already he felt sufficiently well-established to marry - and not just any Danish girl, but Anna Dorothea, the beloved daughter of Ole Bernt Suhr, an extremely prosperous Danish businessman. The notice of the wedding, which had taken place on 9 May in Nyborg, her home town, was published not just in the Newcastle papers but also in the British national press (the Morning Chronicle). The couple were

---

[1] *Asa Briggs: Victorian Cities*

making a clear statement of intent to become part of English society.

Anna Dorothea Suhr had been born in Nyborg in 1827, one of the youngest of a family of thirteen children. We can find a brief picture of her in the memoirs of Johanne Luise Heiberg, one of the greatest Danish actresses of the nineteenth century. Johanne was often invited to Solyst, country home of Anna's uncle, the wealthy and childless Theodor Suhr, and there she wrote of meeting Theodor's nieces, including the 'beautiful, charming Anna Dorothea Suhr, later to be Mrs Erichsen'. Johanne describes Anna Dorothea's generosity, and also her great knowledge of Danish literature, absorbed at the feet of her old grandfather Moller who lived with her family in Nyborg and read to her constantly. This love of Danish literature would later be shared by at least two of Anna's daughters.

Anna never lost her pride in her heritage or her Danish roots. Her will, written in 1904 as she was sorting out her possessions before leaving her home in Tooting for the last time, is an extraordinary inventory of family relics and treasures: she made sure that the 'old teapot on tray (of grandfather Moller)' and Aunt Sannes' 'copper kettle and charcoal dish' would be safe in the hands of her oldest child, Alice. To her son Herman she left an oil painting of the family home at Solyst, and to Dora she bequeathed Aunt Mettis' golden jewellery, and Grandma Suhr's slop bowl, sugar basin and cream jug. Frederick, the youngest, got Aunt Ida's tall grey vase. But Nelly, the unmarried daughter, seems to have been particularly favoured with heirlooms, she was to have the peasant jewellery given to Great Uncle Theodor by that same Johanne Heiberg, great grandmother Suhr's old coffee pot, Great Aunt Charlotte's mustard pot and crystal salt cellars on a silver tray, two pastel portraits of grandfather and grandmother Suhr, a watercolour of the Nyborg town house where Anna had grown up, a small red chalk portrait of her great grandfather and all the other family miniatures and silhouettes. As well as her share of the silver cutlery, carefully divided among all the children and grandchildren, Nelly was to have the old oriental tea set in the drawing room and the 'daily Danish blue tea service.' When Hermann married Anna, he had joined a family with significant possessions and connections.

Anna Dorothea was 21 when Hermann left for England to make his fortune, and 27 when he returned to marry her - perhaps the marriage was arranged to cement an existing family relationship or business opportunity, perhaps it was a love match. After all, they had grown up in different parts of the country. Perhaps Hermann had been sent away to make his fortune before he could be considered as an acceptable suitor. It would have been a long wait for Anna. Either way, it certainly did him no harm to cement his connection to the House of Suhr with this marriage.

Throughout the 1850s, Hermann toiled away in Newcastle, building the firm of Hunter and Erichsen into an enterprise sufficiently prosperous to make philanthropic contributions to various local appeals. In October 1854, a terrible fire swept through the Newcastle docks area. Caused by an explosion at a chemicals warehouse in Gateshead, the blast created a huge firestorm which blew across the river, killing 53 and making some 800 people homeless. Hunter and Erichsen's premises on Sandhill were right in the heart of the blaze and there was tremendous damage to property all along the waterfront from the force of the blast across the river. But although it must have caused great difficulties for the firm, they were still generous contributors, giving ten guineas to the relief fund set up in its wake. The Erichsen children were brought up to believe that it was important to show concern for local issues and try to alleviate suffering in the community. This philanthropic generosity of spirit would, six decades later, cost Nelly her life.

In July 1855 Anna and Hermann, now living in Jesmond Villas, one of the nicer parts of Newcastle, were proud to announce the birth of their first child, a daughter, Alice. Christening her with such an English name, the name of one of the little royal princesses, was a sign of intent - they were presenting themselves as an English family now. Jesmond was a middle-class haven developing in the north of the city of Newcastle, with beautiful and substantial villas built in leafy avenues, and it is hardly surprising that they had chosen to live outside the town centre, as Newcastle was frequently swept by cholera epidemics - being one of the most crowded towns in England, it was particularly susceptible. In 1849 nearly 4000 died across the region, and in 1853 more than 1500 died in the city alone. It was while this epidemic was sweeping the town that it was discovered that for the previous two months a private water company, charging the wealthier residents for a piped supply, had actually been delivering sewage-laden water pumped straight from the River Tyne. Cholera was not the only health problem - in 1865, 500 died in a scarlet fever outbreak.

By the time of the 1861 Census, Hermann and Anna were living with their

St Mary's Terrace, Jesmond

three children - Alice, a son Herman, and a baby known as Dora - at No 1 St Mary's Terrace, Jesmond. The family was prospering - they employed three local women as servants. And here on 9 December 1862, Nelly was born. She was to live in or around Jesmond until she was eight. Their home was the end of a beautiful Georgian terrace of just four four-storey houses, built around 1830 and attributed to John Dobson, the architect of so much that was beautiful in early Victorian Newcastle. You can still see this terrace of houses today, renamed as 14-20 Great North Road.

Three doors away from the Erichsen children lived the brothers Albany and John Hancock, famous naturalists and ornithologists, and founders of the Hancock Museum just across the road. John was a taxidermist, indeed he is considered the father of modern taxidermy, promoting the concept of the dramatic setting, trying to make stuffed animals more interesting to museum visitors. His mount of a falcon attacking a heron which held an eel was one of the famous attractions at the 1851 Great Exhibition. The brothers would have been well known in Newcastle in the 1860s and one can imagine the excitement of the Erichsen children hoping to peep inside their house of curiosities. Albany's interests lay less in birds and more in sea creatures such as sea slugs, which he depicted in extremely intricate and detailed drawings which are still preserved in the Natural History Society's archives in Northumbria. He must have been one of the first artists that Nelly saw at work, and there is a thread running through from the painstaking detail and accuracy of his nature drawings to much of Nelly's work as an illustrator of architecture in her later life.

There must have been many other things about their life in Newcastle that were exciting and stimulating to Nelly and her brothers and sisters: regular trips across the Channel to stay with family in Denmark, perhaps even on Hunter and Erichsen ships, return visits from the numerous relations and trading partners bringing tales of adventure from the high seas, and increasingly their father's involvement in a revolutionary new technology, the telegraph. August 1863 saw great excitement in Newcastle when it was announced that The British Association for the Advancement of Science was to visit the city to hold its 33rd Annual Meeting - and Hunter & Erichsen, showing typical Victorian enthusiasm for scientific advance and new technology, promised the sum of £5 to help stage the event.

It was a good year to be of Danish origin in England - it was in 1863 that the Prince of Wales, later Edward VII, married Alexandra, the daughter of the Danish king, and there followed an upsurge of pro-Danish feeling across the country. However, in Denmark, disaster occurred when its army was defeated in Schleswig-Holstein by the Prussian forces of Bismarck. In February 1864, a national English paper, the Daily News, announced the formation of a 'Relief Fund for Wounded Danes and the families of those killed in battle'. A Committee of Ladies was formed, and its members, although mostly London-based, included Mrs Hermann Erichsen from Newcastle. This shows an impressive level of networking for the wife of Tyneside trader. A more well-known Dane, the London-based surgeon (but no relation) John Erichsen gave £20 to the fund, and Anna herself gave £10. Altogether the fundraising efforts, which continued throughout the year, raised £2,300, a very significant sum, to be forwarded to the Central Committee in Copenhagen. But no sooner had Anna found her place on this committee than she had to withdraw, pregnant with her second son, Charles Cecil. The boy was born at Coxlodge, a smart residential suburb of predominantly detached stone villas, a little further out than their previous family home in Jesmond.

For the next couple of years, the Hunter and Erichsen partnership continued to trade along familiar lines, with press notices of imports of ironware and other goods. But technological innovation, of the kind that would have been presented and discussed at the British Association event, combined with entrepreneurial flair, was about to take Hermann in a very different direction, and lead to a significant change in lifestyle for the whole family.

The discoveries that led to the invention of the telegraph had begun with those of a Danish scientist, Orsted, in the 1820s, but since the 1830s and 1840s had been exploited for commercial use by Samuel Morse in the United States and in England by Charles Wheatstone and William Cooke, who experimented by hanging telegraph wires alongside newly-laid railway tracks. The public rapidly became aware of the power of this invention in 1844 the birth of Queen Victoria's son was announced in The Times, having been communicated 'by the extraordinary power of the Electro-Magnetic Telegraph'. That same year in the United States Samuel Morse was transmitting his famous message 'What Hath God Wrought' between Baltimore and Washington by his own patented method, to be known as Morse Code.

From 1846 to 1870, while Hermann Erichsen was establishing himself in England and setting himself up as a respectable man of commerce, the British telegraph service was in the hands of various private profit-making enterprises. The laying of a cable from London to Paris was announced in 1851 at the Great Exhibition, and over the next four years the number of telegraph messages sent in Britain alone rose from 99,000 to 745,000 per annum. By 1854 120 provincial newspapers were receiving Parliamentary news by telegraph. In 1858 Charles Bright was knighted for laying the first trans-Atlantic cable, and the following year Charles Dickens wrote of the telegraph that *'of all our modern wonders, [it was] the most wonderful'*. That same year, Reuters secured exclusive rights to supply foreign telegrams to all towns in the UK. In 1870, the British Government effectively nationalised all domestic cable companies under the control of the Postmaster General, but the race to win concessions and sign contracts to build international networks continued and created major investment opportunities for entrepreneurs such as Erichsen and his compatriot and colleague, Denmark's principal financier, Carl Frederick Tietgen.

The telegraph had obvious commercial advantages for a country made up of islands such as Denmark. The Danish Government gave a contract to

Hermann Gustav Erichsen

Newall, the Gateshead company whose cable had been used between Dover and Calais, to lay the first cable between Zeeland and Fyn in 1853, and the following year a connection was laid to Sweden. In 1859 a cable was laid across to Heligoland, and then connected on to Cromer in Norfolk - but the cable was cut during the war of 1864. In 1867, with the Danish Government out of the technology race licking its financial wounds, Tietgen stepped in. In the late 1860s Hermann started working as an agent for Tietgen's Danish business interests, one of the pioneers of the telegraph industry in England, and in no time at all he was a major investor and director in the newly formed Great Northern Telegraph Company. He became that company's representative in England until the time of his death and this enterprise led, with one or two ups and downs, to a further improvement in the family's fortunes - beneficiaries of the Victorian telecommunications dot.com boom.Typical of this enterprise was the announcement in the Pall Mall Gazette on 18 November 1869 - that the Russian Government has granted to Mr HG Erichsen of Newcastle-up-on-Tyne and 'some other gentlemen' a concession giving them an exclusive right to lay submarine telegraph cables from the south-east coast of Siberia to China and Japan.

When Nelly was nearly six, definitely old enough and bright enough to be aware of the excitement in the house, her father was one of the prime movers in the laying of the new telegraph cable between Northumberland and Denmark. Two large iron screw steamers - the Archimedes and the Chevy Chase - moored off Robert Newall's Gateshead works for the loading of the cable. Three large tanks twenty-seven feet in diameter and twelve feet deep were built in the hold of the Archimedes and in the centre of each tank was a conical drum eight feet in diameter and tapering slightly at the top. The cable was coiled around from tank to drum and back, with a huge pulley overhead. The cable ran in grooves to a large machine on the deck then again around a revolving drum six feet in diameter and thence to the bottom of the sea. The cable weighed some three tons per mile - as the cable neared the shore line at either side it was changed for an even heavier duty cable stored on the Chevy Chase to protect it against risk of being snared by an anchor - this cable weighed six tons per mile. The vessels left the Tyne at noon on Monday 31 August 1868 and set off for Denmark, laying cable as they went. However the seas were rough and both ships had to be taken to Christiansand in Norway for safety. On the Friday they continued on to Sondervig, making fast the shore end, then splicing it with the mid-sea cable - which operation was 'satisfactorily concluded amid the hearty plaudits of the people'. The cables were floated along by tar barrels, towed ashore by Danish seamen in longboats, then pulled up the beach by horses and placed into trenches cut by local fishermen.

The next day the two ships set out for England again, playing the cable out again, watched from the shore by hundreds of Danes. All went well until the Monday evening when with 250 miles laid, and 100 miles still from England, they were hit by a thunderstorm. They made the brave decision to cut and buoy the cable as soon as land was sighted. On Tuesday morning with Newbiggin on the Northumberland coast in sight they spliced the cable again and the Chevy Chase came ashore, where, according to the Chronicle, Hermann Erichsen led Mrs Newall and the other ladies aboard. Mr Newall reported favourably on the working of the cable, and the representatives of the Danish Government who had been appointed to test it, declared themselves happy. On the Wednesday the sea was very calm and the mid-sea splicing began at six am. Later that evening the Chevy Chase reached land and the cable was spliced to the land cable. The first formal message was sent on the Thursday the King of Denmark, Christian IX, sending a telegraph to his daughter in England, Alexandra, Princess of Wales. The Newcastle Chronicle concluded its account by recording that the Company proposed to continue the line to St Petersburg and on to India. Even if Nelly, at six, was too young to appreciate the technical triumph, or to be on the boat, it must have been a very exciting time in the Erichsen household.

Shortly after the birth of their sixth and last child, Frederick, in 1870, the Erichsen family left the north-east and moved some 300 miles south to London, renting a substantial property known as Leigh House on the Mitcham Road, Tooting Graveney. Hermann's business interests were increasingly London-centred, he was working out of offices in Great Winchester Street in the City of London, the headquarters of the Great Northern Telegraph Company. He now described himself in the 1871 Census as 'Merchant Representative for foreign telegraph companies' and by 1872 he had been enrolled as an Associate of The Society of Telegraph Engineers. His commercial success was mirrored in his economic status: Nelly was growing up in a substantial household which now included a governess, two nursery maids, a cook, two housemaids and a coachman. The family was definitely on the way up.

Whether Hermann just had the good fortune to be in the right place at the right time, resident in England at a time when his Danish connections Suhr and Tietgen needed a British partner for their telegraph plans, or whether he was himself an instigator of the scheme, it is certain that his move into the telecommunications business led to a step change in the fortunes of the Erichsen household. And for his third daughter, Nelly, just eight at the time of the move to London, this new home offered a whole world of opportunities - to train as an artist at one of the world's most prestigious art schools, and to live thereafter with some financial security as an independent woman. It also opened the door into a particular niche of affluent and cultured suburban society that would prove invaluable for Nelly and her sister Alice as they looked for opportunities to fulfil their literary and artistic ambitions.

Not long after we started researching Nelly's Danish roots, we found a website treasure trove. The Suhr Foundation, endowed by Theodor Suhr, had been gathering and preserving family archives since its creation in 1859. In the 1980s it started to catalogue the family tree and every descendant was allotted a specific number and carefully entered into the Family Book. Nelly was K38. Every year a newsletter, 'the yellow booklet' was sent to family members. At some point a website was created and a great deal of effort was made to load up the earlier newsletters, all in Danish of course. But with the help of Google Translate I was able to see that they had in their possession a major collection of Nelly's letters and scrapbooks, more than I have ever been able to find anywhere else.

So, what did I find on the website? Well, in 1983 an architect called Henrik Reimann donated archives which were described in the newsletter as 'among the most interesting the Foundation ever received.' Henrik was the grandson of Nelly's sister Dora. The bequest comprised 94 letters written by Nelly to her mother during her visits to Denmark between 1880 and 1898, also her diaries and sketchbooks. They contained descriptions of the older Suhr generation, their homes, their lives and their life in contemporary Denmark. An extraordinary eyewitness account of this significant family. There were sketches of the various family homes, Solyst, Rosengaard and Kvaekebyegnen. There were also notes that Nelly had taken as dictation from her mother, who was losing her eyesight, being recollections of life at Solyst when Anna was young. The archive also contained letters Nelly had written to Nordic writers including Henrik Pontoppidan, whose work she would later illustrate. It would have been a fantastic resource, and holding the answers to so many questions I had about Nelly.

The first visit to Denmark, described in eight letters, took place over three months in the summer of 1880 - Nelly was only 17, this must have been a brave expedition if she did it alone. The website says that all her visits and experiences were 'delightfully observed and described'. More letters followed in 1888 and 1889, over 80 in all, as she managed another trip including a complete tour of her relatives. This must have been when the photograph of Nelly and Ida was taken. These letters and the earlier ones were illustrated with little drawings - the website even reproduced an example, a small sketch of children playing with a baby pram by a church, dated 1880. She wrote in her diary (translated from Danish by a friend of our family) 'In the morning I went down into the countryside and sketched some cottages...I encountered some children sitting in a little cart, who at first were not at all enthusiastic about being drawn. One little fellow, Frederick Ohlsen, said 'Surely we would deserve some reward'. After that however he became the most forward of the children, collecting others of all sorts and forcing them to stand in the most military positions, as my sketchbook will testify.'

There was a sketchbook entitled 'Round about Rosengaard' full of drawings of the big farm and the nearby village, houses, churches, and characters such as Emil the Postwoman, The Poacher's Daughter, hunters ready to shoot, the gravediggers and many more. Some of these pictures could be directly traced by the Suhr archivist into Nelly's later book illustrations, for example her drawings for 'The Promised Land' by Pontoppidan.

The bundle of letters and drawings apparently also contained portraits of many family members and friends such as the actress Johanne Heiberg, and Mette Gad, Paul Gauguin's Danish wife. It may have been on one of these trips that Nelly bought a painting by Gauguin, which can now be seen hanging in the National Gallery in Copenhagen, donated by her in 1912. Mette and her three children had returned to live with her family in Copenhagen after her marriage to Gauguin failed. Maybe Nelly bought the picture to give financial support to the abandoned woman.

The article reproduced on the website concluded by saying that someone (unidentified) was planning a private publication on Nelly and her works, and a plea went out to relatives living in the UK and US to send more material. The plea was answered by a gentleman called Jasper, grandson of Alice, Nelly's sister, then living in Dorset. In 1986 the Suhr archivist visited Jasper at his home and took possession of another sizeable cache of Nelly's letters to be deposited at the Foundation. This included over 60 letters written by Nelly to her mother from France, Italy and Switzerland in the years 1892-1906, including several on the subject of their young brother Charles' early death in Nagasaki.

Five years later the Reimann family produced more goods for the Foundation's Archive - ten photographs of Nelly's original work - two paintings, several illustrations from the Highways and Byways series and a drawing for "The Emperor's New Clothes'. This in itself is fascinating - when her sister Alice published a translation of the tales of Hans Christian Andersen in the 1890s, Nelly did not have the commission to do the illustrations. So had she started the project but lost out to a better known artist, or simply failed to deliver? I traced the artwork in the Reimann bequest directly back to Nelly's will, as she had bequeathed to her sister Dora 'the old painted family fan, a leatherbound book of sketches done in 1759 by one of our ancestresses, two framed black and white drawings by me, illustrations to 'The Emperor's New Clothes' and 'The Little Mermaid' and any six drawings by me as she may choose from among my Derbyshire drawings now in the possession of Messrs Macmillan &Co St Martins Street or from among the Pisa drawings now in the possession of Messrs JM Dent & Co.'

The following year the Foundation website notes that the papers of Miss Ida Suhr, Nelly's wealthy cousin, had been deposited at the Foundation. As well as numerous letters relating to OB Suhr and his business connections, and a large collection of Ida's correspondence with the literary great and the good of Denmark, there were 40 letters from and about Nelly dating from 1906 to 1918, including 14 very long letters written to Ida by Nelly from Italy, and other letters from her friends in Italy including Janet Ross, who continued writing to Ida from 1911 until 1923. We know from Janet's correspondence with Thomas Lindsay that Ida helped Nelly financially in her later years, these letters, which were probably in English, must have explained how and why this came about.

With this trove of information, which seemed to cover Nelly's adult life from 1880 right up to her death in 1918 and beyond, it is not surprising that Peter and I planned a trip to Copenhagen in 2012. I had started emailing the Foundation two years earlier asking for information about the photographs on the website, and had been sent a copy of the pages I could already see on the website, and an email saying that they did not have any other material. Very strange, I thought, but then I was not part of the family, and it was very much a family website. I tried again using the kind help of Dan, son of Jasper, a family member with a password for the website. Yet again he and I were told that there was nothing to see. It was explained that this was 'in part due to The Suhrske Foundation [having] now rented out all rooms in the building except for two. This required a further reduction of stored family material. The only place we now have written family material is on www.suhrske.com'.

It did not seem to me to be possible that these people could have lost or disposed of the physical archive, which clearly had historical, cultural and national importance beyond my Nelly's life. I emailed the Danish National Archive to see if it had been transferred there for safekeeping but they had no idea what I was talking about. So Peter and I packed our bags and went to Copenhagen. At first things seemed to go well, the sun shone and we were staying in a rather glamorous hotel converted from a warehouse right on the harbourfront. The special thrill was discovering that it was one of Ole Bernt Suhr's warehouses, built by his grandfather in 1805 and still in the family's possession until 1970. Copenhagen was a magical city, the sun was shining and it was easy walking along the harbour front in Nyhavn, and past Hans Christian Andersen's house, to imagine the hustle and bustle of the nineteenth century traders, to picture Tietgen and OB Suhr meeting for coffee and laying plans for Danish economic domination.

We had arranged an appointment with the guardian of the Suhr Foundation, and the morning after we arrived we searched out the old Suhr offices in Gammeltorv, a square that still looks medieval in places, and rang the bell. No-one answered. But then our guide from the Foundation arrived, who looked as mystified to see us in the flesh as he had sounded in our email exchanges, and with a lot of head shaking and sighing, he with as little English as we had Danish, he unlocked the doors. We were shown round the completely empty rooms in the beautiful old building that had once been the head office of the Suhr empire, but was now being prepared as offices for rent. Everything had indeed been cleared out, apart from one or two dusty 18th century portraits on the walls. Disbelieving, I pulled open empty drawers and looked in empty cupboards. Nothing. The poor gentleman who was showing us round had been the guardian of the Foundation when the building had been cleared. He looked very unwell, and unhappy. He told me that some papers might have been bundled up and sent on to the agricultural offices of the Foundation out at a place called Bonderup. Eventually, after a great deal of persistence on the part of Nicholas and his brother Serge, we were invited to Bonderup. We were welcomed warmly and shown up to the attic of the old farm offices, invited to rummage through dusty shelves and folders. Sadly, much remains a mystery. There was no sign of Nelly's letters to her mother from the 1880s or of the original diaries or sketchbooks of her trips to Denmark, or any of Ida Suhr's correspondence. But we found some treasures - a bundle of letters from Hermann to his daughter, written just the year before he died, which were full of warmth, humour and affection. He was not one of those severe Victorian fathers from literature. We found a package containing all the letters written home by Nelly's younger brother Charles as he travelled around the world to Japan, aged just 18. There were many letters Nelly had written to her mother, sometimes on a daily basis, from Switzerland and Italy, through which emerged a much clearer picture of the development of her art from the holiday sketchbook to the professional illustrations for Dent and Macmillan. A poor quality photograph of a pastel self-portrait showing a young, pretty girl with curly hair, a fresh face and a tilted nose. And a peep into the life she lived as a traveller alone, the clothes she wore, the food she ate, the many friends she made. Nelly finally came to life.

Bonderup, property of the Suhr Family Trust

"May we bowl our hoops here?" Nelly Erichsen 1880

Chapter Three: Tooting

"Oh father, will you take us to the Tower tomorrow?" I cried; "and St Paul's" said Dora; "And the Zoological Gardens and the Crystal Palace?" chimed in Bernard and Maude.

"Gently, gently," said father, we cannot do everything at once."

"I am afraid", said Aunt Mildred, "that the dear children must keep any sight-seeing for half-holidays. You know they have a good deal to learn, and we must not waste the opportunity of being in London. Madamoiselle comes tomorrow, so that they may commence in French at once, and I should like them to work for two or three hours each morning. At four o'clock I have arranged for them to join the dancing class at M. D'Egville's that their time will be well filled up. You know, my dear Francis, that you left it all entirely to me to settle as I thought best."

"Not tomorrow", we cried in dismay. "why we never dreamed of beginning lessons at once. We thought, of course, we should see a little of London first."

"I think it is a little sharp upon them, I must say", said father. "I quite meant to have taken them about first."

"How could I tell that you were going sight-seeing, like country folks," said Aunt Mildred, rather scornfully. "nobody thinks of going to places like the Tower and St. Paul's now. If you must go somewhere, do go to the picture galleries or places where people go."

"Why, my dear Mildred, what do you take us for? Country folks: why I should think that is just what we are, and going to see everything are we not children - British Museum, Thames Tunnel and all?"

Extract from "We Four" by Mrs Reginald Bray, published in 1881, illustrated by Nelly Erichsen, aged 19.

It is very easy to get to Tooting, South London nowadays, on the Northern Line, but it is much harder to imagine what it must have been like when eight-year-old Nelly arrived there. You emerge from the underground station onto a busy crossroads and the parades of fried chicken bars, off licences and charity shops seem to stretch out before you. But sometimes you just have to look up at the dates on the gables to realise that behind the tacky facades, there are buildings that have survived the arrival of the railway line and the depredations of German bombers and property developers. The Wheatsheaf pub, an unmissable red brick edifice, was built in 1892, so Nelly will have seen it being built. The London Fire Brigade Station is Edwardian. And the two churches, Holy Trinity and St Nicholas, where so many of Nelly's family and friends were baptized, wed and even buried, are still in use.

The Erichsen family was just one tiny part of a huge wave of immigration into London - during the 1870s, almost half a million people moved into the city and its suburbs, and not surprisingly, the provincial-born middle classes seemed to feel most comfortable at the green belt edges. Having left leafy, suburban Jesmond, the family chose to live in an area of London still relatively rural and affluent in feel, but with easy transport links into the City where Hermann was to pursue his new career as a Company promoter and director.

Little is known of the early history of Tooting Graveney, a small Surrey parish in the shadow of both Streatham and Mitcham, now known as Tooting Broadway. Not being part of London, it was much less described or documented. A short distance away to the north beyond the fields, was another small rural village, Tooting Bec, taking its name from its ownership by the beautiful Normandy Abbey, Le Bec Hellouin. In the years before the urban revolution, the two villages were agricultural, supplying the ever-increasing needs of nearby London, and the main road to London was their economic lifeline. In Thackeray's 'Vanity Fair', Tooting is where Rawdon Crawley sends his laundry. Development beyond farm buildings was limited prior to the 19th century - some Georgian villas were built, as out of town residences for London's wealthy or noble families, but the area mostly comprised undulating countryside, farms and orchards. In the thirty odd years that the Erichsen family called it home, it turned from what was still a country village into first an affluent suburb and finally a busy urban redbrick sprawl.

In 1912, the historian and novelist Walter Besant wrote romantically of the land he remembered south of London before the coming of the train and the tram: *'When the ground rose out of the great Lambeth and Bermondsey Marsh it opened out into one wild heath after another Clapham, Wandsworth, Putney, Wimbledon, Barnes, Tooting, Streatham, Richmond, Thornton, and so south as far as Banstead Downs…between the heaths stretched gardens and orchards…..'* but, he goes on to say, when the roads were improved enough to make driving easy and pleasant, the City merchants followed, building big houses and driving in and out of London every day in their carriage and pair. Hermann would have been just one of these City merchants. These houses did not need accompanying agricultural estates to support the inhabitants, just substantial gardens with greenhouses, a lawn where the family could take tea or play croquet, a carriage drive, stabling and room enough for friends at weekends.

Nelly's first experience of London was peeping out of the high windows of the nursery of Leigh House on the north side of what is now Tooting Broadway, close to the vicarage belonging to the church of St Nicholas. This is the property you can see on Victorian maps, a sizeable detached house in its own grounds, demolished and built over long ago. Her father kept a coach and horses to travel into town, and had enrolled his oldest son Herman at Harrow School. All the girls and the little boys were being home-educated, by a governess, Marion Reid, who had moved down with them from Newcastle. The household also included a nurse, a young nursery maid from Geneva, a cook who had come with them from Northumberland, two housemaids, and the coachman. Charles would in time be sent to Marlborough, Frederick to Rugby. They were all to be brought up as young English gentlemen.

Nelly, however, was to be home-educated, as were both her sisters and most Victorian middle class girls. After all, there were very few high quality day schools for girls to be found in London in the 1870s. The Taunton Commission, reporting in 1868, had said that there were only thirteen girls' secondary schools worthy of note in the whole of England. There was one well-known girls' school in South London, in Blackheath, established earlier in the century by the Misses Browning, who were aunts of the poet Robert Browning. It was called the Academy for the Daughters of Gentlemen and it offered an unusually broad education (but, not unusually, no science). Pupils included the sisters Elizabeth and Millicent Garrett, both of whom were to become pioneers of the women's movement, Elizabeth as the first woman to qualify as a doctor, and Millicent as an early leader of the suffrage movement.

The problem for the vast majority of middle class girls was that their parents saw no point in spending money on educating daughters who would then be turned onto the marriage market and would not need to support themselves. Indeed, '*A lady, to be such, must be a mere lady and nothing else. She must not work for profit, or engage in any occupation that money can command, lest she invade the rights of the working classes who live by their labour.'* Thus wrote one Margaretta Greg in her diary in 1853 - but already many women were challenging this philosophy. Just the previous year Florence Nightingale, as yet unknown but deeply frustrated with her lot, had written an unpublished autobiographical novel *'Cassandra'*, in which she spoke of the intolerable life of a lady of leisure - looking at prints, doing needlework, reading little books and going for drives. *'The vacuity and boredom of this existence are sugared over by false sentiment.'*

Miss Buss, headmistress of the North London Collegiate School, which she herself had founded at the age of 23, later wrote '*The terrible sufferings of the women of my own class for want of good elementary training have more than intensified my earnest desire to lighten, ever so little, the misery of women brought up 'to be married and taken care of' and left alone in the world destitute.'* Women who failed to find, or to keep, a husband who would look after them, were often left in real financial difficulty once their parents had gone, because they had no means of supporting themselves.

As a consequence, the demand for better education for girls of all classes was slowly gaining momentum. On 1 May 1848 the Reverend Frederick D Maurice, a professor at King's College London, opened Queen's College for Girls in Harley Street. This was the first institution in Britain where girls could gain serious academic qualifications. His early students included the educational pioneers Mary Frances Buss and Dorothea Beale. He had started the practice of giving evening lectures for ladies the year before and was encouraged by the popularity of the courses. Queen's College was a girls' school by day, offering paid tuition to pupils over the age of 12, and provided free evening classes for young ladies in maths, geography, Latin, history, theology and philosophy. This latter was seen as a means to improve the educational standards of women seeking to train as schoolteachers and governesses - Maurice's sister was herself a governess. The following year saw the opening in London of Bedford College, the first undergraduate college for women, and an establishment set up and managed by women. Elizabeth Jesser Reid, the founder of Bedford College, was so appalled by the general educational standards of the young ladies who joined, that in 1853 she set up a girls' school nearby.

Generally speaking, the daughters of middle class families such as the Erichsens went to poor quality small boarding schools or, more often, stayed at home with governesses, who were often untrained and expected to teach nothing more than French, music, drawing and deportment. But although Nelly's first governess had come from Newcastle, by the mid 1870s she was being taught by a young woman, Jeanne Lador, who came from Geneva. Her education now included proper instruction in both French and German, taught by a Swiss governess, who would have been more competent, in languages at least, than most of her profession. Nelly was already bilingual, speaking both English and Danish with her family. She also spoke Swedish, capable of translating the playwright Strindberg for publication in England in the 1890s, and was proficient in Latin and Greek. She kept up her German as well, although she later admitted to struggling to hold conversations with German professors. At some point, she taught herself Italian. As well as being accomplished linguists, the Erichsen daughters were extremely well-read. Their mother had been an avid reader of Danish literature, from Hans Christian Andersen, whose first collections of fairy tales had been published when Anna was a little girl in the 1830s, to the modern realist novelists such as Henrik Pontoppidan.

There was much else to amuse and stimulate the intellect of a lively and intelligent girl growing up in London in the 1870s. The Great Exhibition, originally opened in Hyde Park in 1851, had now relocated to Crystal Palace, (the area taking its name from the exhibition halls themselves) and these buildings also housed schools of art, literature, science and engineering. This was easily reached by train direct from Balham, a very short distance from Tooting, and a trip to the exhibition could be combined with a wander through the pleasure grounds, a picnic by the lakes and a look at the full-size models of dinosaurs. Nelly and Anna would have enjoyed teasing their little brothers Charles and Frederick with tales of these monsters coming alive. Nelly also enjoyed wandering around the regular art exhibitions, noticing the increasing number of female artists: Barbara Bodichon, Henrietta Ward, Anne Mary Howitt and others.

Further afield, the Natural History Museum did not open to the public in South Kensington until the 1880s, but the British Museum, London Zoo and the National Gallery were increasingly popular with the British public and would definitely have been on the itinerary of any self-respecting governess seeking to educate her charges. Even when there was no educational purpose, there was still skating or carriage rides in the park or train trips into the country, amateur dramatics, parlour games and the theatre. Once a year the streets of Tooting thronged with people heading for Epsom Racecourse - Derby Day had captured the public imagination and even if you weren't going to the races, you turned out to watch the punters who were. The narrow roads became congested with every type of transport, all pulled by horses or donkeys: wagonettes carrying parties of office workers, hansom cabs, landaus, dog-carts and donkey carts. The less well-behaved children of Tooting would wait for the slow straggling return from Epsom and lie in hiding behind the parapets along the house roofs, to squirt the racegoers with water pistols and pea shooters.

When the weather was not suitable for outings, Nelly and her siblings may have been confined to the nursery or schoolroom, but at least by the 1870s there was fun to be had indoors. The tide had really turned in social attitudes to children, more interest was being taken than ever before in the education of the young, in the experience of childhood, and in the creation of educational materials such as books specially written for children and young people to read. Less than five miles away, in Chelsea, another young girl was growing up in very similar circumstances. Beatrix Potter, who thirty years later would become one of the world's most famous children's authors, was brought up on a diet of Aesop's Fables, The Pilgrim's Progress, Uncle Tom's Cabin, Edward Lear, Lewis Carroll and Sir Walter Scott. She was also home-educated, like Nelly, and when she was not reading, she was experimenting with art and design, using colouring books and copying books. Children's illustrated books became highly desirable to the materialist and aspirational Victorian parent, and artists such as Kate Greenaway and Walter Crane set very high standards and were much in demand. In a world of thick London smog and gaslight, where photographs were black and white and usually fuzzy, the magic of a brightly-coloured picture book to be read by the nursery fire must have been absolutely captivating.

The decision not to send a daughter to school did not imply poor parenting. Looking back on her childhood in Cambridge in the late 1890s, another artist, Gwen Raverat, the granddaughter of Charles Darwin, wrote '*There was a strong theory that day schools for girls were Bad; so...we girls were condemned to the dull confinement of the schoolroom at home, under a series of daily governesses...the upper classes did not approve of day schools, though boarding schools for older girls might sometimes be allowed. They were all kind, good, dull women; but even interesting lessons can be made incredibly stupid, when they are taught by people who are bored to death with them, and who do not care for the art of teaching either. But of course if these ladies had had any ambition they would not have been teaching us, but would have made a career of it by teaching at a school.*

'But, anyhow, there was always Miss Mary Greene's Wednesday drawing class, which was the centre of my youthful existence. I lived in those days from Wednesday to Wednesday; for it was not only that the drawing was an ecstasy, but that Miss Greene's warm generous appreciative nature was a great release and encouragement to me.'

Nelly would have understood these sentiments. After all, she came from a well-educated family; her mother's relations in Denmark seem to have moved comfortably in a world of artists, writers and intellectuals. She may have envied her brothers their opportunities at public school. But at some point in her teenage years, like Beatrix Potter, like Gwen Raverat, she discovered a love of art, and an extraordinary natural talent. And crucially her parents allowed this talent to be nurtured and developed by one of the greatest art teachers of the day, John Sparkes. By 1880, Nelly had left the schoolroom far behind and was heading off to the Royal Academy Schools in Piccadilly.

There were other influences at play which encouraged Nelly and her family to cultivate her artistic ambition. At some point in the early 1870s, the family had moved up the road to the smarter end of Tooting, and had taken up residence in Grove Cottage, Upper Tooting, closer to Balham railway station. The train was an easier way to commute to the City and the family's carriage had gone, but the 1881 Census shows that the household was still quite substantial with five domestic staff including a nursery governess, who had been working for them for at least ten years, as had the family cook. Anna had two maids to help manage and clean the house, and a page was employed to run errands and deliver messages. By this time, Charles and Frederick were both away at boarding school, and Nelly and Anna certainly no longer needed a governess, so it is not clear why Jeanne, from Geneva, was still with them. Herman, the oldest son, had completed a degree at Trinity College, Cambridge, and was living at home studying to be a barrister, while Alice, Nelly's oldest sister, was living around the corner in Tooting Bec Road, married and with a young family of her own.

Alice had married Edgar Lucas, the son of a neighbouring family, at Holy Trinity in Upper Tooting in July 1875 when she was just 20. Edgar was one of a family of fourteen children, a dozen of whom survived into adulthood. The founder of this impressive dynasty was Joseph Lucas, quite a character in his own right. Nelly's portrait of him, painted in 1890, shows a wonderful white-haired gentleman with a strong nose, piercing blue eyes, marvelous whiskers and the knowing smile of a man who has seen a great deal and achieved even more. At the date of this painting he was already nearly 80, but had another dozen years to live, dying in 1903 at the ripe old age of 92 and leaving nearly £80,000 in his will, a sizeable fortune, as much as £5 million today. A solicitor by profession, he lived in Stapleton House (eventually demolished to make way for what is now Stapleton Road), local legend said that he kept two eagles in cages in his garden. He was a pillar of the community and Churchwarden of the newly built Holy Trinity church from 1858 to 1879. His family origins can be traced back to a prosperous firm of millers and fullers in Hitchin, Herts and for many generations the family were Quakers. Joseph was a remarkable man, the eldest son of a farmer who lived at Stapleton Hall, Hornsey, he went to Edinburgh University and qualified as a solicitor in 1833. Two years later he married his cousin Sarah, who had family with property in Upper Tooting. In the year that they married, Sarah's uncle died, leaving them the Tooting property, where they were to live for the next sixty-eight years.

Joseph Lucas, a pastel by Nelly Erichsen

Joseph Lucas practised law in Surrey Street off The Strand. Of the sons, his eldest surviving son Frederick joined him in practice, and so also did his second surviving son Edgar, born in 1845. Edgar had been educated at the very recently founded Brighton College, where he was a contemporary of the controversial thinker and writer Edward Carpenter, and both these young men, high academic achievers, went on to Trinity College, Cambridge. Edgar returned to London, qualifying as a solicitor in 1872, and shortly afterwards he met and fell in love with the newly-arrived Alice Erichsen, Nelly's older sister, ten years his junior.

This wedding must have been a wonderful occasion for the Erichsen family. Alice was marrying into the affluent, professional English middle class. Nelly and Dora, aged 13 and 14, would have been among the bridesmaids. The witnesses were the two fathers, Hermann Erichsen and Joseph Lucas, supported by another Tooting neighbour, Alexander Macmillan, and Edgar's friend Edward Carpenter, who stood as best man. All four signatures can be clearly seen on the marriage certificate. Carpenter was already making his name as a socialist writer and proponent of adult education, and later would also be known as an advocate and practitioner of free and homosexual love. This friendship between Edgar and Edward persisted for many years, marking Edgar and Alice out as a couple with unusually liberal persuasions. Carpenter's openly homosexual lifestyle, combined with his radical opinions, might have led many old friends to distance themselves but there is a letter in Carpenter's archive in Sheffield dating from 1908 from Edgar to his old friend 'Chips', inviting him to visit next time he was in London.

And the other witness at the wedding? Alexander Macmillan was the founder of one of the most famous and rapidly growing publishing houses in London. Although born into a very humble family in Scotland, with little formal education, Alexander had followed his older brother Daniel to live in Cambridge where they had started the firm of Macmillan, initially focusing on the work of the Christian Socialist set, including Charles Kingsley who wrote 'The Water Babies', and Tom Hughes, of 'Tom Brown's Schooldays' fame. In 1863 Macmillan was appointed publisher to Oxford University, and this may have prompted the decision to loosen his ties with Cambridge and move his whole family to London. He chose to live in Tooting. By this time, Alexander Macmillan was one of the best-known publishers in London, regularly corresponding with writers such as Tennyson, Mrs Gaskell, Caroline Norton and Matthew Arnold. He wrote all his correspondence in his own hand and it is clear from the archives that he read practically every manuscript he was sent.

In Streatham Lane (now busy Tooting Bec Road, but then a quiet tree lined avenue), was a house called The Elms. In the 1850s this was a ladies' boarding school but in 1863 it was bought by Alexander Macmillan, who rechristened it Knapdale, in honour of his ancestral clan home in Scotland. The Macmillan family was to live there for the next twenty-five years. Alexander described it as *'a nice quaint old house, with a very pleasant garden so retired and countrified and yet so accessible.'* Macmillan told friends and visitors to come to the house via 'a railway that goes from the West End (Victoria Station) to the Crystal Palace'. Although it was in a London suburb, yet there were *'gypsies and tea on the common when we first went there'*. The elm trees were a feature of the place; Macmillan wrote *'I am getting to find them unendurable since they have given up the murderous habit of shying down big branches at people's heads.'* There was also a mulberry tree, which Macmillan believed had been planted by the philosopher John Locke, on a visit to Lord King, his biographer, who had lived on the site. Unfortunately the tree blew down in 1886.

Alexander had a large family, as by the time the Erichsens arrived in Tooting, he was looking after not just his own four children by his first marriage, but four more of similar ages belonging to his brother, both Daniel and his wife having died and left them in Alexander's care. The eight Macmillan children were of similar ages to the Erichsens, and thoroughly enjoying their life at Knapdale, playing tennis and croquet and, according to Alexander, just running about in the gardens. His older daughter Margaret, later Mrs Louis Dyer, recounted her memories of her father reading aloud to them around this time from his manuscript copy of Charles Kingsley's 'The Water Babies' - *'how we all sat spell-bound, more than 40 years ago! That nursery scene is still vivid, and the keen joyousness of my father's face and voice as he read. In those early days, although such a weight of responsibility hung upon his shoulders, he was always bright and buoyant in my recollection.'*

Knapdale House, Tooting

Knapdale House can still be seen on Tooting Bec Road, next to St Anselm's Roman Catholic Church. It is in use as a Christian Education Centre - Alexander would be happy that it was being used for religious purposes, as that had been his hope when he moved from the house, gifting it to the Church, although he may find it harder to swallow that it is now in Catholic hands. It is closed to the public, and the original building seems to be in good condition, if a little institutional. There is still a sweeping semi-circular driveway with two entrances and a high wall protecting the house from the traffic on the main road. Sadly, the garden behind the house, where the Macmillan children played croquet and then sat and discussed art and literature with their friends the Lucases and Erichsens, is now a tarmac-covered playground for a Roman Catholic primary school. But when I visited recently, the playground was full of small children in mulberry-coloured jerseys, which seemed really to be the next best thing. I had been loitering suspiciously in the driveway taking photographs when a kind young man who worked at the Centre came out to ask my business. He was only too happy to show me around the downstairs rooms and offered me a pamphlet on the history of the house, but there were no traces of the wonderful Macmillan family to be seen.

When he lived in Cambridge, Alexander had regularly come up to London for dinners with his favourite authors. Now, these 'feasts of talk, tipple and tobacco' were held at Knapdale. Alexander entertained lavishly; guests included Thomas Huxley, Lord Tennyson, Charles Kingsley and the historian JR Green (who stayed there for weeks at a time while writing his most famous work, his 'History of the English Peoples'). Macmillan hosted annual 'All Fools Day' dinners; either at Knapdale or the Garrick Club, and signatures visible on the menu cards include Robert Browning, John Millais, Matthew Arnold, Henry Sidgwick, and John Morley. The reputation of Knapdale as 'the place to be invited if you wanted to get published' continued for many years: from 1878-1881,Thomas Hardy brought his wife Emma to live at No 1 Arundel Terrace, on Trinity Road in nearby Wandsworth in an attempt to get himself more noticed by literary London. Hardy visited Knapdale several times, where he met other writers including Arnold and Tennyson he was at a garden party at Knapdale when a thunderstorm hit, and the guests had to take shelter, an incident he used in *'The Laodicean'*. Hardy's widow claimed that a scene in *Jude* was inspired by Alexander's daughter Margaret Macmillan showing Hardy a view of the sunset out of a window with a mirror when he was unwell. He never forgot the great care Alexander Macmillan had taken when rejecting his first, anonymously submitted manuscript of *'The Poor Man and The Lady'* - *'You see I am writing to you as to a writer who seems to me, at least potentially, of considerable mark, of power and purpose. If this is your first book, I think you ought to go on. May I ask if it is, and - you are not a lady, so perhaps you will forgive the question - are you young?'*

Margaret Dyer describes everyday life for families such as the Erichsens and the Macmillans in Tooting at this time: *'on week days, prayers were at eight or soon thereafter, and breakfast at half-past, as an early train had to be caught at Balham station'.* Alexander worked in London six days a week, coming home for dinner at seven. But on Sundays, with his bright scarlet coat, or perhaps a brown velvet coat and cap, he led his family first to church, then for a long walk, and then they shared dinner at three. Thereafter guests from London would call, and they spent time either in the garden or the library and drawing room, until tea was brought to the dining room table. The evenings were given over to reading aloud - the Bible or poetry, and hymn singing. Alexander sang Scottish folk music, not particularly well but with great enthusiasm - and despite their religious upbringing, the parents did not insist on sticking to bible readings, but encouraged the family to read widely. A great friend from Cambridge days, Alfred Ainger, wrote of Knapdale *'In its large leisurely rooms, or in its spacious old world garden, there gathered together informally the men and women of note and the young promise of the day authors, poets, painters, English and French, whether they came from Oxford or fresh from the ranks of the Impressionist Artists'.*

In July 1871, just as the Erichsens were moving into nearby Leigh House, Alexander's wife Caroline died, leaving him with sole responsibility for the eight children between the ages of 12 and 20. It must have been a terrible blow. But in the autumn of 1872, at the age of 54, he re-married - a much younger woman, Emma Pignatel, a schoolfriend of Louisa Cassell, the family governess. If this seems to modern eyes rather rapid, there is no evidence that it caused any family difficulties. In 1878 he wrote charmingly to Leslie Stephen, father of Virginia Woolf, after Stephen's remarriage: '*I may venture to congratulate you on following my example in restoring a shattered home with a new sweet centre of woman life. Whatever their wrongs and rights, they are very essential to our home life - these same women.'*

Emma Pignatel was 29, twenty-five years his junior, and one of four daughters of a French father and English mother. She had been born in Livorno, Italy, and then brought up in Cheshire, and undoubtedly exercised a cosmopolitan influence on the family. Mrs Dyer wrote *'We had known very little of foreigners or foreign travel. My father had once been to France, and constantly declared that nothing could ever induce him to leave England again. It was characteristic of him that after this vehement assertion he was persuaded in the year following his marriage to make his first journey to Italy, humorously professing himself subject to the irresistible will of another.'* I suspect that Emma was delighted to find herself living close to another family of continental origin, the Erichsens, and that this helped the friendship along. Alexander's second marriage produced two more children, Mary and John. The family began to take regular holidays - in 1873 they travelled to France, and in 1874 to Whitby on the North Yorkshire coast, which was to become a favourite part of the country for the family and their friends, including Nelly. The older children continued to enjoy life around Tooting, and their relationships with the Lucas and Erichsen families became more than just acquaintanceship. Maybe they all met at church on Sundays, maybe the fathers shared the daily train journey to London, but the ties between the three families became increasingly close. In 1879 Edgar's sister Margaret married Alexander Macmillan's second son George.

The closeness of these three families, Erichsen, Lucas and Macmillan, all living within a few yards of each other in Upper Tooting, attending the same church, sending their sons to the same Cambridge college, playing at the same tennis parties and sharing family dinners, and now linked by these two marriages, opened up for Nelly as she reached adulthood a network of contacts in the world of publishing and literary life which subsequently she was able to draw upon for inspiration, hospitality and commissions. For instance, in 1881 at the time of the Census, Frederick Sandys, a prominent pre-Raphaelite painter, was staying at Knapdale. Meeting visitors such as these must have been inspirational for the 18-year old Nelly, as she started out as a student at the Royal Academy Schools. There was literary as well as artistic inspiration: if your neighbours regularly entertained Alfred, Lord Tennyson, John Ruskin, Thomas Hardy, Charles Kingsley, Matthew Arnold, Lewis Carroll and Henry James to dinner or tea, it is likely that their published works would be very familiar to you. Nelly lapped it up: she was inspired, if not a bit starstruck, by the people she met. Among her prized possessions, guarded all her life and carefully listed in her will, were two particular treasures: a copy of 'Becket', a now-forgotten play by Tennyson which he had autographed for Nelly, and a framed photograph of *Tobias* and the *Angel* by Perugino, which had been given to her by another Victorian pin-up and friend of Macmillan, John Ruskin, who greatly admired this particular painting.

Perhaps it was one of Macmillan's friends who introduced the family to John Sparkes as an art tutor for Nelly. At a time when all young ladies were encouraged to learn to draw and paint, but only as a pastime, an accomplishment, Nelly's talent had singled her out for extra attention and coaching. And the Erichsen family aimed high in the tutor they found for her. John Charles Lewis Sparkes was born in 1833, in Brixton, the son of a corn chandler, and received his initial art training in Guernsey under Paul Naftel, a prolific water-colourist. He studied further under James Mathews Leigh, who had his own private art school off Oxford Street, and then joined the Royal Academy Schools. Leigh advised him to become a teacher, and in 1853 he entered the newly founded Art Masters' Training Class, in the Government School at Marlborough House. Just a year later he took charge of the art classes set up by the Rev Robert Gregory (later Dean of St Pauls) at the school of St Mary-the-Less in Lambeth. This was the beginning of the well-known Lambeth School of Art, which began to attract students from all over the country and abroad. In 1873 Vincent Van Gogh lived briefly in Lambeth, and it is possible that he attended drawing sessions at the art school.

One of Sparkes' particularly attractive qualities was the interest and encouragement he gave to young women artists. In 1868 he had married Catherine Adelaide Edwards, then 26, and an accomplished artist in her own right. She had been a pupil at Lambeth and then at the Royal Academy Schools, exhibiting in the Summer Exhibition under her maiden name in 1866 and 1868, and also at the Grosvenor Gallery and the Dudley Gallery. She continued to paint and illustrate for the next twenty or so years, which was unusual, as many women ceased to work professionally once they married. She provided illustrations for several books and periodicals (including The Illustrated London News, Cornhill and The Graphic) and also worked as a tile painter and designer for Lambeth Pottery.

It may have been due to his wife's encouragement, or genuine enthusiasm on his part for encouraging female talent, but according to the Entry Register at the Royal Academy in the 1870s and 1880s, John Sparkes was not only a very frequent sponsor of new students, but also by far the most prominent sponsor of young women. This bias in favour of women students was to survive his death: when Sparkes died he left his whole estate to the RA on the instruction that it was to be used to fund scholarships for female students. It was definitely time for some positive discrimination in favour of women. In the twenty-five years from 1865 Sparkes sponsored over 80 students, nearly half of whom were women. Among them, aged just 17 in 1880, was Nelly Erichsen. Perhaps he had been teaching her at the Lambeth Schools, perhaps he had taught her as a private pupil. But his encouragement must have been just as crucial to building Nelly's self-confidence as the love of her parents and the enthusiasm of her well-connected neighbours.

It was a search for Nelly in the electronic archives of The Times which revealed to us the Macmillan connection. The search brought up the usual long list of advertisements and reviews of the various publications which she had illustrated, but listed alongside all the reviews was the funeral notice for Alexander Macmillan, the publisher. Among the family mourners, and the great and the good of the literary world noted in The Times - the likes of John Morley and Henry James - were Miss Nelly Erichsen, her older brother Herman, her eldest sister, Mrs Edgar Lucas, and her friend Miss Fanny Johnson. Nelly's name seemed very high on the list for a casual contributor of illustrations to lesser known Macmillan volumes. It seemed mysterious, and even more so when we noticed that her name fell among the family group of Macmillans. A hurried look back at the Ancestry records made clear just how and why Nelly had managed to get into print, into book illustration, into magazine writing. Sometimes it is not just what you know, but who you live next door to, that counts.

Peter and I had been playing around with Nelly and her family and friends for seven or eight years before the idea of writing a book about her took hold of me. I had never considered the possibility of being a writer, although I have always read for pleasure - to me the highlight of many long days working in the City in the 1980s was the chance to read a book during my forty minute tube journey from Kew Gardens, where I always got a seat, to Monument. While everyone else struggled to manage the flapping pages of the Financial Times in a crowded tube carriage, I just did not have the length or strength of arm to hold anything larger than a paperback. There were many days when the idea of staying on the line to Upminster to get to the end of the story seemed greatly preferable to fighting my way up through the streets around Bank for another long day in the office. Working late into the evenings on a regular basis meant I always got a seat on the way home as well. Thus I travelled with the great Victorian novelists, taking Dickens, Trollope, and especially George Eliot with me every day, and then I turned to history and biography. But it was a novel read slightly later in life that for some reason hooked me into thinking that I needed to tell Nelly's story.

AS Byatt has always been my favourite modern author, if I had to choose I think Possession would be the one twentieth century novel I would take to a desert island. 'The Children's Book', published in 2009, with its sweeping survey of Edwardian intellectual life and its terrible descent into the Great War, allowed me to see Nelly afresh, made her come alive as someone who had really existed and had experienced the world Byatt described. In so many ways Byatt's characters seemed to belong in Nelly's life as well, their concerns were those shared by Nelly's friends and families, and their artistic endeavours matched her own. Take this description: 'This was the Wellwoods' third midsummer party. Their guests were socialists, anarchists, Quakers, Fabians, artists, editors, freethinkers and writers…'. If this was Byatt's imagination, it is peopled by the social set that Nelly would mix with in the 1890s, the likes of Bertha Newcombe, George Bernard Shaw, the Lucas and Johnson families. And this seems to be an exact description of Nelly's great friend Fanny Johnson: "She liked to be busy, she was the acting secretary of many groups, the local theosophists, the local Fabians, the Winchelsea and District Dramatic Society, the Circle of Watercolourists, and a group which worked for women's suffrage.' The novel namechecks Edward Carpenter and Graham Wallas, people with whom Nelly had actually attended family parties and been on outings to the country.

And Byatt's glorious, rich, enveloping prose helped me to imagine the world in which Nelly lived and the interiors she inhabited: 'The parlour had dark green Morris & Co wallpaper, spangled with scarlet berries, and a Morris set of spindly Sussex settle and chairs, with rush seats. There were woven rugs on a dark floor and high shelves of orderly books.' I know that if the unconventional Alice and Edgar Lucas had invited me into their grand new house in Elm Park Gardens, Chelsea in the 1900s it would have looked just like that.

Chapter Four: Nelly Enters The Royal Academy

"To the President and the Council, we the undersigned students of the Royal Academy do hereby respectfully and earnestly petition that rearranging the schools of this institution you will reconsider the question of granting us a life class for the study of the partially draped figure. We beg to lay it before your notice that almost all of us rely on the profession we have chosen as our future means of livelihood. Therefore a class which is considered so essential to the training success of male students must be equally so to us. We venture to hope that the separation of male and female students in the upper schools of the Academy may have removed an important objection against the granting of our request."

Petition to the President and Council of the Royal Academy, 1883. Signed by 64 female students of the RA, including Nelly Erichsen.

When Nelly Erichsen walked through the doors of the Royal Academy in Piccadilly in April 1880, aged only 17, she was entering an institution in crisis. Founded in 1768 at the prompting of a group of prominent artists and architects who were concerned that Britain was falling well behind Continental Europe in artistic endeavour, it had first opened on 2 January 1769 in temporary rooms in Pall Mall with Sir Joshua Reynolds as its president. For most of the next century, it held its position as the pre-eminent training school for artists in Britain. Its founders had petitioned the King, George III, with a financially viable scheme *'the establishment of a well-regulated School or Academy of Design, for the use of students in the Arts, and an Annual Exhibition, open to all artists of distinguished merit.'* The clever idea was that the profits from the Exhibition would fund the training school. In fact, the King had to subsidise the Academy for the first twelve years, but since that time it has always been self-supporting, and tuition was offered free of charge. In its heyday, famous students had included Turner,

A Hard Day's Labour

Soane, Rowlandson, Blake, Lawrence, Constable, Wilkie, Etty and Landseer.

However, a century after its foundation, the Academy was facing major threats which it was struggling to resolve. Its teaching methods had changed little in the hundred or so years since foundation, and it was now seeing competition from new ideas and fashions. The Pre-Raphaelite Brotherhood, founded in 1848, had fallen out dramatically with the art establishment, as personified by Sir Charles Eastlake, President of the Academy. Not only were the Schools under pressure to modernize their approach to art training, to take more notice of the methods being used on the Continent, for example, but they were also having to deal with the increasingly loud demands of women to be treated equally with men. New schools were being founded elsewhere, the most famous of which was The Slade in London, where men and women were taught on equal terms. To the great and the good who governed the Academy, the attempt to contain the challenge of the female art student was a proxy for the much larger shifts in the art world that they could not hope to control.

The very fact that Nelly had been admitted to the Schools despite being a female was a sign of the pressure the Board found itself under - times were changing. It had not been the intention of the Founders that the Schools should be a male-only preserve, indeed the original Foundation petition to the King, in 1768, had two women signatories, Mary Moser and Angelica Kaufmann, both well-known professional artists of the time. Unfortunately, the Instrument of Foundation seemed to make the assumption that all students would be male: 'XXV No student shall be admitted into the Schools, till he hath satisfied the Keeper of the Academy...of his abilities'. And for most of the next century, women did not challenge the assumption, sending their works to the Summer Exhibition for display, but not attempting to be admitted as students. However, by the 1850s, ambitions were beginning to surface. In 1856 Barbara Bodichon and Anna Mary Howitt, early campaigning feminists, set up The Society of Female Artists from their headquarters at Langham Place in central London. They were not just pursuing some point of feminist principle: it was based on a very practical concern that women needed to be trained as professionals in many fields to become self-supporting. In 1859 a letter was sent to all Academicians and published in The Athenaeum magazine pointing out that as 120 ladies had been successful exhibitors at the Summer Exhibition in the previous three years alone, 'the profession must be considered as fairly open to women'. But in fact as the 1860s arrived, the door to the Royal Academy Schools remained firmly closed. The stumbling block seemed to be that the Council could not imagine male and female students working together in the Life Schools. Victorian prudery was holding back progress.

Nelly and her fellow women students remembered with gratitude those who had fought the battles that made it possible for them to attend the RA, and in particular a Miss Laura Herford. Back in the 1850s Laura was a student at Sass's Academy who wished to join her fellow male students as they progressed to the RA Schools. Herford decided to challenge the authorities: in 1860 she submitted one of her works to the Schools with an application, signed only "L. Herford." A return letter, addressed to "L. Herford, Esq.," admitted the recipient to the Academy. When the Academy realised its mistake, it was simply too embarrassed to withdraw the offer, and Laura was duly enrolled. Four female students were admitted the following year, and six in 1862, and after this slow start the number gradually increased to about twelve a year - but only for the antique and painting schools, not the Life Classes. The Establishment tried to fight back, and for a short while later in the 1860s even succeeded in getting the permission revoked for several years until some element of separate accommodation could be provided. But the tide had turned against the men in charge.

Even after women were grudgingly admitted to the Schools, they had to continue to fight to receive equal treatment in the hierarchy of the Academy. There might be female students, but there were no female teachers or academicians. In 1879, the year before Nelly entered the Schools, Elizabeth Thompson, later famous as Lady Elizabeth Butler, creator of scenes of battle and military life, commercially successful and beloved of Queen Victoria, was beaten in the ballot to become an Associate by just two votes. In 1887 the artist WP Frith wrote defensively that *'Whether we shall have female Academicians or not depends upon the ladies themselves; all the honours the Academy can bestow are open to them.'* Writing in 1914, in 'The Inner Life of the Royal Academy', George Leslie RA teased that the *'Members considered the difficulty of the treatment of women after they had been elected; for instance, they might choose to come to the banquet, possibly one solitary lady would come? Would she have to be escorted into dinner? And if so, by whom?'* The difficulty appeared insuperable, and no woman was admitted as an Academician until the election of Dame Laura Knight, long after the First World War, in 1936, by which time the world had turned upside down.

Entry to the RA Schools was free to anyone who passed the admission test. There were no academic qualifications required, so the fact that Nelly had not had any formal education did not count against her. To apply, all she needed was a letter of recommendation, from a recognised art master such as Sparkes, and then to submit a finished drawing, two feet high, of an undraped antique statue, or, if of a torso, with a head and a hand or foot. Once the Keeper approved her initial drawing, Nelly was admitted as a probationer, and given three months to prepare a portfolio of drawings for submission to the Council. In early 1880 Nelly received her 'bone' - an ivory disc that guaranteed admittance to the Schools, on which was engraved her name and date of admission. Nelly signed up for what was then a seven year studentship, but in 1881 it was reduced to six years, divided into two terms of three years, with Upper and Lower Schools of Painting and Modelling. Students were not required to attend for the full six years - no records were kept of leaving dates - and it was presumably left to the discretion of the student when he or she felt that they had finished their studies, or needed to move on for personal or financial reasons.

Most artists will have prepared for their entrance assessment at a private fee-paying school, such as Sass's school in Bloomsbury, or Leigh's (later Heatherley's) in Newman Street. By 1895 there were over thirty private art schools in London alone - some of sufficient reputation, such as the Slade, to stand as rivals to the Academy. There is no such school listed by Nelly's name in the admission records, so for Nelly to win a place without this additional training, one of only ten admitted to the School of Painting that term, and at such a young age, would have been a source of enormous pride to her family, and would have given her some considerable cachet among the talented literary and artistic figures at the Macmillans' garden parties.

Once admitted, Nelly was taught to draw principally by copying from an extensive collection of plaster casts, mostly Greek and Roman statues, and some from Renaissance masters such as Donatello and Michelangelo. She attended classes and lectures on perspective, and there were also courses on painting, chemistry, sculpture and architecture. If she had been a man, she would have then joined the Life School, where models, male or female, were alive and naked. For this is where the Royal Academy was in danger of lagging behind other 'upstart' art schools - the governing body was really struggling to cope with the demands of female students, as it was considered completely unsuitable for them to be allowed anywhere near a naked body of either sex. When Elizabeth Thompson had entered the Schools in 1866, she had had to go elsewhere to find a class studying the undraped female model, and worked there on alternate days. Gertrude Massey, a contemporary of Nelly, complained of the problems of being denied access to the nude. Writing in the 1930s, she complained *'It was only after a serious fight on our part that we could snatch as much as one inch of freedom. For instance, every problem in art can be discovered in the human figure, and so a careful and thorough study of the nude is a practical and very necessary method towards rapid and genuine progress in art. In our days, however, girls were expected to paint portraits, still-life groups, landscapes and all that sort of thing, but we were certainly not expected to study from the nude. In fact it was almost a crime to mention the word nude; and although acquainted with our personal anatomies, we were supposed to accept the conventional point of view that women had no legs. They had heads, arms and feet, apparently linked together by clothes. Between the head and the feet there was a mysterious something heavily clothed.'*

Massey tried to enrol in classes run by the highly respected Sir Hubert von Herkomer in Bushey, who claimed to offer the same teaching privileges to male and female students (unless the female students were married) but he *'refused point blank even to glance at my work and told me bluntly to go home and make puddings.'* This lack of opportunity to study and improve may explain why Gertrude's surviving work, although very popular with the Victorian Royal Family, mostly seems to consist of miniature paintings of babies and dogs. Gertrude's husband Henry Massey later became the proprietor of Leigh's Art School in Newman Street. Her autobiography 'Kings, Commoners and Me', published in 1934, is an amusing read once one gets past the namedropping…she enjoyed the humour of the young art students, including the notice they pinned up: 'Artists' models are not always as bad as they are painted.'

Throughout the Victorian era, controversy raged over the use of live, naked female models for either sex of artist. In England, where the female nude was rarely depicted in publicly displayed art, it was felt unnecessary to waste much time on the skill of life drawing. In 1873 a copy of the relevant RA by-law was pinned up outside the Life Room: it stated that *'none but Members of the Academy or Students of the School shall be admitted when the female model is sitting, nor shall any student under twenty years of age (unless he be married) be allowed to study from that model.'*

Women continued to petition for their own life classes throughout the 1870s. The petition of 1883 was drafted by the female students, and Nelly's name is among the first ten signatories on a list of more than sixty. The frustration of being admitted as a student on equal terms with the men, but then being forbidden access to one of the most interesting and valuable resources on offer, the Life Class, was too much for her to bear without protest. Appended to the petition were letters of support from a number of well-known, established painters including Kate Perugini (the daughter of Charles Dickens); the four well-loved Montalba sisters, all of whom were successful exhibitors at the RA; Helen Allingham, one of the most famous water colourists of the Victorian era; Louisa Starr, the first woman to win the Gold Medal at the RA; and Marie Spartali, perhaps the greatest female artist of the Pre-Raphaelite movement. The signatories made the case that these women were serious artists, hoping and needing to make a livelihood from their talents, and therefore requiring proper training. The issue was debated at length by the Council of the Academy in December 1883 and approved by eight votes to two. But over the Christmas holidays the opposition gathered its forces and when it came back to a vote at the all-male General Assembly in January it was dismissed by twenty-four votes to nine. Nothing was to change until 1893, seven years after Nelly had left, when it was grudgingly resolved to allow female students to draw from a male model undraped except around the loins. It took another year to agree the exact manner of the drapes: *'ordinary bathing drawers, and a cloth of light material 9 foot long by 3 foot wide, which shall be wound round the loins over the drawers, passed between the legs and tucked in over the waistband' and to prevent accidents 'a thin leather strap shall be fastened round the loins in order to ensure that the cloth is kept in place.'*

Despite these frustrations, Nelly was a diligent student. She travelled up to town every day from Tooting, catching the train from Balham station to Victoria, her sandwich lunch wrapped in wax paper, her art materials in a stout canvas bag, then a twenty minute walk up Buckingham Gate, past the front of the royal Palace and across St James' Park - Victorian London at its best - her head full of ambitions and plans. From 1771 until 1830, the Schools had been housed in Government buildings in Somerset House on the Strand. They were then squeezed into the National Gallery on Trafalgar Square, until splendid new purpose built accommodation was opened on Piccadilly, at Burlington Gardens, where the Academy moved in 1868 and remains to this day. The newly-

60 THE ROYAL ACADEMY EXHIBITORS

Engleheart, Thomas—*continued.*
1778. 102 A small bust in wax.
103 Three medallions; do.
28, *St. James's Street.*
1779. 89 A model in wax.
1780. 294 Portrait of a lady; model in wax.
295 Portrait of a gentleman; model in wax.
Richmond, Surrey.
1786. 370 Portrait in wax.

ENGLEHEART, William F. S. Miniature Painter.
7, *Shepherd Street, Mayfair.*
1801. 758 Portrait of a lady.

ENOCH, G. ... ... Architect.
4, *New Basinghall Street.*
1850. 1163 Garden front of a design for a Gothic Villa.
1165 Entrance front of a design for a Gothic Villa.
The Hall, Grove Lane, Camberwell.
1852. 1169 Elevation: Villa at Dover.

ENTHOVEN, Miss Julia ... Painter.
The Gable House, Sydenham.
1889. 1035 Poppies.

EPINAY, D', Count Prosper. *See* D, vol. ii, page 307.

EPINETTE, Mdlle. ... ... Painter.
6, *St. James's Terrace, N.W.*
1881. 1183 Ella, youngest daughter of the late Wm. Hepworth Dixon.

EPPS, N. ... ... Painter.
12, *Claughton Road, Birkenhead.*
1872. 516 At Townshend House.

EPPS, Miss ... ... Painter.
20, *Devonshire Street, Portland Place.*
1874. 962 My doll's picnic.

ERCOLE, Signor Alcide Carlo. Painter.
31, *Grosvenor Street, Grosvenor Square.*
1857. 1175 Mrs. Dickens.
1858. 83 Capt. R. Gosling.
826 Miss Adelaide Stringer.
837 Mrs. F. Fuller.
15, *Langham Street.*
1859. 382 Ophelia.
1860. 483 Ivory and ebony.
1861. 564 Guiderius. "O sweetest, fairest lily!"—*Cymbeline.*
14, *Cockspur Street.*
1864. 17 Mrs. G. Grisi.
16, *Russell Place.*
1865. 174 The Marchioness of Northampton.
562 Miss Rosalind Northall Laurie.
1866. 558 The Hon. H. Brand.

ERICHSON, Miss Nelly...... Painter.
Upper Tooting.
1884. 1558 The deserted homestead.
2, *New Court, Lincoln's Inn.*
1885. 469 A descendant of the Danes.
541 "No, truly, she is too disdainful."
1062 Briars and brambles.
1693 A study.
1888. 634 Miss Margaret Macmillan.
3, *Trafalgar Studios.*
1891. 462 The magic crystal.
1390 The street end.
1892. 956 "Out of the deep have I cried unto thee."
1142 Going home.
1893. 1054 Phyllis.
1894. 338 The churchyard path.
384 Flower o' the elder.
908 Miss Cecil Lucas.
1896. 107 Miss Rosamond Lucas.
1897. 1692 The emperor's new clothes.

ERLAM, J. ... ... Architect.
16, *Green Street, Grosvenor Square.*
1825. 971 Design for a cenotaph.
41, *Park Street.*
1828. 41 Gateway at Exeter, Devon.

ERLAM, J. S. ... ... Architect.
Bloomfield Road, Maida Hill.
1842. 1131 Design for a Catholic chapel.

ERLAM, S. B. ... ... Architect.
20, *Green Street, Grosvenor Square.*
1815. 850 Design for a naval pillar, to commemorate the achievements of departed Heroes, whose gallant exploits are the boast of England and the admiration of the world.
40, *Brook Street.*
1817. 984 View of the interior of the Egyptian Hall, Mansion House.

Excerpt from 'The Royal Academy Exhibitors', her name is wrongly spelled again!

built top-lit north-facing studios, plus an impressive collection of galleries and a lecture theatre, allowed the students far more space and meant that they could work throughout the year with only a two month summer break. The entrance to the School was in an alley between Burlington House and Burlington Arcade off Piccadilly, through swing doors guarded by the porter, Mr Osborne. These opened onto a large irregular corridor adorned with plaster casts, where Nelly and her fellow students spent their lunch hour. The first set of classrooms were those of the Architectural School. Next came the Life School room - 'men only' in Nelly's time, laid out with a throne area for the model and a horseshoe of seating for students. Then the Upper Painting School, the Preliminary and the Antique, in all of which men and women did mix. These classrooms had recently been enlarged at a significant cost of £25,000 but were still considered slightly unsatisfactory, although they provided the students with every kind of plaster model - men, women and children, draped and undraped, still life casts, and pictures borrowed for copying from the Dulwich and Diploma Galleries.

The female students were generally perceived to be a good addition to the Academy by the time Nelly arrived - they fitted in well, and were seen as 'pinafore-aproned and neat', preferring to eat packed lunches at the morning break rather than playing billiards, as the men did. *'The girls, it must be confessed, work very hard and well, numbers of them have taken medals over the heads of boys…they are more attentive to the teaching of the Visitors than the generality of the boys, though for the most part they lack the self-reliant conceit which so often characterises the brightest geniuses of the male sex.'* The author of this 1889 article in The Graphic magazine went on to say *'as a general rule, the prettier the girl, the better the study. Girls are very receptive of careful coaching, and it may be that a pretty girl, as she passed through her art training, when the teachers are men, received decidedly more attention than falls to the lot of her plainer companions; it is not quite fair, but I am afraid it is inevitable.'* I hope this says more about the author than about the rest of the teaching staff.

However, The Graphic noted: *'Women's rights are fast becoming 'men's wrongs' if half of what one hears is to be believed. How the ladies claim the rights of both sexes, how they insist on their own privileges and throw themselves on the chivalry of the men to obtain theirs, taking possession of the best seats, contrary to all recognised custom, while all the time they 'never had a chance' - and above all never failing to give the men clearly to understand that they consider them a selfish, an ineligible lot: such are some of the charges constantly brought against them. I confess I tremble as I record them, but gallantry must yield to truth.'*

Actually, although the men complained that the girls won too many of the prizes, the statistics show that between 1880 and 1901 two out of every five male students won prizes, but less than a third of the women.

The students enjoyed a good social life, with clubs, hockey and tennis tournaments, fancy dress balls and drama productions. But that of course was not the principal purpose of the Academy, which was to turn out professional artists. The author of The Graphic article felt that the standards were slipping in the second half of the nineteenth century. *'The liberal patronage that was given to living artists during the 'fifties and 'sixties tempted a vast number of young aspirants to take up art as a profession, many of whom, it must be confessed, might better have been otherwise employed.'*

Nelly was one of a talented intake, but still she stood out from the crowd. The most important event in the students' calendar was the annual prize giving ceremony on 10 December, the Academy's birthday. The Schools awarded various prizes and medals to the top students in each of their disciplines - painting, sculpture, etching and architecture. During Lord Leighton's presidency throughout the 1880s, including the years when Nelly was a student, these ceremonies were particularly brilliant affairs, as Lord Leighton would address the students and invited audiences. The ladies wore evening dresses - and the prizewinners' work was put up in the galleries for the audience to view afterwards. In 1884 Nelly Erichsen was awarded the first prize, the Silver Medal, for her "Drawing of a Head from Life". Tellingly, she was the only female prizewinner in a list of 18 names. Sidney Paget, who went on to become a leading magazine illustrator including the original Sherlock Holmes stories for Strand Magazine, was also a medal winner that year. Nelly won two prize medals in all, a silver and a bronze, and they remained among her most cherished possessions, bequeathed to her brother Herman in her will.

Silver medal awarded to Nelly by the RA for the second best drawing of a statue

Her other successful contemporaries in the Painting School included William Henry Gore, also recommended by Sparkes and a pupil of the Lambeth Schools, William Margetson and his future wife Helen Howard Hatton, and a young Tom Roberts, who became one of Australia's most famous artists. Tom had come over to study from Australia and spent three years at the Royal Academy. When he left, he took home with him an autograph book of sketches by his fellow students which now resides in the archives of the National Library of Australia. Nelly's simple line drawing of a woman with a hoe is probably one of her earliest surviving works. It is a very small grey wash painting, less than 8 inches tall, but beautifully detailed. There is no romanticism in the depiction of the woman as she walks home from a long day in the fields, the sun setting behind her. Her face is lined and thin, her arms strong. And the frame that Nelly has created around the image itself is beautiful and unusual. It is a very different vision of country life than the chocolate box fantasies of her slightly older contemporaries, Helen Allingham or Kate Greenaway.

For many hopeful students, admission to the Academy was a crucial step on the path to becoming a commercially successful artist, but that was just like winning a ticket to compete. Even gaining medals was not enough; one of the best ways to launch a career was to be successful at the Summer Exhibition. Following its move to Burlington House, the RA had been able to develop its two main annual exhibitions into the major public attractions required to ensure that the organisation remained self-financing. The Winter Exhibition was a display of well-regarded works by famous artists, not necessarily Academicians. It seems to have been mounted as a worthy, educational display but nonetheless enjoyed decent visitor numbers. 25,000 was not an untypical attendance. But the Summer Exhibition, which still flourishes today, was an altogether different affair.

By the time Nelly was a student the Summer Exhibition was hugely popular with the public. On the first public Opening Day in 1882, no less than 7,569 people paid to attend. The queue reached across the courtyard and spilled out into Piccadilly. There were 377,814 paying visitors that season in total (compared to an average attendance nowadays over ten weeks of just 100,000), in addition to the various holders of free tickets. These included Academicians, students and the Royal Family (for whom a half day was set aside when no

A Woman with a Hoe

public visitors were allowed in until noon so that Queen Victoria could tour the exhibition rooms.) The Prince of Wales was invariably a visitor, and the Exhibition was established as a part of the London "season". WP Frith's great painting *'The Private View of the Royal Academy'* was painted in 1881 and exhibited in 1883 - this showed the Queen attending, accompanied by an extraordinary array of the great and the good - Gladstone, Trollope, Millais, Huxley, Oscar Wilde, Lillie Langtree and Robert Browning, as well as a portrait of the recently deceased Disraeli - included as a special request from Victoria, who could not bear to think that her favourite Prime Minister was missing the event. Maybe to compare the array of power, talent and celebrity in our current experience, you might think of the Royal Box at Wimbledon for the Men's Final. But you would be wrong, the RA Private View was a more glittering occasion.

For the RA, the income from the Summer Exhibition was considerable, around £40,000 in 1881 came from the paying visitors and from the sale of nearly 130,000 catalogues. The scale of this income can be judged against the total salary bill for permanent staff at the RA at the time of just under £2000, of which £325 was the annual salary of the Curator of the Schools. For artists it was an enormous advantage to be selected. Those who exhibited regularly at the Academy's exhibitions could be elected as members of the Royal Academy, entitled to put RA after their name. In 1885, more than 9,000 works were submitted of which two thirds were rejected, but Nelly had four paintings accepted and hung on the walls that year - her best single year - and she was only 22. It must have felt as if a career as a professional artist was within her grasp.

Nelly was learning to draw and paint at a time of major upheaval in the professional art world, which created opportunities that would not have been open to her even fifty years earlier. The second half of the nineteenth century saw major commercialisation underway - the rise of the art dealer, the critic and the art historian, the launch of specialist and illustrated magazines, and an increasing curiosity on the part of the public about the lives of the famous artists. Painters became celebrities in their own right. There were many more patrons and private collectors, and crowds flocked to see all the big public exhibitions and galleries, with increasing sales not just to institutions but also to private homeowners, making the practice of some form of art a reasonable career prospect, at least for a few. But it was highly competitive, and for the few who became household names, there were many hundreds, men and women, who failed or simply gave up. As a woman, to try to join this struggle was particularly daunting and took a particular determination and willingness to make sacrifices. But Nelly was not to be discouraged.

Amidst all the excitement and controversy occasioned in the art world by movements such as the Pre-Raphaelites in the 1850s,the French Realists and then the Impressionists in the 1890s, the protests of women artists seeking to be taken seriously were often drowned out. Although by the middle of the nineteenth century there were at least six galleries in London holding regular open exhibitions, and several major regional locations such as the Walker Gallery in Liverpool, these were all generally felt to be discriminatory against females.

The opening of the Slade School in Gower Street in 1871, as part of University College, had created more opportunities for women to receive art training, as women were admitted and given access to 'half draped nudes' for figure drawing practice. But, as Nelly was only too aware, women were still failing to gain acceptance in the higher echelons of the art establishment. The blatant discrimination being shown was despite the obvious commercial success beginning to be enjoyed by female painters - in 1876, Ellen Clayton was able to fill two published volumes on the subject of 'English Female Artists'. In 1880, Louise Jopling noted gleefully that there was talk of limiting the female intake to the RA Schools because the women were winning too many prizes. But while women were struggling to gain entry to the RA, many talented men were being urged to avoid its 'stultifying discipline'.

Whether it was due to preference, or to lack of technical training, many of Nelly's female contemporaries avoided the more ambitious genres, instead carving out niches in domestic or maternal subjects, flower painting, pets and family portraits, or prettified rural scenes. They felt constrained to stick to what they had been taught, they were less willing to take risks, perhaps feeling that by choosing art as a career, they had already taken enough chances with their respectability. And they did not move with the times. In 1908 Anna Lea Merritt wrote, wistfully perhaps, of her feeling that she was left behind by developments in the art world '*I have not acquired the latest impressionist style, which so ably represents things as seen from a motor car at full speed. I have been obliged to sit for many hours daily in freezing wind, and later in burning sun, looking long and carefully at flower and leaf*'.

I can imagine that Nelly, lugging her portable easels, macintosh squares and umbrellas around Tuscany and the English countryside, would have felt the same. There is nothing impressionistic about Nelly's incredibly careful, detailed and timeless illustrations.

'You ask my views upon art as a profession for a girl of talent. It seems to me that if a girl has talent enough there is always room for her at the top, and this might apply to every profession. Every profession is overfull, art, as well as everything else, yet I believe that there is, and always will be, room for those with exceptional gifts. I however believe that no one is justified in taking up art as a profession who does not love it so devotedly that it is the irresistible impulse of life, apart entirely from the desire of gaining money.'
Louisa Starr (1845-1909), in an interview

'The Extra-Woman Problem'
In April 1895 The Strand magazine published an article by a Mr J. Holt Schooling of the Royal Statistical Society which examined the results of the National Census of 1891. He was particularly interested in the 'various random statements' being made at the time 'about the extra females in this country, such as "there are three women to every man", etc.' His calculations did indeed show that in every age group, women outnumbered the men, but often the difference was negligible, with only a one per cent difference in the numbers under the age of 20. But for ages 25 and older his figures showed that there were 1,116 females for every 1000 males, and as the population aged, this gap widened. The best bit about this excellent article, which appears to have been written with absolutely no hint of irony or humour, is the extraordinary conclusion Mr Holt Schooling draws. It is worth quoting in full, as I could not do it justice if I tried to paraphrase:

"The total number of extra women is over one million, and more than one quarter of the total excess is in respect of women aged 25 to 34, viz 268,291 surplus women at these ages. But it has occurred to me to make some test of quality as well as quantity, and I have gone carefully into the matter of the respective brain weights of man and women.....the male brain weighs on average 48 ounces and the female brain 43 ounces, giving an excess of five ounces of male brain....there is still a substantial predominance of male brain at the best period of life (20 to 54), despite the marked numerical excess of women at those same ages: in all there are in the same country 559 tons of male brain...in excess of female brain...and until these 559 tons of extra male brain become very appreciably fewer, it is not at all probable that the possessors of the heavier brains will be able to fully endorse certain current opinions as to the equality of men and women - even if it were desirable to bring to terms of equality personal-

ities that are and must always remain essentially different and non-equal."

It is good to know that the Royal Statistical Society had such a clear grasp of the issues. It was indeed the case that the surplus of women was becoming a serious social and economic problem of the Victorian period– exacerbated by male emigration, military service and a higher male mortality rate. In 1851, the census showed that there were 365,000 more women than men - and 29 per cent of women over 20 were unmarried. In total there were some 2.75 million unmarried women. The number continued to rise by 1861 there were three million unmarried women, and in 1871 3.25 million. Men, after all, had the liberty to put off marriage until they could afford to support a wife, and then to look around at what had most recently arrived on the market. Women rarely had any choice in the matter. So, even if women could never be equal to men, there was still an urgent need to educate these surplus women to be self-supporting. Especially as their brains were apparently so small.

Sketch for an invitation to a party at the Royal Academy drawn by Nelly Erichsen

Chapter Five: A Career Takes Off

In 1881, Griffith & Farran, a small London firm, published a children's story book called '*We Four*', written by a Mrs Reginald Bray and containing eighteen illustrations by a nineteen-year-old Nelly Erichsen. The book is an adventure story about a small motherless family, three girls and a boy, who have to leave the countryside they love and move to London. Reginald Bray, the author's husband, was a lawyer and was to become an eminent judge, but at the time his wife was writing children's books, he would have been a friend of Edgar Lucas. They had overlapped at Trinity College, Cambridge, and he now lived near Tooting on Wandsworth Common, making an easy connection between Nelly and Mrs Bray through Alice Lucas, Nelly's oldest sister and Edgar's wife. Like her contemporary Beatrix Potter, Nelly must have been practising the skills required to illustrate a book since she had first started to read and to draw, and now she was being given the opportunity to show what she could do. Amazingly I tracked down a copy of the American edition of this book in a second-hand bookshop in West Cornwall, Connecticut - the works of this small publishing house in St Paul's Churchyard had been advertised and sold across America by EP Dutton, a much larger firm. Nelly's illustrations are simple, naïve, with an intricate monogram signature, but there they are in print! Holding this small cloth bound volume in my hand felt special to me, I can imagine how very exciting this must have been for such a young woman, to see her name in print on the title page.

When she was not attending classes at the RA, Nelly took the opportunity to travel to broaden her portfolio. She spent at least one long summer in the early 1880s visiting Denmark, staying with the Suhr family in Copenhagen and among her relatives at their various country estates. She filled her sketchbooks with local scenes, children playing in the street, workers on her uncle's farm, fishermen at the docks. After months struggling through London fogs and

Illustration by Nelly Erichsen to "We Four"

winters, the fresh air of the countryside blew away the cobwebs and brought colour back into her life. She also travelled by train to the north of England, probably with the Macmillan family, particularly George and his new wife Margaret, and worked on the North Yorkshire coast. Sitting alone in the open air with her paints, brushes and easels, at such a young age, must have been a brave thing to do - many of her female contemporaries confined themselves to interior work, such as portraits, particularly of babies, dogs and cats, and still life studies. In an age when young girls were to be chaperoned and protected at all times, Nelly was not afraid to make herself conspicuous, and to cope with the vulnerability and exposure this entailed.

By 1883 she was sufficiently confident and competent to exhibit her work in public. Her first success was at the Royal Society of British Artists - a painting called *'Past Work'*, on sale for nine guineas, say £500 in today's money. Her second was at The Society of Women Artists - *'After the sun is set'* with a £6 price tag. The next year she again had a painting in the RSBA exhibition, entitled *'Midday Sun'*, and three at the SWA *'A weedy corner'*, *'A Neapolitan Boy'* and *'A green pool'*. That year also saw a major breakthrough, her first hanging at the RA Summer Exhibition, *'The Deserted Homeland'*. These titles suggest that at this stage Nelly was creating typical Victorian narrative paintings - rural subjects, landscapes with or without people, perhaps conveying a soft social message *'Past Work'* might have shown an elderly worker, perhaps now destitute, and *'The Deserted Homeland'* may have been drawn from Nelly's recent stay in war-torn Denmark. The social message is an important element in her work: *The Woman with the Hoe*, sketched for Tom Roberts, is highly realistic in its portrayal of the hardships of rural life.

Encouraged by her family and well-connected friends and capitalising on the first rate tuition she was receiving, Nelly soon became a prolific exhibitor at the Royal Academy Summer Exhibition, apparently concentrating on this venue rather than the lesser known galleries. Between 1884, only four years after her admission to the Schools, and 1897, she had sixteen paintings accepted and hung, at a time when many artists, particularly women, struggled to be seen at all. Furthermore, she was sufficiently established as an artist to work from rented studios - initially her work for the Summer Exhibition was submitted from an address in Lincoln's Inn Court, a popular location for many artists. This is evidence that she was determined to establish herself as a professional.

The family was supportive of this show of independence, proud of their daughter's prodigious talent, although it marked a departure from expected behaviour. After all, both her older sisters took the more conventional route of marrying and starting families, Alice living just round the corner from her mother in Tooting, and Dora eventually marrying a Danish relative and returning to Denmark. But by the 1880s Nelly was joining an ever-growing network of professional women artists who lived and worked apart from their families and struggled to be self-supporting.

This determination to forge her own independent career is even more striking when it is put against the backdrop of a family tragedy that must have shaken her confidence and created huge pressure to return to the family fold. Her younger brother Charles Cecil, just two years her junior, left Marlborough School in 1883 and chose not to go to Oxford or Cambridge but to pursue a career in the telegraph industry, following in his father's footsteps. In May 1882 he had been admitted into the Society of Telegraph Engineers and Electricians as a student and a few months later he set out for Japan on the steamship Seine, to work on the Great Northern Telegraph's operations there. It would have been a thrilling opportunity for such a young man, he was only eighteen years old. But just a year later the family learnt that he had died of fever on the ship on his way to Nagasaki, Japan, on Thursday 13th September 1883, and was buried there. Ironically, the news probably travelled rapidly to Tooting via the telegraph wires that Hermann's firm was installing. Sudden deaths of young men were all too common: within a few years the three families in Tooting were to lose Charles Erichsen, Charles and Samuel Lucas, and Arthur and Malcolm Macmillan, as well as the babies Alister and William Macmillan. But for this boy to have died so far from home and from his family must have been particularly hard to bear. I can only begin to imagine the shock and grief the family must have felt. Alice Lucas named her baby daughter, born that same year, Cecil Veronica, but that sad tribute must have been a tip of the iceberg of pain being endured. Charles' gravestone still survives in the Oura International Cemetery at Nagasaki cemetery, the archivist there tells me that it looks expensive, made from imported white alabaster with impressive iron fixtures. It seems strange to me to think of these gravestones surviving at Nagasaki, when 40 per cent of the buildings and so many thousands of people were destroyed in 1945. I wonder if Hermann felt to blame for sending his boy on such a journey, I wonder if Anna ever forgave him. Nelly was in her third year at the Royal Academy. At that age, just 21, she must have felt she was beginning to lead a separate life, but this would have pulled her back into the family as they struggled to come to terms with their loss.

Two years later Nelly left the family mourning behind and was emotionally ready to stride off into the world again. It was her close association with the Macmillan family which afforded her a truly significant opportunity to get her name known in literary and artistic professional circles, and she was still only 23. Macmillan's publishing house had first launched a monthly journal, Macmillan's Magazine, in 1859, and in 1883 it created a second title 'The English Illustrated Magazine'. This was also issued monthly and sold for a shilling, under the editorship of J Comyns-Carr. It was squarely aimed at the family market - nothing that would shock the Victorian matron, a mixture of fiction, travel and celebrity portraits, and lots of pictures. In 1886, a front-page featured article was 'A North Country Fishing Town', which Nelly had written and for which she had produced the artwork. The piece - eight pages of text and drawings - was well-reviewed when it was published, with praise for both the writing and the illustrations. Her portrait of one of the principal subjects of the article, a fisherman named Joe Verrill, was reproduced as the frontispiece of the magazine in an engraving by Octave Lacour, well-known in his trade. This was a great achievement for such a young woman: after all, this is a magazine that published original writing by Thomas Hardy and Henry James, and drawings by Walter Crane and Kate Greenaway. She must have been enormously proud to see herself in print and in this company.

Joe Verrill, from a drawing by Nelly Erichsen

Nelly sets her scene '*down on the very edge of the North Sea, thrust out on rocky ledges washed in winter by the salt foam*'. The tiny town she is describing, but never names, is Staithes, half way between Whitby and Redcar on the North Yorkshire coast, at that time a bustling town of 1400 people and 80 fishing boats. Her scene opens by plunging us into the action, set on the beach before dawn, a confusion of noise and lanterns as the fishermen prepare to set sail. During the day while the fleet is away, the young women gut fish or wash their linen in the stream and the young men prepare the nets and paint their boats. Then round the headland return three fishing boats and the population of the town rushes to greet the returning sailors. The fish buyers arrive, the sale is concluded, and the fish are prepared for despatch in barrels from the train station. The railway has only reached that far north for a year, before that the carrier's wagon had to take the fish twelve miles over the hills to Whitby. Nelly's piece is sentimental about the sturdy fisherfolk, but does not underplay the difficulties of their isolated and dangerous life. '*No people can be more kindly*'. I love to think of her getting up in the dark and wrapping herself up against the cold, carrying a lantern and standing on the shore with the wives to watch the boats go out. She was not one for sitting indoors painting flower arrangements or kittens, and her willingness to experience the life of her subjects and live among them shows how brave and independent she could be.

Nelly was staying a mile away from the sea, in a farm above the town, in the autumn and winter of 1885. '*The first few weeks of my stay were too much taken up in exploring the country round to leave time for more than casual intercourse with the human element of the place, but by the beginning of October, when I had settled down to work and my solitary easel was daily set up on the beach, or in the steep and somewhat evil smelling paths about the town, the old folks became interested, made hospitable advances, and before long had adopted the unfamiliar settler as almost one of themselves.*'

The first to approach her as she worked were the old gentlemen, too crippled by rheumatics to go out to sea, who wandered the town all day. They must have been fascinated by this attractive young woman from the south sitting at her work all day. The first to speak was Auld Billy. '*For a long time he simply stared like the others, but one day being I suppose cordially inclined, he suddenly thrust both hands into his pockets and uttered a mysterious guttural sound, very loud at first, but which gradually died away into a kind of feeble piping whistle. Then he took one hand out of his pocket and laying it gently on my shoulder said, in a tone of remonstrance and surprise, 'Thou hast a new jacket on, honey.' That was all. But he seemed perfectly satisfied that he had said quite the right thing, and toddled off chuckling softly to himself. After that we were fast friends and he never passed without emitting his inarticulate greeting, and making some friendly but totally irrelevant remark.'*

Nelly struck up a friendship with one part of the Verrill family (she noted that generations of intermarriage mean that there are only three surnames in the town) and was interested that they claimed to have Danish roots, a point she could use to forge a bond. Nelly was not always alone during her stay - the first time she had met Joe she and her friends, probably the younger generation of Macmillans, were wandering on the rocks, and had engaged Joe in conversation.

Nelly's tale is full of interest and she writes it well and humorously, capturing the precarious and dangerous existence of the community - the story of the mother and child nearly washed away when their house flooded, who had to be rescued from the roof of an overlooking house, the infant with a scar on his chin from when he was hit by a coble (a local fishing boat) blown through the window in a storm while he was sitting on his mother's lap. Nelly became a regular visitor to Joe Verrill's house at teatime for hot tea and griddle cakes, chatting to Joe's wife while the latter prepared supper. When Joe came home they ate and talked, while his family prepared and mended his nets, and Nelly read to them extracts from the local newspaper '*selected with some difficulty from the collection of hideous accounts of cannibalism at sea, wrecks and outlandish disasters of every description, that seem to fill its columns.'* Then Joe would walk Nelly back to the farmhouse where her simple supper was waiting. Nelly writes that she has run out of space in her article to describe the other characters she met. Perhaps she was hoping for a commission for a second piece. Throughout her prose is light and humorous, yet sympathetic to the folk she had met, never patronising. This is the first time I had heard Nelly's voice, and what a delight it was. So now Nelly effectively had two strings to her bow: she could try to sell her paintings, a precarious way to make a living, or she could earn more regular money writing and illustrating for the book and magazine trade. For a dozen or so years she explored both options.

For fourteen years, the Erichsen, Macmillan and Lucas family lived as neighbours and friends, sharing family happiness and griefs. The first change came in 1885 when Alexander Macmillan left London, taking with him his two older unmarried daughters, Nelly's friends Olive and Margaret, and of course his young wife Emma and their two small children, John and Mary. He donated his beloved house Knapdale to the Diocese of Southwark, rather than see it be pulled down and covered over by the speculative development which had changed so much of Tooting since he had first arrived there. He moved his family to a large country estate, Bramshott Chase, near Haslemere but the three families remained close, linked by the two marriages and the surrounding friendships.

By 1885, Nelly was busy and successful, working out of her studios in New Court, Lincoln's Inn, with four paintings at the Summer Exhibition: *'A Descendent of the Danes', 'No, truly, she is too disdainful', 'Briars and Brambles'* and *'A Study'*; one at the Institute of Painters in Oil Colours: *'Daughters of toil'*; and one at the SWA: *'Staithes'*. It is frustrating that no trace of any of these paintings remain, but not untypical of the fate of women's work at this time, probably made of cheap materials, not collected in galleries, not protected or preserved. My search to find these pictures continues and I would be delighted to hear from anyone who thinks they may own or have seen an Erichsen. The first painting may have been historical, but may just have easily have been a portrait of an Erichsen or Suhr relative with obvious Danish characteristics, blond hair, blue eyes. Perhaps it was a portrait to remember her brother Charles. The second exhibit takes its title from a line in 'Much Ado About Nothing': it is the phrase that opens the scene of the deception to be practised on Beatrice, so we can imagine the poor heroine hiding in the shrubbery, eavesdropping on Ursula and Hero as they teasingly discuss Benedick's supposed love for her. The works of Shakespeare were one of Nelly's passions, both her friends George Bernard Shaw and Thomas Lindsay mention having conversations about Shakespeare with Nelly.

Nelly was now attracting the attention of the critics, and published reviews allow us to catch glimpses of her work, to imagine what it might have been like. In January 1886, her painting *'Daughters of Toil'* was reviewed in the Cornish press, by a critic mysteriously convinced that all serious art at that time was likely to be of Cornish origin: *'Although the title does not say as much, the subject we assume to be an unmistakeably Cornish one. Two homely, honest-looking women, wearing characteristic 'gooks', the younger carrying in one hand a length of fishing net, in the other a string of pilchards. These latter look altogether too 'stagey', as also does the wooden pail, tub, or whatever it is the elder woman carries on her head this being an especially anti-Cornish feature. Otherwise there is a reality, and an air of general truthfulness about the picture, which we greatly like, which also indicates artistic powers considerably beyond the general run, and which, in connexion [sic] with Cornish subjects, we trust Miss Erichsen may yet employ to even still more successful pictorial account'.* Of course, it is always possible that Nelly had not painted this with Cornwall in mind, particularly as she had spent the previous autumn in North Yorkshire. It is much more likely that this is a painting from her time among the fishing community in Staithes.

Not long ago, one of Nelly's better known works from this period in her life came on to the market, and as the auction was being held at the other end of the country from us, in Scotland, we took a chance and bid for it 'sight unseen'. It arrived a few weeks later immaculately padded and packaged, and much larger than we had realised, some three feet wide by four feet tall. Until then we had made do with a small Bridgemans reproduction hanging above the spare bed, and I had assumed, without checking, that it would be the same size. This was 'Golden Hair', a striking pastel composition, showing a young girl with long blonde hair in a white dress in profile, at first sight she seems to be eating an apple. The girl's face is almost hidden by her long free flowing hair, the light is shining from behind her right shoulder, illuminating her sash and her sleeve, which is trimmed with fine lace. When you look closer, it is a lemon she is holding, and she has an orange in her other hand. The quality of the pastel is breathtaking - there is no doubt that Nelly's art has the power to summon strong emotion, and this is another image which has often been commercially reproduced. The price tag on this when originally exhibited at the Royal Society of British Artists in 1888 was £20, a sign that Nelly was becoming more ambitious, and more commercially successful.

After we carefully unpacked the picture it was immediately obvious that time had not been good to it. Behind the glass we could see that the sketch had several small tears in the paper. Although these were not so obvious that it spoiled the image, we felt we owed it to Nelly to see if we could get it restored, concerned to prevent any further damage. And so we found the patient and talented Lisu, ten miles away from us over the Cotswold hills, working out of a huge sunlit studio full of giant presses, inky bottles and jars. In the next few weeks we learnt more about the mysterious problems of pastel deterioration and decay than we probably wanted to know and none of it was good news. Under the glass, the condition was even worse than we had imagined. There was mould on the surface, and the paper had become brittle and acidic. At some point someone had tried to stabilize the original by attaching it to a canvas backing and then nailing it to a wooden stretcher underneath the frame, and that made the task of repairing the tears even harder. It needed some retouching in places, but the worst issue undoubtedly was to discover whether it could be separated from its canvas backing. Throughout Lisu was unbelievably patient, and explained every step and every option to us in great detail. I got the distinct impression that for every hour she worked on the project, she had worried and thought about it for at least two.

The first step was to cut the pastel off the stretcher, above where it had been nailed to the sides, and carefully separate it from the canvas. Luckily it had not been glued down. Then she was able to clean the surface mould, sterilize and fix the surface. The tears had to be mended from underneath using wheat starch paste and Japanese tissue. Then the hardest part of all - to re-line the picture. As the surface was too delicate to be touched, this had to be done by laying the canvas gently on top of the lining and placing the dampened sandwich onto an enormous suction table to pull the pieces of paper together and hold them flat as they dried. This was to ensure that the pastel made contact evenly with the lining with no bubbles or bumps. It took all night to get it dry and set, over 20 hours, with Lisu checking on it during the night. It finally dried at 5am. She then retouched with Sennelier pastels, in itself a historic tribute as Sennelier first started grinding colours to sell to Parisian artists at his studio on Quai Voltaire, just a few steps away from the Ecole des Beaux Arts, in 1887.

There are many places you can find a reproduction of Golden Hair on the web. Most recently it has been posted on Pinterest by a young man living in Tbilisi, Georgia, labelled by him as the 'Young Cersei Lannister', as he thinks she looks like the scheming, megalomaniacal character from Game of Thrones. I suppose that art speaks to every generation in a new way, and if Nelly's art can strike a chord across so many cultures and generational gaps, and in such a surprising way, I am glad that in Lisu we found someone who could help us preserve it with so much love and care for at least the next century.

Now Nelly discovered that she had a real talent for portraiture, and her family and friends were the immediate beneficiaries. In the Royal Academy Summer Exhibition of 1888, Nelly exhibited her first named portrait, *'Miss Margaret Macmillan'*. Margaret, the oldest daughter of her family neighbour Alexander Macmillan, was five years older than Nelly, and was shortly to marry Louis Dyer, an American Classics scholar. The painting was described as 'promising' in a review.

The following year, 1889, Nelly's art hung alongside that of the well-known Louise Jopling at the Grosvenor Gallery, in an exhibition of Women Pastellists. The 'Women's Penny Paper' published a review by Bacheliere…. *'Miss Nellie (sic) Erichsen sends a very nicely done portrait of a good-natured looking old gentleman.'*

This may well be the portrait of Canon Atkinson, now held by The Pannett Art Gallery in Whitby. Nelly was now moving easily between different media, oils, pen and ink, and pastels, and was equally successful in both. But the end of the year was marked by more family sadness: in November Nelly's little niece Estelle, Alice's youngest daughter, died, aged only 18 months. Poor Nelly sat by the little girl's deathbed and drew her pretty face, coloured in pastels, nestled against the pillows, for Alice and Edgar to keep. I cannot imagine a harder or more heartbreaking task. The family still own this portrait.

Estelle Lucas, deathbed portrait

Estelle's death was not the only tragedy to hit the three families in 1889. In July of that year, their world was shaken by the mysterious disappearance of Alexander's oldest son, Malcolm, while climbing Mount Olympus in Greece. Unlike his younger brother George, Malcolm had never settled to the family publishing business, and had never married, but was known to be very clever and widely read, with a passion for all things Hellenic. He was 37 when he died and no trace was ever found of the body or of any of his possessions. It was assumed that he had been murdered by local brigands, who were known to be haunting the area at that time. It was a terrible blow to Alexander in the final years of his life. One cannot help but wonder whether the complete disappearance of a man with 'Hellenic passions' who never married, leaving no trace at all, might not be more suggestive of someone who wanted to vanish for his own reasons. The tragedy pulled Nelly even closer to the Macmillan family, even after they left Tooting. At the time of the 1891 census she was staying with them and a large family party at Bramshott Chase. She was a particular friend of Olive Macmillan, now Mrs Norman MacLehose, who was close to her in age and staying at the house at the same time with her husband and small children. They had sad experiences in common now, both had lost a beloved and close brother abroad.

In 1890, Nelly exhibited work at 'The Society of British Pastellists' at the Grosvenor Gallery. The work was reviewed in 'The Musical World' as follows: *'...ever so high in the air, we find the 'Allotment Gardens' by Miss Nelly Erichsen (no 91), of which the colour and the composition are, to say the least, creditable. Since the painters of such scenes most generally fail in one of these features, when not in both, this instance of artistic knowledge should not go by unnoticed.'* This level of critical sarcasm, frequently aimed at women artists, was not uncommon, particularly around the lesser exhibitions.

On 6 December 1890, just three days before Nelly's 28th birthday, Hermann Erichsen died, aged just 62. Not a very great age, even in those days. He died a relatively wealthy man, with a personal estate valued at nearly £11,000, or just over £1 million in today's money, despite the fact that in the late 1870s he had suffered some personal financial misfortune which had required him to go through bankruptcy proceedings. But his reputation had survived untarnished and his obituary listed his directorships including the Chairmanship of The China and Japan Telegraph Company, and board positions in The Tramways Union Company, The Central Borneo Company and The Telephone Company of Ireland. He was decorated by the Danish Government with the Silver Cross of the Order of the Knight of Dannebrog.

Of Hermann's six children, by 1890 only Alice had married and was living in a villa called Netherfield on nearby Tooting Bec Road with Edgar and their five surviving small children, four girls - Rosamund, Phyllis, Cecil Veronica and Helga, and their only boy Frank. His wife Anna stayed on in Grove Cottage for more than ten years, surrounded by the rest of the family including, from time to time, Nelly. But for all the suburban development of Tooting in the 1880s and 1890s, the creation of the Public Library, the Camera Club, the Conservative Association, the lawn tennis and the cycling, the writer and critic Walter Besant made the point that south of the Thames there was no cultural centre no university, no theatres, no clubs, no grand public buildings, and only one picture gallery of any note, in Dulwich. *'It must surely be a disadvantage', he wrote, 'for a young man who would pursue a career in art not to live among people who habitually talk of art and think of art'.* If it was a disadvantage for a young man, it must have been crippling for a young woman. Around this time, perhaps tasting freedom after the death of her father, Nelly moved across the river to Chelsea.

Nelly took a lease on Number 6, Trafalgar Studios in Manresa Road, just off the Kings Road. This was a purpose-built block of 15 units, constructed only 12 years earlier, and full of artists, male and female, just like her. It must have been exciting and liberating to be so independent, and yet part of a community of like-minded professionals in London's art world. Here she was right in the heart of a community of young artists, many of them women, and right next door to a particular friend, Dora Noyes. Dora, christened Theodora, was one of three sisters who never married and yet lived a full and busy life. The three sisters traveled often to Italy, spoke Italian fluently and were fascinated by Italian culture. Dora had been admitted to the Royal Academy Schools one year after Nelly, another recommendation of John Sparkes, so they had been friends for some years. Both Dora and her sister Mary signed the 1883 petition along with Nelly to beg permission for women to study nudes.

Hermann's death did not seem to slow down Nelly's output and it was from the studios in Chelsea, perhaps inspired by her new friends, that she submitted *'The Street End'* to the 1891 RA Summer Exhibition, as well as one of her better-known works, *'The Magic Crystal'*, which still survives today, having changed hands at Christies in 2005. It is very different from anything else of hers I have seen, distinctly Pre-Raphaelite in style, and, it has to be said, my least favourite of her paintings, although the very poor reproduction on the web may do it a disservice. Germaine Greer writes '*The Pre-Raphaelite movement attracted women…. the archaic postures, with bodies obscured by period costumes, backgrounds simplified by patterning, were well within the competence of women whose training had been strong on patterning and portraiture and weak on construction, movement and dynamic.'* The two figures in *The Magic Crystal* are stiffly posed, with none of the movement and grace seen in Nelly's pastoral canvases but it demonstrates her willingness to experiment, and, I suspect, to produce work which she hoped would be commercially successful. But it does not do justice to her talents for realism or beauty. The critic Bacheliere, however, writing in the Woman's Herald, thought it was 'excellently rendered.' Other women hanging at the Summer Exhibition this year included Anna Nordgren, Louisa Starr, Margaret Dicksee, Anna Lee Merritt and Kate Perugini.

Nelly was to exhibit eight more times at the Summer Exhibition over the next six years. One of the few paintings known to have survived, and probably her largest canvas, was *Going Home,* 1892. Four feet deep by six feet wide, this is a beautiful rural scene, set in a quiet village at sunset, the plough horse team being led past a churchyard with a distinctive lychgate, two girls walking home from the corn field, a sheaf of wheat under one arm, a small child with striking blonde curls dawdling alongside. This painting survives, and has changed hands several times. In its lyrical beauty, the painting could be accused of romanticising rural life, but surely she can be excused for creating such a stunning piece of work. At this time, it was common for the huge new populations of townsfolk to feel romantic, wistful, about country life. Buying this size of blank canvas would have been an extremely ambitious undertaking for Nelly, it was unusual for female artists to attempt such large projects. I wonder if she spent part of a gift from her father's estate on buying the canvas. Even Lady Elizabeth Butler's famous and elaborate war paintings, such as *Quatre Bras*, were little or no bigger than this.

Over the next few years, Nelly successfully submitted some more family portraits to the RA including three of Alice Lucas's daughters: Cecil, Phyllis and Rosamund Lucas. She had a particular gift for pastel portraits of children, and her extended family were the beneficiaries of this talent. They have survived handed down through the generations: little Frank Lucas in his sailor suit is hanging on a wall in a doctor's house in Sheffield, and although George and Helen Brimley Johnson recently went to auction, Helga Lucas is on a descendant's wall in a Dorset cottage. And poor little Estelle has been kept safe in a family attic in London, perhaps a bit too sad to hang on a wall, but still with her great nephew looking after her.

Nelly's paintings and pastels draw on many typical Victorian feminine themes children, pastoral scenes, quotations from literature. But her work, never insipid, seems most powerful when she paints the country life, and the family and friends she loves. Her portraits are truly stunning. One such is the pastel portrait of the Reverend Canon Atkinson of Whitby, a portrait hanging today in the Pannal Art Gallery in Whitby. Atkinson was well known to the Macmillan family, and Nelly must have met him and painted this portrait while staying with George and his wife Margaret at Danby Hall. We tracked it down and went to see it one snowy day while we still lived in Yorkshire, and had the pleasure of sharing what we knew of Nelly's life and her connections with Atkinson and the Macmillans with the staff. This was the first time we had seen The North Country magazine piece, shown to us by the particularly helpful and welcoming curator. Back then we thought it might be the first of several such expeditions to see Erichsens hanging on gallery walls. But we never found another. The portrait was bought and displayed in Whitby because Atkinson was a local hero, not because Erichsen was thought a collectible artist.

Nelly painted many scenes of rural life, of which a few survive today, we catch occasional glimpses on the web, and often with confusing titles. For instance there is a painting or pastel which changed hands somewhere under the name of 'Cheesemaking', but possibly it is also known as 'In the Dairy', and another called 'Fishwives'. A lovely pastel of an old man returning home from the fields with his scythe over his shoulder, "A Hard day's labour', recently passed through an auction house in Scotland and we were lucky enough to buy it. Nelly's work did not always get a mention in the major reviews of the bigger exhibitions, but when it did, the review was usually complimentary: *"'Out of the Depths have I cried unto thee' - a group of life-sized figures giving thanks in church, evidently after a shipwreck. Rare thing, the members of the congregation are nearly all men. Her work, like that of Miss Anna Nordgren, seems to show all the boldness of the North in its execution"* (Woman's Herald, May 1892 Women at the Royal Academy, review by 'Bacheliere'). This is an interesting review, implying as it does that Nelly's Danish roots might be evident in her style, and that made it distinctive and attractive. Nordgren had been born in Sweden, and was some fifteen years older than Nelly. She was certainly better known than Nelly, but with a very similar number of paintings hung at the RA Summer Exhibition.

By the mid-nineties it seemed that the tide had turned and that women were finding it slightly easier to get their paintings displayed at the major galleries.

The Englishwoman's Review in the summer of 1894 remarked '*The critics have decided that the Academy this year is even worse than usual, but from the women's point of view it is one of the best and most promising that has been noticed in this Review. Women are more largely represented and their canvases better hung than hitherto, and many of their pictures have attracted well-merited attention.'* The review specifically mentions Nelly: '*Flower of the Elder' is the best of Miss Erichsen's three exhibited pictures. Face and flowers are realistic, and fiercely painted, harsh and almost too strong in colour; but the faults are on the right side in this as in her other pictures, and there is none of that femininity so often noticeable in the manipulation of women's work.'* All these reviews of women's art seem sadly reminiscent of Dr Johnson's remark about the preaching of women, which reminded him of a dog walking on its hind legs 'It is not done well; but you are surprised to find it done at all.'

In the 1841 census, 278 women in England described themselves as artists but by 1871 this had risen nearly fourfold to 1,069. The remarkably high level of talent being demonstrated by these women, and the emergence of their professional aspirations, became a subject much debated in the press. In 1857 Barbara Leigh Smith (later Bodichon), an early campaigner for women's rights, published 'Women and Work': *'there is no reason at all why a woman should not build a cathedral if she has the instruction and the genius'*. However, it must have taken enormous reserves of self-confidence and bravery to persist in a world where women were expected to take the subservient role in family and economic relationships.

In 1859, Bodichon's friend Jessie Boucherett, and her other friends in the group of campaigners know as the Langham Place Ladies, formed the Society for Promoting the Education of Women ('SPEW"). A SPEW pamphlet of 1879 set out *'to show that it was a matter of necessity that nearly half of the women in the United Kingdom should maintain themselves, and that women, properly trained, may become useful members of the body politic.'* There was a crying need to widen the employment possibilities for middle class women beyond those of governess, ladies' companion or seamstress all of which were hopelessly underpaid. It was possible to make significant money as a professional artist men such as Millais and Val Prinsep became very wealthy indeed (in a good year, Millais earned as much as £30,000). The commercial art world was given a further boost by the patronage of Queen Victoria and Prince Albert - it became fashionable to collect art, and to patronise British artists in particular.

Anna Lea Merritt, an artist who painted Bodichon several times, wrote sadly about the difficulties posed for women artists - in 1900 in an article in Lippincott's Magazine she wrote *'the chief obstacle to a woman's success is that she can never have a wife'*. The difficulties for women wishing to make a career in art were never-ending. The commercial need to cultivate a following by producing a regular flow of work did not suit women artists, whose career trajectory was likely to be more erratic than a man's. Other problems particularly affecting women would include a lack of moral or financial support in some of the more traditional Victorian families, the cost of raw materials, minimal access to professional models, the difficulty and mess created by working from home without a studio (as opposed to, say, professional writing, which can be put away in a moment when visitors come to call) right down to the obstacles of using public transport. Louisa Starr's daughter, writing in the twentieth century, commented that Louisa's father *'did not like Louisa going alone to the RA and getting out of the buses quite unprotected, but he knew that [her mother] had other ideas on the subject!'*. No wonder that some of the only professional women painters who broke through the barriers came from artistic families, or were married to artist husbands. Without these supportive males, the art world could appear dauntingly masculine *'the guilds and brotherhoods often had an all-male, pipe-smoking style of camaraderie which made life awkward.'* [2] The late nineteenth century invented the idea of an artistic Bohemia, rejecting class division and other social mores. But the more unconventional it became, the more daunting it was for Victorian women. Women had to take a huge risk to reject 'ladyhood' to become artists.

Gertrude Massey had just managed to get her foot on the lowest rung of art training, when her father died, leaving her in dire financial straits. A friend of her father funded one further term at art school, but as she wrote *'If I lunched, I went short of paints - if I bought paints, I went short of lunch.'* She scraped a living by painting greetings cards and calendars, and began to have some success selling portraits, but it was not until she married Henry Massey in 1890 that she received the help she needed : *'I owe practically all my art training to him.'* She eventually became a highly successful painter of miniature portraits, working on commission, often for the Royal Family, and completed over 800 such paintings in all.

Many single women would have struggled to make ends meet on what they could make from their art. At the end of the 1880s, the artist Sophia Beale

---

[2] *Women in the Victorian Art World ed. Clarissa Campbell-Orr*

Golden Hair

Canon Atkinson

Going Home

Magic Crystal

wrote to Millicent Fawcett *'I pay rent and taxes £130 - I have nothing but what I earn by painting, teaching and writing, and naturally have to work exceedingly hard.'* When Nelly's father died, his money all went to support his wife, so Nelly had no obvious source of private income, and she never had a home of her own - she was constantly moving between friends and relations' houses or boarding houses. Other women in her position set up home together to share their meagre resources, offering financial and, crucially, emotional support to each other. *'Women could do together what it was hard or impossible to do singly: in particular they could travel abroad or live away from the parental home.'* [3]

Distinct connections were now drawn by commentators between women's success as artists, and the growing campaign for political equality. On 7 May 1892 the leading article in the Woman's Herald was the defeat, by only a small majority, in the House of Commons the previous week of the Women's Suffrage bill. The review of the RA Summer exhibition, in the same newspaper, began *'When two women have eight pictures in the Academy and one seven, when in the very first room of the gallery there greets one full length portraits by the hand of a woman, one thinks of the smallness of Wednesday's majority and is fired into action full of hope.'* Progress was being made, but it was painfully slow for women hoping to be treated as equals in the professional art world.

Nelly's paintings usually sold for perhaps eight or ten guineas a piece, not really enough to make a living. So not surprisingly by the early 1890s she was making further experiments with book and magazine illustrations as an additional source of income - and by 1900 this seems to have been her major occupation, although she continued to take commissions for portraits and painted family members. After 1897 there are no more exhibits by Nelly at the Summer Exhibition or any reviews of her art elsewhere. She was only 35 yet seems to have put her paintbrushes and pastels away, only occasionally getting them out for portraits of young nephews and nieces.

Later in life Nelly's friends wrote that she suffered from depression and it always had an impact on her ability to work. Did she give up painting because she discovered that editing, translating and illustrating books was easier or more profitable, after all it required no initial outlay for paints or canvases, and publishers could be persuaded to pay in advance. Did she get discouraged that her exhibition successes were not translating into a stream of commissions? Having such a great talent and then letting it lapse might seem sad, even

---

[3] *'Women in the Victorian art world' ed. Clarissa Campbell Orr*

cowardly. On the other hand, she had chosen a different sort of life which offered more freedom, more opportunities. For the next couple of years as she built her reputation as a book illustrator she worked at a phenomenal pace, travelling and drawing all over Europe, hardly lacking in either energy or determination. Was this her choice, her new passion? Or a way of masking her disappointment that her paintings had not brought her fame and fortune, or even a regular, reliable income?

Luckily, by the 1890s, there had been major advances in the freedoms allowed to middle class women attempting to live independently. Society began to accept that unmarried women could travel on buses, trams and trains without chaperones, they could enter restaurants and stay in hotels, they could shop in department stores and establish their own clubs and societies. But it could still be very hard for some women to assert independence. As the African explorer Mary Kingsley (born the same year as Nelly, and a friend of the Macmillan and Johnson families) was to write *'My life can be written in a very few lines…it arises from my having no personal individuality of my own whatsoever. I have always lived in the lives of other people, whose work was heavy for them…it never occurs to me that I have any right to do anything more than now and then sit and warm myself at the fire of real human beings.'* Mary suffered from an over-bearing father and a highly conservative family, but after the death of her parents she managed to escape to another continent in search of adventure.

Nelly may have failed to climb onto the bandwagon of financial success as a painter, but the other developments of the late Victorian age - the explosive growth of the book publishing industry, the massive popularity of the illustrated periodical magazine, and the expanding middle classes' thirst for travel and tales from abroad were all to open up new possibilities for paid employment. *' She lived on the cusp of a new century near the end of the elderly Victoria's rule at a jagged moment when women were emerging in fits and starts from the clutter of artifacts and expectations that had made the Victorian parlour so stifling.'* [4] As the youngest and the unmarried Erichsen daughter, and having given up on a career as a professional painter, Nelly could easily have retired to spend her spinsterhood in the parental home, looking after her widowed mother, and playing the role of the universal maiden aunt. But she chose to keep her independence, to find other sources of work and to travel. It was a brave and potentially lonely decision.

---

[4] *A Voyager Out, the Life of Mary Kingsley. Taken from the Introduction by Rosellen Brown.*

'Going Home', our favourite of all Nelly's work, now belongs to us, we bought it as a late and highly extravagant wedding present to ourselves at an auction at Sothebys in 2009, and it hangs in our double-height hall in pride of place. It is a stroke of luck that we even have a space big enough to show it off - at four foot by six foot it was clearly not designed to hang in a typical Victorian terrace or mansion flat, of the sort where Nelly's family all lived. Just getting it put up was a labour of love and of engineering, involving several strong men, scaffolding, ropes and pulleys and a process of balancing on bannisters and planks that I could not bear to watch. We had it specially lit and it certainly makes a conversation piece. For many years we asked guests to vote on whether it was rural England or Denmark. The thatched cottage, the lychgate, all seemed to Peter to say England, but the children are so blonde, and the women's elaborate white bonnets so distinctive and unusual that I thought it might just as easily have been a village in Denmark. And we continued to have this family debate for some seven or eight years, with me scouring the web for pictures of traditional Danish headgear, for example, to try to prove my theory. Then one evening the whole story was solved, in less than an hour. Peter had been skimming through the copies of Nelly's letters to her friend Thomas Lindsay written in the early 1900s, and in the middle of a debate the two writers were having as to the identity of William Shakespeare, as mildly topical among certain literary folk then as it is now, he had come across a particularly sweet passage. Nelly was very clear on where she stood on the subject:

'After spending six months once at Welford-on Avon, a delicious village four miles out of Stratford, and finding 3 Jakes (Jaques) and 2 Audreys in the village, and hearing the people express their shrewd ungainly thoughts in the language of Corin and Silvius, I have never had a particle of doubt. I was present there too at a gravedigger scene, as like the one in Hamlet as peas to peas. From my campstool in the churchyard I overheard the two grave-diggers at work close by my side. My attention was fixed on my palette and canvas and at first their voices reached me only as a murmur. Then finally a skull (only I hardly think it had 'lain 9 years in the earth') was thrust on a spade just under my nose and upon my word the gravedigger apostrophied it so like his prototype in Denmark that I could not but exclaim "Alas poor Yorick!'. The fact is that all that part of Warwickshire breathes of Shakespeare not only as the burger of Stratford but as the poet, and intelligent residence there leaves one without a doubt. The names of the villages come in to The Taming of the Shrew, the dialect of the country folk is that of the clowns, and so on ad infinitum.

'The cottage where I lived had a meadow called Quinneys Ley and it had belonged to Shakespeare's Quinney. The other meadows were called Abraham's Bosom and The Green-Field - all good names!....'

So, Peter said, what do we know about Welford-on Avon? I looked it up, and there in front of me on my laptop, quite extraordinarily, was a photograph of the lychgate from our painting. Welford is a small pretty village just a few miles from Stratford, and turns out to have been a popular and well-known spot for Victorian artists with its rural setting by the river, its thatched roofs, its black and white half-timbered cottages, and, of course, its medieval lychgate. The date of Going Home, exhibited at the RA in 1892, suggests that Nelly spent some time staying here in 1891, the year after her father died. If she really came for six months, as she told Lindsay, she was quite determined to escape responsibility for looking after her widowed mother.

The next day we drove to Welford, somewhere we had never been before, and it turned out to be just 20 miles from where we lived. It is still a remarkably picturesque village, despite the main road through the middle of it, and we quite easily found the church with its lychgate which seemed to be in remarkably good condition and exactly as painted by Nelly. She had taken some liberties with the composition of the picture, as it is impossible to sit where she would have sat across the road to do her sketches and not include the village church, but the main focus of her painting is the interaction between the people and the carthorses, the buildings around are deliberately vague. However, she must have sat on the little patch of grass which is still there, outside some thatched cottages which certainly have not changed in the last 150 years, and drawn the scene that hangs on our wall.

Was there any record of Nelly's stay? My next step was to track down the Welford and Weston Local History Society and I received a wonderfully warm and enthusiastic response from Brad, the Chairman, who I met with his wife Anne in their beautiful double-fronted Georgian house in the village. Another delightful encounter that Nelly had created for me - yet again I was poring over old records and photographs in a stranger's house, and then wandering the rather damp lanes of Welford, a mecca for Victorian artists, wondering where Nelly had stayed. Surprisingly, the lychgate which caused us to say, 'that clinches it, this is the place', actually only dated from 1969, less than 50 years ago. The original that Nelly painted dated from the end of the 1300s but in 1966 it had to be dismantled because it was unsafe. Fortunately for all concerned when it was rebuilt in 1969 it was a careful replica, exact in measurements and design. The timbers were apparently selected with great care from slow growing 300 year old trees and chosen for 'character, strength and limitation of splits'.

Illustration by Nelly Erichsen, for The Idler Magazine, Vol. XIV

Chapter Six: The 1890s
The Rise Of The New Woman

'I have sought to put on the stage for the first time (as far as I know) the highly educated, capable, independent young woman of the governing class as we know her today, working, smoking, preferring the society of men to that of women simply because men talk about the questions that interest her and not about servants and babies, making no pretence of caring much about art or romance, respectable through sheer usefulness and strength, and playing the part of the charming woman only as the amusement of her life, not as its serious occupation.'
George Bernard Shaw, writing to a friend about his play "Mrs Warren's Profession", 1896

In the early 1890s, perhaps liberated by the death of her father, Nelly began to assert herself even more strongly as a self-supporting professional woman. Spending six months in lodgings in a mini-artists' colony in Welford-on-Avon was part of this process. She was turning 30 and had completed her studies at the Royal Academy with two major prizes tucked under her belt. She had exhibited a string of paintings at the prestigious Summer Exhibition and elsewhere, several of which had earned appreciative, if not effusive, reviews in national art journals. Perhaps even more importantly, she had a growing social confidence, derived from her relationships with the inter-connected Macmillan and Lucas families, and she was ready to make her own life. She looked for the moral support to be garnered from friendships with other like-minded single women, and with wider circles of men and women enjoying each others' company on the grounds of intellectual and common interest, rather than participating in some matrimonial speed-dating circus. She was now living at a time where unmarried women began to enjoy unchaperoned friendships with the opposite sex, could live alone, travel on trains at home and abroad, use bicycles, eat out, and join societies and clubs. The world was changing fast and Nelly took full advantage of these new freedoms.

Through her neighbours in Tooting, Nelly had become close to a family of Cambridge intellectuals, relatives by marriage of the Macmillans, called the Johnsons, and in particular one Fanny Johnson, at one time headmistress of Bolton School for Girls, and her younger brother Reginald Brimley Johnson, with whom Nelly would work on several books as an illustrator and then as an editor and translator. The three Johnson sisters, Harriet, Fanny and Alice were all highly independent and politically active, as well as supporters of the campaign for women's rights. Around the same time, one of Nelly's new artist friends, Bertha Newcombe, introduced her to a whole new world of Fabian socialist intellectuals, with very different ideas about society and morality. In particular she was to meet the predatory bachelor George Bernard Shaw.

The 1890s is the decade in which interest in 'The New Woman' as a concept captured the public's imagination, dramatised on the stage by Shaw and in novels such as the very shocking 'The Woman Who Did', by Grant Allen, and Gissing's 'The Odd Women'. A few years later, 'Ann Veronica', by HG Wells and EM Forster's 'Howards End' would draw the same portraits for an even wider reading audience. These characters were depictions of women who were educated and politically active, who struggled to be self-supporting, and who were prepared to take sexual risks. Nelly's friend Alice Johnson had been one of the first five students admitted to Newnham College Cambridge when it opened in 1871 and went on to become a biologist, just like Ann Veronica herself. Somewhere between the 1850s, when Barbara Bodichon and her friends were campaigning primarily to be taken seriously as potential wage earners and professionals, and the 1890s, the challenge seemed to have broadened, if not switched, to the possibility of the New Woman as an intellectual partner for a man and a sexually active creature, either inside or outside the bonds of marriage.

Another such woman was Bertha Newcombe, a few years older than Nelly, and as one of the first women admitted to study at the Slade School of Art, one who already knew her way around London and its art world. From what we know of her personality and subsequent history, she was certainly independent and forceful of character, prepared to live her life right at the boundaries of what was acceptable for a young unmarried woman. She was well-placed to join the London circle of artists, writers and political thinkers, her entrepreneurial father Samuel having taken a house in Cheyne Walk, a prestigious address close to the Thames in Chelsea. Bertha lived there right through the last decade of the nineteenth century until the First World War. She was also secure financially, as on his death her father left a substantial estate of some £25,000, so she was more than capable of supporting herself. Meanwhile she and Nelly were working in studios only a few hundred yards apart off the Kings Road in Chelsea, exhibiting at the same galleries, and both producing work which avoided the trap of appearing too feminine, too easy for the critics to scorn. Bertha was politically aware and would become an active supporter of the women's suffrage campaign, although never a suffragette. In many ways her life ran in parallel courses to Nelly, and as Nelly accepted her friendship, I believe she accepted her way of life.

There are no surviving images of Bertha in the 1890s, but her friend the Fabian writer and campaigner Beatrice Webb described her thus: *'She is petite and dark, about forty years old but looks more like a wizened girl than a fully-developed woman. Her jet-black hair heavily fringed, half-smart, half-artistic clothes, pinched aquiline features and thin lips, give you a somewhat unpleasant impression though not wholly inartistic. She is bad style without being vulgar or common or loud - indeed many persons ... would call her 'lady-like' but she is insignificant and undistinguished.'* Back in the early 1890s, Bertha had joined the growing Fabian Socialist movement, and in 1892 this led her into a life-defining experience. She was asked to paint a portrait of one of the movement's leading lights, George Bernard Shaw, and the painting was to be known as 'The Platform Spellbinder'. Shaw was certainly impressed with the painting, and with the artist, but poor Bertha fell heavily in love with her subject, a mistake that threatened her position within Shaw's circle, and a distraction that held her back professionally. She nursed this passion for many years although it seems never to have been reciprocated, despite the attempts of mutual friends at various times, to promote the match. Bertha, believing herself to have been jilted, would never fully acknowledge Shaw's later marriage to Charlotte Payne-Townsend and she resisted the couple's subsequent attempts to befriend her.

In the early 1890s, Shaw was becoming well known as a public speaker, critic and pamphleteer, but he was not yet famous as a playwright. His first public success, *Arms and the Man,* would not be staged until 1894. The portrait Bertha painted of Shaw is reproduced in several places, including in Shaw's *'Sixteen Self-sketches'*, published in 1949, with the unkind caption

'Portrait by Bertha Newcombe, spellbound'. For many years the painting was lost, believed to have been destroyed in the Second World War, but in 2012 was discovered during a spring clean at Ruskin College, Oxford, and was last heard of hanging in the Labour Party Headquarters in London.

We know exactly when Shaw first met Nelly. On 24th April 1893, Shaw noted in his diary *'…went to Bertha Newcombe's where I found Wallas* [Graham Wallas, a prominent Fabian] *and a Miss Erichsen who attracted me considerably. They went presently and I was left with Bertha, to whom I read a bit of my play'.* Bertha should have taken the hint: the play on which Shaw was working at that time was 'The Philanderer'. Three weeks later, Shaw made up a party with Nelly, Wallas and Bertha to visit a beauty spot near Haywards Heath. He met Nelly and Wallas at Victoria Station and they travelled down by train. Bertha and Charlotte McCausland, another painter, met them off the train and they walked to Sherlock's Cottage to dine. *'Then we went out and sat under a tree for a time. Finally we started for Three Bridges. We soon left Wallas and Miss McCausland behind; and soon after Miss Erichsen sat down and said she would wait for Bertha's return. Bertha came on with me and put me into the High Road for the station.'* One can imagine that Nelly felt the need, or took the hint, to let her unhappy friend Bertha have time alone with the maddeningly indecisive Shaw.

By 1895, Shaw was under pressure on all fronts to marry Bertha. The Easter of 1895 was spent in a party including the Webbs and Bertha at the Beachy Head Hotel, near Eastbourne. Bertha had been specifically invited by Beatrice Webb who believed she would make a suitable wife for Shaw. But Shaw was not to be bullied or shamed. In fact, the most significant event of this holiday in his own eyes, according to his letters, appears to have been his attempt to master the bicycle *'after a desperate struggle, renewed on two successive days, I will do twenty yards and a destructive fall against any professional in England. My God, the stiffness, the blisters, the bruises, the pains in every twisted muscle, the crashes against the chalk road that I have endured and at my age too. But…. I will not be beaten by that hellish machine.'*

There are no mentions of Nelly in Shaw's diaries for the next couple of years, but they must have stayed in touch. On 4 February 1896 he visited Nelly in her studios in Manresa Road to read from his latest draft of 'You Never Can Tell' but was annoyed to find that she had with her a companion her friend from Cambridge, Fanny Johnson. Shaw clearly thought that Bertha had told Nelly that he was not to be trusted alone with women. He pondered the event for several days before writing to Bertha: *'Your attempt to discredit me with NE has had a most ludicrous upshot. On Monday she invited me to afternoon tea. I washed and brushed myself most carefully and went. When I got there, lo! A chaperon, a sly little woman who was drawing N on millboard. N's introduction clearly meant 'I am sorry to disappoint your evident hope of finding me alone; but I have no intention of trusting you to that extent.'. Naturally our constraint was fearful. Presently the little woman began to smile slyly as she surveyed us with confidential good nature. She hurried up the tea, and then, before we could intervene, nodded at us in a 'I know you want to get rid of me' way; snatched up her things and deserted her hostess, leaving us in the most miserable confusion and consciousness. For an hour & a half we clung to Wagner, Shakespeare & other topics (including you); and I tried hard to behave myself, although the breaking off of the end of the sofa reminded me rudely that I had lapsed in to the habit of sprawling and lolling. However, we parted on fair terms with an understanding that I might turn up on Monday afternoons when I had nothing better to do. I must get her to take me to the Grafton Gallery: your departure is a serious blow to me in the matter of picture seeing…I have finished the first act of the play*[5] *with another extraction, this time under gas. Nellie [sic] is disgusted at it.'*

Nelly handled the rather unsavoury and highly conceited Shaw with great aplomb. I can imagine her irritation when the man broke her sofa. Shaw tried to give the impression that Nelly was one of the new generation of modern girls who appeared willing to take risks with the opposite sex but who found that when it came to the point, their middle-class upbringing seemed to get in the way. Leaving aside the several obvious reasons why unmarried women at that time might have been nervous about indulging in sex outside marriage, I think it much more likely that Nelly could see Shaw coming a mile off and was quite capable of fending him off without the need for a chaperone. She must also have been well aware of how Bertha would have reacted to any flirtation. After all, Nelly was over 30, and had been mixing freely and unchaperoned with male art students since she was 17. I think it more likely that Shaw had his considerable vanity piqued by finding that Nelly did not seem as susceptible as Bertha did, and decided to spin the tale in a way which would show himself in a more amusing light.

There would have been many things about Shaw which Nelly would have found interesting as she built her career - at several stages in his early life as a journalist, Shaw worked as an art critic. He was the art critic of The World from the spring of 1886 to autumn 1889 and in 1885-6 he also contributed an

---

[5] *'You never can tell' set in a dentist's office*

art column to Annie Besant's Our Corner. He found the experience uncomfortable: *'I once gave up a valuable appointment as picture critic to a prominent weekly journal because I was asked to write flattering notices of the pictures painted by the proprietor's friends regardless of their merits, the argument being that as I was welcome to do the same for my own personal friends, I could not be so churlish as to refuse to do as much for my employer. Later on I obtained an equally desirable appointment but had to give that up also, because the proprietress of the paper insisted on interpolating over my signature ecstatic little raptures about minor Academy pictures by painters who invited her to tea at their studios....'*[6] They also shared a love of modern European drama which Nelly would tap into as she developed a second career as a translator and editor later in the decade.

Shaw began to use Nelly as one of his several female shields against the persistent Bertha - pretending to flirt with Nelly to annoy or deflect his pursuer. The following month he wrote to Bertha *'Miss Erichsen has gone off to Cheshire to paint a portrait. She offered me one date at the studio but I could not go.'* But we know from his diary that he had in fact called on Nelly again in early March, which he chose not to mention to Bertha. When Shaw first met Bertha Newcombe he was 36 and she was 35 - Nelly was just 30. They seem to us too old to be behaving like lovestruck, flirtatious teenagers - but perhaps their behaviour illustrates that they had only recently escaped from the restraints of Victorian convention and family and begun to live independent lives - this was their 'adolescence', if adolescence is the time in one's life when one experiments with emotional and sexual freedom. It would have sounded shocking to Victorian matrons for Nelly to offer to entertain Shaw alone in her studio, even at the age of 30 - hence the mutual embarrassment revealed in his half-serious letter to Bertha. But I suspect she was more mature than Shaw.

The relationship with Bertha and Shaw seems to have had limited impact on Nelly's professional development or networking, and from the records it does not seem that she chose to get any further involved with the Fabian movement. Much more useful was her connection to the Johnson family, including Fanny, the apparent chaperone in Nelly's room when Shaw came for tea, a niece of Alexander Macmillan. Like Nelly she was a bluestocking, self-supporting but with no formal education, and she never married. She dedicated herself to the causes of women's education and women's rights, a pioneer struggling on behalf of the women who would come after, to secure for them access to opportunities that she herself had never been offered. The relationships between the

---

[6] *'Shaw: An Autobiography extracted from his writings' ed Weintraub*

Johnson and Macmillan families were complex and longstanding, with their origins in a Cambridge bookshop. Fanny's grandfather William had a similar life story to Alexander Macmillan - he was the son of a baker, but educated himself to the point when at the age of 30, already a noted classical scholar, he acquired Llandaff House School, in Regent Street, Cambridge. The school thrived under his ownership and this house was the Johnson family home for the next 80 years. At some stage Nelly made two paintings of the house, and these are still in the possession of one of the descendants.

Fanny's father William Farthing Johnson was the third of William's four children. The children inherited their father's intellect and love of learning - William Farthing studied at Corpus Christi College but as a Baptist was not able to gain his Cambridge BA until after the 1857 University Act opened most degrees to non-conformists. He succeeded his father as headmaster of Llandaff House School in 1851 and became a notable Cambridge figure, serving as a Justice of the Peace for many years. Fanny's maternal grandfather, Augustine Gutteridge Brimley, married in succession two sisters, first Hannah and, after her death, Harriet Gotobed, and had four children: George, Caroline, Harriet and Fanny. The second daughter Harriet married William Farthing Johnson in 1851. She was a great lover of literature, and acted as matron and teacher at Llandaff House. Meanwhile in the same year her older sister Caroline married their brother George's closest friend Alexander Macmillan. Thus the Johnson children, including Fanny, were first cousins to the Macmillan children.

Fanny Eliza Johnson was born to William and Harriet on 30 November 1855, the third of eight children. Like Nelly, she was educated at home, although her brothers and some of her sisters were sent away to school, but the house where she lived was, after all, a centre of academic and literary pursuit in Cambridge. When she was 16, the hostel for girl students which was to become Newnham College was set up very close to their house. All the Johnson family were keen supporters of emancipation and educational rights for women. Fanny's first employment as a teacher was at Nottingham High School in 1877 at a salary of £100 per annum, then in 1881 she moved to Croydon School.

In 1888 Fanny was appointed headmistress of Bolton High School for Girls in the north-west and would stay there for six years until ill-health forced her to retire. It had opened in 1877, backed by local subscriptions, and had already seen several changes of headmistress. When Fanny arrived, there were 54 girls and 3 assistant teachers, plus four visiting teachers. Fanny kept an excellent log of events at School, and set about reforming the syllabus, introducing more poetry and reading lessons in the lower school, as well as more practical science lessons. In her second year, she exploited her family contacts at Macmillans to obtain a present for the School library of 68 volumes of stories, poetry, biography and travel writing. Miss Johnson played piano for the girls, performed in school dramas and organised school trips. But she also believed in training the girls to be 'useful, serviceable women' and pupils spent time making toys and clothes for the local infirmaries and children's homes. A kindergarten was established and she drew up plans to raise the numbers to 100, including encouraging girls to stay on until they were 18. Fanny was conscious that the position of women in society was changing: 'Every girl should look forward to the possibility that she may have to earn her own living.' No girl could be certain of marriage, she said, and 'even marriage does not always mean being provided for without exertion.' Wise words.

Above all, Fanny believed in raising her girls' academic aspirations and ambitions. She put them forward for the Cambridge Senior local examinations, and within the year the first pupil would win a place at Newnham College. Plans were developed for much larger new school premises which were officially opened in May 1891, by Mrs Millicent Garrett Fawcett. Millicent was the leader of the National Union of Women Suffrage Societies and the sister of Elizabeth Garrett Anderson, the first female to qualify as a doctor in England. In 1868 Millicent had written an influential article for Macmillan's Magazine on the importance of higher education for women, which had publicised the campaign to found Newnham College. She was married to a Cambridge professor, Henry Fawcett, and the Cambridge academics were always well-connected to the Macmillan publishing empire. The service at the Bolton High School opening ceremony was conducted by Canon Atkinson from North Yorkshire, presumably also known to Fanny through her links with the Macmillans. Fanny certainly believed in calling in favours.

Milicent Fawcett was a famous figure for those who followed the cause of women's rights, and would have been especially well-known to the girls at Bolton School as the mother of the celebrated Philippa Fawcett. In the summer of 1890, Philippa, a student at Newnham College, had sat the University of Cambridge mathematics examination and had beaten the highest scoring male undergraduate of the year, traditionally known as the Senior Wrangler, with a mark 13% higher than his. The winner of the title of Senior Wrangler was always well-publicised in the British press, so this marked a massive triumph for those who supported the cause of education for women, at a time when many were arguing that women could never compete with men. A Newnham College student recorded in her diary: *'The great event of the year was Philippa Garrett Fawcett's achievement in the Mathematical Tripos. For the first time a woman has been placed above the Senior Wrangler. The excitement in the Senate House when the lists were read was unparalleled. The deafening cheers of the throng of undergraduates redoubled as Miss Fawcett left the Senate House by the side of the Principal. On her arrival at the College she was enthusiastically greeted by a crowd of fellow-students, and carried in triumph into Clough Hall. Flowers, letters, and telegrams poured in upon her throughout the day. The College was profusely decorated with flags. In the evening the whole College dined in Clough Hall. After dinner toasts were proposed: the healths drunk were those of the Principal, Miss Fawcett, her Coach (Mr Hobson) and Senior and Junior Optimes. At 9.30 p.m. the College gardens were illuminated, and a bonfire was lighted on the hockey-ground, round which Miss Fawcett was three times carried amid shouts of triumph and strains of "For she's a jolly good fellow."*

Fanny had been in the University Senate House when the results were announced and on her return to Bolton had described the scene to the excited and inspired girls. Then she and a number of the girls had written to Philippa with personal congratulations.

When Fanny left the school in 1894 after a spell of ill-health, she took some time to recover before embarking on a tour of Italy. In the autumn she returned to give a lantern slide lecture to the Old Girls on her Travels, complete with photographs and sketches. Did she encourage Nelly to visit Italy as well? Perhaps they went together, Nelly helping and advising Fanny on the sketching? She then took a house in Chelsea where she lived for some years with her brothers Rex and Augustine, not far from Nelly's studios. In the 1901 census she described herself as an author and, impressively, as head of the household. In 1902 Llandaff House in Cambridge was sold and Rex married. Fanny went back to Cambridge and moved to 1 Millington Road, to live with her brother William and her sister Alice named Ramsay House after their grandfather's birthplace. William, who was an extremely well-respected mathematician and philosopher, was widowed in 1904, and Fanny and Alice looked after his two small boys.

Fanny spent her time in Cambridge writing and working for good causes, with a particular interest in German literature, as well as adapting dramatic scenes from history as school play scripts. In the 1920s her pageant plays were published by Bowes and Bowes. She remained active politically, with controversial views on equality that she was happy to express in print: a letter to 'The Freewoman' magazine in 1911 included the great line 'Might not the advice to go home and mind the baby sometimes be applied to fathers?' This enthusiasm brought responsibility as she was appointed press secretary of the Cambridge Women's Suffrage Association from 1912 and remained actively involved, keeping its presence alive in the press throughout the war. The CWSA had over 500 members. She was also active in the Labour Party and the Women's International League.

There is a glimpse of Fanny in the memoirs of Frances Partridge, a member of the Bloomsbury group, who was taught Logic at Cambridge just after the First World War by Fanny's brother William. Frances thought that William (Willy, as he was known) had a brilliant mind and knew that he had been an influence on Maynard Keynes. She describes him as very shy but affectionate, and a born teacher. He invited his students to join him at home for musical tea parties, and Frances was allowed to turn the pages for him while *'his tall gaunt sister Fanny stands listening with a plate of cucumber sandwiches in her hand.'* [7] Fanny died in 1943 at the grand old age of 87.

Meanwhile, Nelly was building her skills and contacts in the world of publishing. Her introduction to both the Macmillan and Dent publishing houses came through her family relationships. She was not the only one to find an outlet through Macmillan's - her sister Alice translated some fairy tales of Hans Christian Andersen for her brother-in-law George to publish in the early 1890s. These translations were very popular and went through many re-prints in the United States as well as Britain.

Through her friendships with the Johnson family, Nelly also established a professional relationship with the firm of Joseph Dent, another up and coming publishing house established by a maverick autodidact. Nelly would continue working with Dent, and arguing with him about royalties and promotions, until she died. Joseph Malaby Dent was born in 1849 in Darlington, the tenth child of George Dent, a housepainter. *'I was a complete dullard at school, succeeding in*

---

[7] *F Partridge: 'Memories'*

nothing, not even learning to spell (I cannot do it yet), and I left it to go to work at the age of thirteen. I was, as I have always remained, a very desultory, dreamy 'feckless' sort of boy, absent minded to a degree, naturally indisposed to think consecutively or to express my thoughts clearly.' His early education was basic but he learnt to read, and then to love literature. In his memoirs he wrote "*When I was about ten or eleven years old ... I formed the habit of reading which has never since been broken.*"

At the age of thirteen, Dent was apprenticed to a printer; shortly thereafter, he moved within the workshop to acquire more complex skills as a bookbinder. He moved on to work for a Mr Rutherford in Darlington, until the latter went bankrupt. Undaunted, in 1867 at the age of just 18 Dent went to London to finish his apprenticeship at a small bookbinders off Cheapside. Driven by huge ambition, he soon determined to set up his own bookbinding shop.

Dent quickly gained a reputation for fine craftsmanship; he realised that his fine leather bindings put to shame the unattractive Victorian typography of the sheets they bound. But the business continued to struggle, and 1887 marked a particularly low point for Dent - his premises burnt down and his wife died, leaving him with a handful of children to support. Far from deciding to give up the fight, this seems to have spurred him on to greater entrepreneurial effort. In 1888, picking up some second hand printing machinery from a press that had failed, he took premises in Great Eastern Street, London and founded the firm of J. M. Dent and Company (the name was changed to J. M. Dent & Sons in 1909). Dent's first publication, Charles Lamb's *Essays of Elia,* was edited by Augustine Birrell and illustrated by Herbert Railton. It was followed in 1889 by Goldsmith's *Poems and Plays* and then by editions of the works of Jane Austen, the Bronte sisters, Geoffrey Chaucer, Daniel Defoe, Maria Edgeworth, Henry Fielding, Samuel Johnson and Lord Tennyson. These early editions of great classic works, known as 'The Temple Library', were produced in limited quantities on handmade paper and enjoyed some commercial success.

In 1893, the bookseller Frederick Evans suggested that Dent publish a series of pocket volumes of William Shakespeare's works. Recognising the potential demand for cheap editions of the classics, Dent established a second imprint in 1894, the Temple Shakespeare series, and appointed a young Shakespearean scholar, Israel Gollancz, as chief editor. The series eventually included forty volumes that were sold for one shilling a volume, with illustrations by Walter Crane. Over the next four decades, the series sold over five million copies, *"the largest sale made in Shakespeare since the plays were written,"* Dent claimed. Other series followed: Temple Classics, Temple Dramatists, the Lyric Poets series, and the Temple Biographies. By 1895, Dent had published about three hundred volumes and paid off all his debts.

'In lordship over golden words lay secular power, to override even origins, class or accent. In that guise had destiny beckoned JM Dent toward the kingdom of books, and without ever learning to spell he became an influential bookman. He was small, lame, tight-fisted, and apt to weep under pressure, a performance that could disconcert authors and employees. When his temper had risen like a flame he'd scream; the scream, one employee recalled, was what broke men's sprits. His paroxysms were famous; a Swedish specialist thought of prescribing a pail of cold water for Dent to plunge his head into.... Dent's ungovernable passion was for bringing Books to the People. He remembered when he'd longed to buy books he couldn't afford. Yes, you could make the world better. He even thought cheap books might prevent wars.' [8]

In 1894, the ambitious Dent commissioned a young and unknown literary editor, Reginald Brimley Johnson, to produce a six volume set of the novels of Miss Susan Edmonstone Ferrier, a Scottish contemporary of Jane Austen. The illustrator, presumably suggested by Johnson, was Nelly Erichsen, and this is the first time we can see her seriously tackling a new career, that of professional book illustrator. The novels are social comedies even the editor, Johnson, writes in the preface *"The stories are themselves in no way impressive, and can with difficulty be retained in the memory; but the minor characters stand out clear and well-defined, they 'are persons with whom we are delighted to meet, sorry to part, and certain to meet again.' In a word, 'they are excellent company'."* Nelly's drawings are few - only two in the first volume - but distinctive and amusing.

Reginald Brimley Johnson, some three years younger than Nelly, was the youngest of William Farthing Johnson's six children, hence a nephew of the Macmillans and brother of Nelly's friend Fanny. He was born in Cambridge in 1865 and graduated from Corpus Christi College in 1886. His first publications for the up and coming publisher Dent in 1891 were editions of the essays and the poems of Leigh Hunt. Prior to this he had managed to get some of his own poems published, but they had no commercial success and from then on, he concentrated on a career as a literary editor. His first books for Dent were both illustrated by Herbert Railton, Dent's first illustrator. By the time he came to edit the Ferrier novels, Railton was becoming quite a well-known artist, and Nelly would have been less expensive. However she had experience

---

[8] *The Sinking Island, Hugh Kenner, referencing Ernest Rhys' autobiography*

in commercial illustration as well as an impeccable artistic training.

The nineteenth century saw a revolution in the form of the illustrated book. At the beginning of the century, the picture book was for the very privileged few. The only way of reproducing an image was through the use of copper-plate engravings, which required very skilled craftsmen. But within fifty years, the demand from the better educated, better off middle classes for books with pictures led to the introduction of new techniques which were to change the landscape and offer many more opportunities to artists and engravers. The 1850s and 1860s saw a golden age of book illustration with facsimile wood engraving reaching perfection and even the best-known British artists feeling that they needed to explore the technique. Ruskin wrote about it, Lord Leighton and other stars of the Royal Academy contributed line drawings to novels, and Whistler illustrated magazines. By the 1890s the technology had improved sufficiently for photo-engravings to be an alternative form of illustration, but the line drawing was often preferred for added style and clarity. Photography would pose a particular problem for some types of book: everything in the photograph illustrations looks grey, depressing and foggy. It is certainly not what you want in a travel book, for instance, and Dent knew this.

Dent believed from the outset that his books would sell better if they looked beautiful and this often led him to seek out some new and unusual illustrators. One of his first commissioned artists was the young, unknown, Aubrey Beardsley. Beardsley's drawings for Dent's edition of La Morte D'Arthur, *'The achieving of the Sangreal'*, were so admired that Dent decided to put on an exhibition of some of the original black and white drawings commissioned for his publications. The publisher hired the Institute of Water Colour Painters' rooms in Piccadilly for two months in the autumn of 1894 - the same year that Nelly had provided the illustrations for Dent's edition of the Susan Ferrier novels and the exhibition created *'a great deal of interest and drew public attention to our work, so that we received many suggestions for books and a considerable addition to our business'. Dent wrote 'There were drawings by several men whose work was exceedingly interesting and whose names are now well known. Among others were…Arthur Rackham, Walter Crane etc, but some did not fulfil the promise of the work there exhibited.'* The name of the illustrator began to be included as an additional selling feature by Dent and other publishers when advertising new publications, and when critics wrote their reviews, they often mentioned the artist by name as well.

Title page of The Promised Land, published 1896

In 1896, Dent seems to have had a brainstorm and diverged violently from the narrow commercial groove he had been following. He published two of the newly-written novels of Henrik Pontoppidan, a Danish social realist who in 1917 was to win the Nobel Prize for Literature but at the time was completely unknown in England. The works chosen were the first two volumes of a great trilogy, *'Emanuel, or Children of the Soil'* ('Muld', or 'Sod', in Danish) and *'The Promised Land'*. The translations were by Nelly's eldest sister Alice, formally named as Mrs Edgar Lucas, and the books contained some thirty illustrations, including headpieces and beautifully intricate 'arts and crafts' style frontpieces, by Nelly.

There had only been one previous translation of Pontoppidan into English, in 1890, from an unknown publisher, so he could hardly be classed as a popular novelist for the English-speaking public. It would be fascinating to know how Alice and her sister Nelly, relatively unknown to the literary world, persuaded the cautious Dent to take the commercial risk, outside his usual run of popular classics. For a start, the writer was still alive and the books were very recent - there must have been royalties to pay, not Dent's usual line at all. The letters that survive between Alice and her later publisher at Macmillans show us a very uncommercial and hesitant author: so it must have been Nelly's powers of persuasion that swayed Dent: the beginning of a distinctly combative relationship between the two of them that lasted her lifetime.

The novels tell the story of an idealistic preacher who leaves Copenhagen for the country and marries a local peasant girl. They recount his descent into insanity; set in a rural landscape, they deal with political and religious questions of the day. Pontoppidan was radical in his views and opposed to the increasingly dictatorial nature of the Danish state at the time. *Emanuel*, the first volume, has a preface written by Nelly, which makes clear that she was sympathetic to many of the author's social and political concerns and proud of her Danish heritage and political freedoms. She wrote *'the Constitution of 1849, ... was then the most free of any in Europe. This gave [the Dane], among other things, Religious Liberty, Manhood Suffrage, Free Education, a Free Press and Parish Councils. The outburst of popular enthusiasm at this juncture was immense.'* Nelly was able to draw on visits she had made to the more remote areas of Denmark in which he had set his novels to find sources for the illustrations.

There were very few reviews of the novels published in the literary press, but what there were, must have been encouraging: a review of Emanuel in the Glasgow Herald in May 1896 said *'Among the many Scandinavian works that have late appeared in an English dress, few have worn it with a more charming air'.... 'a really excellent version for which we have to thank Mrs Lucas, while the delightfully quaint and delicate illustrations of Miss Erichsen give it exactly the setting that a fastidious reader would desire.'* The critic goes on to compare the writer to Mrs Gaskell and concludes *'It is not very far from being a work of real genius.'* The Pall Mall Gazette gave a similarly favourable response to the second volume, *The Promised Land. 'Mrs Lucas' easy bright translating and Nelly Erichsen's dainty graceful illustrations add greatly to its charm.'* A review in 'The Friend of India' commented that the illustrations had been created 'during a late trip to Denmark', which obviously added to the authenticity of the piece. However, the reviews of The Promised Land, the second volume, were more mixed. Danish angst and misery was not proving to be everyone's cup of tea. A review in The Spectator complained that the intricacies of Danish politics made the plot too complicated to follow, and that the Scandinavians seemed to have a 'lax attitide' to marriage. The third volume of Pontoppidan's trilogy dealt with a popular religious gathering at a Danish folk-school and it was never published in England - it may have been that even Alice and her sister thought this would be too unfamiliar a setting for a British audience - or maybe the first two volumes had not been a commercial success and Dent finally called a halt.

Nelly's preface to Emanuel is one of the strong pieces of evidence we have of her liberal political persuasions. She might have petitioned to be admitted to Life Classes at the RA in the 1880s, but that was where her enthusiasm for public protest seems to have ended. Throughout Nelly's life, the cause of votes for women was one of the principal topics of debate and evoked strong passions in both directions. The Eligibility of Women Act, which finally gave women the vote in the United Kingdom, was only passed in the month that Nelly died. Not all women had wanted the vote. Many educated and politically active women, even as they struggled in their own lives for financial independence and social freedom, drew a line at political equality. In the summer of 1889, the well-known novelist Mrs Humphrey Ward organised and published 'An Appeal against Female Suffrage' which stated 'We believe the emancipating process has now reached the limits fixed by the physical constitution of women.' Mrs Ward was a great supporter of women's education and of their right to work, indeed, like many female contemporaries, she had taken up writing to support a hopelessly insolvent husband and her son, but she believed that women should concentrate their moral and intellectual powers in making a practical contribution to society: trying to participate in the cut and thrust of the political world would damage their character and weaken their moral natures. Famous signatories supporting her manifesto included Lady Randolph Churchill, mother of Winston; Mrs Leslie Stephen, the mother of Virginia Woolf; Mrs Alma-Tadema, wife of the painter; Mrs Arnold Toynbee, widow of the economic and social reformer; and Mrs Matthew Arnold, wife of the poet, the range of opposition to the cause illustrating just how confusing the debate was.

Even Shaw's great friend Beatrice Webb got herself into a public muddle over the issue. As she put it: *'In the spring of 1889 I took what afterwards seemed to me a false step in joining with others in signing the then notorious manifesto, drafted by Mrs Humphrey Ward and some other distinguished ladies, against the political enfranchisement of women, thereby arousing the hostility of ardent women brain-workers …when pressed by Frederick Harrison and James Knowles to write a reasoned answer to Mrs Fawcett's indignant retort to this reactionary document, I realised my mistake. Though I delayed my public recantation for nearly 20 years, I immediately and resolutely withdrew from that particular controversy. Why I was at that time an anti-feminist in feeling is easy to explain, though impossible to justify. Conservative by temperament, and anti-democratic through social environment, I had reacted against my father's over-valuation of women relatively to men; and the narrow outlook and exasperated tone of some of the pioneers of women's suffrage had intensified this reaction…..*

But at the root of my anti-feminism lay the fact that I had never myself suffered the disabilities assumed to arise from my sex. Quite the contrary; if I had been a man, self-respect, family pressure and the public opinion of my class would have pushed me into a money-making profession; as a mere woman I could carve out a career of disinterested research.'

The response that Mrs Webb referred to, from Milicent Fawcett, was supported by more than 2,000 women, including Nelly's friends Fanny and Alice Johnson, and several women artists including Louisa Jopling, Evelyn de Morgan and Margaret Dicksee. But it was not signed by Nelly, nor by any of her immediate family. In the 1890s, the Women's suffrage movement was still a generally law-abiding group, content to campaign through letters to the press and annual petitions to Parliament. It wasn't until 1898, when Emmeline Pankhurst founded the Women's Social and Political Union, that the suffrage movement became known for acts of militancy and civil disobedience very different from Mrs Fawcett's Suffrage Society in which Bertha Newcombe and Fanny Johnson had found a home.

There is plenty of evidence in the early 1900s that Nelly shared her friends' radical views on suffrage, although she was probably not a supporter of the more militant tendency led by the Pankhursts. Certainly her friend in Tuscany, Janet Ross, who was fervently opposed to both the suffragists and the suffragettes, found Nelly's attitude provoking and often teased her about it. But there had been progress: in the 1890s Nelly did have a vote - if only as a ratepayer in Manresa Road for the London County Council Elections, a right which had come into existence in 1889.

1896 saw the death of Alexander Macmillan. At the grand old age of 77 he died peacefully at his London home in Portland Place, and was taken by special train from Waterloo to be buried in Bramshott's little churchyard. The coffin, covered with white and purple flowers, was carried from Liphook station in an open cart lined with ivy and evergreens. Nelly went to the funeral, standing alongside notables such as Henry James, John Morley and Sir George Grove. The Macmillan publishing house continued to grow from strength to strength under the stewardship of his son George, who Nelly knew well, and of his nephews Frederick and Maurice. Between them they would continue to run the firm in London until all three died within a few months of each other in 1936. Maurice's son Harold took time out to pursue his political career, culminating in six years as Prime Minister in the 1950s and 1960s, but returned to chair the

The Loch of Romach, published in the Pall Mall Gazette

business until 1974.

Nelly continued to pick up odd artistic commissions here and there: in October 1895 her illustrations accompanied Mrs Kate Terry Gielgud's short story, *'The Loch of Romach'*, published in the Pall Mall Gazette. The Christmas edition of The Sketch in 1896 includes a lovely drawing to accompany a rhyme 'Come guard this night the Christmas pie…'. She even produced three pen and inkwash sketches which were reproduced in a children's story, Tormentilla, published in 1898 by the Society for Promoting Christian Knowledge. But this would not have been enough money to live on. Meanwhile, Nelly's family circumstances were changing. A couple of years after Hermann's death, her sister Dora married a Danish cousin, Olaf Suhr - and went to live with him in Denmark, where her two daughters Xenia and Sylvia were born. Now Anna was rattling around in Grove Cottage with just her two surviving sons Herman and Frederick, while Nelly was increasingly absent, preferring independence in her rooms in Chelsea. Being the only unmarried daughter would in most families have meant that she was required to return home and give up ambitions and independence, but in fact Nelly refused to conform. Herman had taken his degree at Trinity College, Cambridge and then qualified as a barrister, but he was lame in the leg and happy to stay at home being looked after by his doting mother. His record in the alumni records of Cambridge explained: *'In his early days he was of fine presence and great muscular strength, and but for an accident to his leg at his preparatory school would have probably been a prominent athlete. That physical handicap, as all else, he bore with exemplary fortitude. As his sister, the late Miss Nellie Erichsen, the artist, once said to the writer, "It is impossible to upset Herman. If you cut off all his limbs he would go on smoking his pipe: if you took that away he would whistle."'* But Grove Cottage was too big now that the family was shrinking, when there were more modern and convenient homes being built just around the corner.

Eric Bligh writes '*…on one side of Tooting Common, a patient of my father's, a speculating builder, had begun to build many roads of good-sized red-brick houses, all exactly alike. A uniform row faced the Common, and they were supposed to be of more material grandeur, for they had a room on each side of the front door.*' This development included Elmbourne Road, marked out in 1888, and in 1896, this is where Anna and three remaining unmarried adult children, Herman, Nelly and Frederick, moved, to one of these attractive double fronted red brick houses. The house was called 'Woodlands', number 92 on the corner of Elmbourne Road and Louisville Road, facing the Common. The new houses were part of the Heaver Estate, covering a stretch of land which had still been farmland and meadow when the Erichsens arrived in Tooting in 1871. All these streets are still there, and the name Heaver survives on the sale boards of a local estate agent. While Anna stayed with her daughter Dora in Denmark, Nelly was left in charge to supervise the house move, get the carpets laid, and hire a cook. The latter was a particularly delicate task, and Nelly wrote to her mother to say that she had interviewed one May Hickman, who she thought would do - she had nearly five years' experience, was prepared to do housework and even willing to try baking. Best of all she would take £18 even though her previous post had paid £20. However, 'she might have a temper, I think'. Meanwhile Nelly was painting her niece Rosamund, making sure that brother Herman was fed, and looking after the cat. Two years later Herman finally did marry, quite late in life, and went to live with his wife Justinia, known as Tina, in a mansion flat on the Hammersmith Road, Fulham. They had no children. Anna and Frederick continued to live on in Woodlands for several more years but in 1904 Frederick also married the widow of a barrister from Liverpool, Sara Elizabeth Woollright, who had two young daughters. It seems likely that they had been introduced through Herman, who may have been in practice with Woollright before the latter's death. Fred moved his new family around the corner to 22 Tooting Bec Gardens, and within a few years Anna, whose sight was failing, moved to Chiswick, to a house where she could be looked after by Florence

Carter, perhaps the same woman who had worked for Anna as a housemaid ten years earlier.

Nelly's social circle in London in the 1890s was not extensive, although she had her studios she still spent much of her time with her family and her old friends from Tooting. If she had opportunities to join the wider Fabian set as an active political campaigner, she chose not to take them, preferring to concentrate on her work and her career. But as the new century approached she was about to embark on a phase of her life which would take her to Italy and beyond, and would introduce her to a more cosmopolitan set of British and American expatriates, among whom she would settle and with whom she would spend her final years. Travel books were becoming hugely popular with the British public, and Nelly, with her facility for languages, her relative independence and her experience of travelling alone, was an obvious candidate to illustrate and contribute to these works.

It was February 2004, our first Valentine's Day together, and Peter and I had decided to spend a weekend in Amsterdam. Meanwhile, the Nelly story was beginning to take hold and our curiosity about her American friends Rose and Evangeline, and their unconventional relationship, was nagging away. There were so many assumptions and questions about the nature of their affair, and it was hard in the context of the early years of the twenty-first century to judge what was going on. So when it started to sleet and we dodged into a second hand bookshop with a sizeable English language section, a large paperback volume - 'The Worm in the Bud, The World of Victorian Sexuality' by Ronald Pearsall - seemed to leap off the shelf into my hands. As had become my habit, I started thumbing through the index, looking for any familiar names. And there, utterly extraordinarily, were the words 'Erichsen, Nelly, translator… p194'. This was at a time when no-one outside our family (or hers) had ever heard of Nelly, as far as we knew. And yet it turned out that this reference to an encounter between Nelly and George Bernard Shaw had been taken from Michael Holroyd's definitive biography of the playwright.

Pearsall was describing the occasion when Nelly had invited her new friend Shaw to visit her studios, but then out of Victorian modesty, failed to seize the opportunity this might have presented for a flirtation, or more. At first we hoped to place the meeting against the backdrop of a longer romance, to find letters or confessions of secret passions, but we were disappointed. In fact, the reference in 'The Worm in the Bud' to Nelly's relationship with George Bernard Shaw, supported by entries I found in his diaries and in a letter to their mutual friend Bertha

Newcombe, seemed initially to confirm Nelly as the archetypal Victorian spinster, terrified of being left alone with a man. But the more I learnt about Shaw and his predatory relationships with women, and the more I thought about Nelly's determined experiments at independence at that time, the more impressed I became by her self-confidence and deft handling of the man.

Sometimes our quest for Nelly took us down blind alleys: and sadly the Holroyd biography was one of those. Pearsall had shown us that there was a connection with Shaw, so we went to the three volume biography of Shaw looking for more information. In Volume I of Holroyd's great work, 'The Search for Love', we did indeed find a reference to Nelly Erichsen in the index, with the extremely puzzling addition of the name 'Leonora' in brackets. But something had gone wrong here...index compilers can make mistakes. According to Holroyd, Leonora was the code word Shaw used for a young lady he had a flirtation with in London in January 1879. Shaw wrote in his diary 'Made the acquaintance of the Lawson family on 5th [January] and met Leonora on the 11th.' Holroyd continues 'From Leonora he preserved a pressed flower together with an odd note: 'these flowers were plucked from the garden of a millionaire by one of his would-be brides as a memento of a sweet prelude to a "might have been".' That was all Holroyd said on the subject. I spent a long time in the British Library puzzling this and scouring the GBS archives, letters and diaries for more clues. I discovered that there are acres and acres of written material on Shaw and every possible combination of subject - Shaw and politics, Shaw and literature, Shaw and women being the most common. Although I could see Shaw's references to meeting Nelly in diaries and letters, no-one else had thought the Leonora incident worth researching. Had there really been this early contact between the two of them? But then common sense prevailed: Nelly was only 16 in January 1879, she was living at home with her parents in Tooting. And I am not aware that she knew any millionaires or anyone called Lawson. Shaw himself records that he met her for the first time in 1893. I think the index just got muddled. But if I had not spent so long in the Shaw archives, trying to prove that Nelly was Shaw's lost love, I would not have become so fascinated by the sad tale of Bertha Newcombe.

Poggio Gherardo

Chapter Seven: Translations

In 1899 a new publishing house, Messrs Duckworth & Co, announced in the press that they had arranged to issue a series of modern plays, to be edited by R Brimley Johnson and N Erichsen. Duckworth & Co had been set up by Gerald Duckworth, stepbrother to Virginia Woolf and previously an editor at Dent. Duckworth was a great fan of new theatre, and the publicity for the series stated that aim of the series was *'to represent, as widely as possible, the activity of modern drama - not confined to stage performance - in England and throughout the continent of Europe. It so happens that, though translations seem to be more in demand every day, the greater number of the Continental dramatists are at present little known in this country.'*

The announcement lists some ten plays, including Strindberg's 'The Father', which was to be translated by Nelly herself. *'The work of translation has been entrusted to English writers specially conversant with the literatures represented, who, in many cases, are already associated in the public mind with the authors they are here interpreting.....the volumes will contain brief introductions, bibliographical and explanatory rather than critical.'* At that time Strindberg was very little known in England, and he was struggling with the major disadvantage of writing in a language that hardly anyone could understand.

The year before, in 1898, Reginald Brimley Johnson, known to his friends as Rex, had tried to set up his own publishing firm, and had become engaged to be married to a young woman called Gertrude Blogg. Gertrude was one of three sisters living with their mother in the Bohemian area of Chiswick called Bedford Park, she worked as secretary to Rudyard Kipling. One of her sisters, Frances, was shortly to become Mrs GK Chesterton. But in the spring of 1899, tragedy struck - Gertrude was knocked down and killed by an omnibus. That same year, Johnson published Chesterton's first book, *'Greybeards at Play'*, which was a commercial success, but after Gertrude's death their relationship foundered, perhaps because it brought back too many unhappy memories for

Johnson, and Chesterton, just about to hit the big time, found a new publisher. Rex had missed a golden opportunity, and after winding his business up, reverted to offering editorial services to other publishers, such as Duckworth. Nelly, who had experience of translating modern European authors for the increasingly experimental reading public, and had shared this enthusiasm with George Bernard Shaw, encouraged Rex to look beyond the over-used British staples to the Continent, and to drama in particular. They pitched their idea to Duckworth and found a very receptive audience.

The list of translators signed up by Nelly and Rex is an impressive one: it includes Arthur Symons, the poet and critic; William Archer, the well-established drama critic who had helped to launch Shaw's career; Constance Garnett, a prolific translator of the Russian language who would later work on Tolstoy and Turgenev; and Lucas Malet, the pseudonym of Mary, daughter of Charles Kingsley, a successful if somewhat scandalous novelist and cousin to her namesake, Mary Kingsley, the African explorer. These individuals were all known personally to Nelly and Rex, in some cases through Nelly's connection to Shaw, indicating the impressive literary and creative circles in which they were now moving.

The Father is a controversial play for Nelly to have chosen. The Introduction to this edition is signed just with an enigmatic 'W', perhaps written by William Archer, theatre critic and translator of Ibsen. The tone of the play is clear from the opening sentence of this preface: *'The shadow of the exceeding sorrow of living which, in these latter days, hovers over the world-wide realm of letters has settled in deep darkness upon the literature of the far North.'* The writer goes on to note that Strindberg is the most pessimistic of living pessimists. Furthermore, Strindberg was not just pessimistic, he was a misogynist, '[who] has come to hate womankind with a hatred, not unreasoning yet most intense and implacable.' It does not inspire enthusiasm in the casual reader.

The plot revolves around the conflict between a husband and wife whose marriage is failing, and who fight to the husband's death over the education of their daughter. It explores highly topical subjects, which may explain the play's appeal to Nelly: the education of girls, and the legal rights of a husband over a wife, contrasted with the psychological power the woman can choose to wield, which in this tragedy brings about the husband's insanity and death. Nelly must have been intrigued by the couple's conflict over the daughter's education - is it better to be educated away from home, as the girl's father suggests, and given the opportunity to become a teacher, thus able to support oneself in case no husband comes along, than to stay at home doing nothing more than practising art, especially if the talent is of dubious quality?

The general reaction to the play was predictable - the review in The Scotsman called it 'As dreary a piece of reading as this age of literary worship of the ugly has produced.' It adds that 'Mr (sic) Erichsen's translation has every appearance of being faithful to the original' and predicts that it will not find favour with many theatregoers. The review in the Dublin Daily Express is even worse: '… if this play did not stick in one's nostrils, it would be laughable; and we wonder what Messrs Duckworth and Co are about. …of Mr R Brimley Johnson we are aware, as an editor of everything and anything. Of the other editor, N. Erichsen, we do not seem to have heard before.' The Pall Mall Gazette called it 'The Literature of the Madhouse' but did add that it was 'powerful in its gloom and subtle in its psychological aspects'. None of the reviews ever questioned whether N. Erichsen might in fact be a woman.

In fact, despite this extremely disheartening reception, Nelly's translation of The Father was particularly successful: reproduced by other publishers including those across the Atlantic, it stayed in print for at least 25 years. A booklet printed by Duckworths for private circulation to mark the firm's 50th anniversary remarked on several books from the first list 'that fifty years later are still in good demand, among them….a translation of The Father'. Unlike some of the other plays on Duckworth's list, The Father has survived and is still occasionally performed today.

One of the other playwrights featured in the collection was Archer's translation of the Belgian, Maurice Maeterlinck, with three plays "Alladine and Palomides', 'Interior' and 'The Death of Tintagiles'. Among Nelly's treasured possessions, listed in her will, was an unbound but autographed copy of a later work by Maeterlinck, 'Aglavaine et Selysette'. It has to be said that the chances of any of these plays being performed in England was exceedingly slim, they were not aimed at the commercial market, but were of interest to the intellectual and modernist community. It could be that Nelly and Rex were dreaming ahead to a time when amateur, repertory or experimental theatre companies would look for more avant garde material to perform. It was also an age which saw frequent tours by foreign theatre companies who could access the English stage much more easily. However, if this was the moment at which Nelly could have settled into a quiet life in London as a translator and editor of foreign literary works, it did not happen. For by the time The Father was published in England in 1899, Nelly had fallen in love with Tuscany, and the countryside around Florence in particular, and travel writing and illustrating had become her main passion.

The quest for Nelly had begun with Peter's discovery of the artwork she had created in 1900. The drawings were clearly labelled, in Nelly's handwriting on the back of the pictures: "Florentine Villas". This turned out to be a rather unusual offering from the House of JM Dent, published in 1901 as the equivalent of a coffee table book, and Nelly's illustrations accompanied text by the Queen Bee of Anglo-Tuscany, Mrs Janet Ross. It seems likely that the drawings had never been returned to Nelly after Dent had used them for the print. They are not listed in her will although she carefully distributes among her family some drawings she did for a volume on Derbyshire published by Macmillan, and for a book about Pisa she had co-written for Dent. She possessed two copies of the actual book, a small version left to sister Alice and the 'deluxe' full size version bequeathed to brother Frederick. But the drawings that Peter acquired must have remained the property of Dent, the publisher. I don't know where they were kept between 1900 and 1999, when Peter bought them, but I suspect it was somewhere dark and dingy, probably on a shelf in a printworks.

I had only known the man I was going to marry for a few weeks, when he arrived at my house carrying a large dusty parcel and started telling me Nelly's story, as much as he knew at that time. When he left he asked me to keep them safe, and I pushed them under my bed, where my three small children would not find them or use them for colouring practice, their clear black outlines looking very tempting. The drawings have been precious to us ever since, offered as a proof that Peter trusted me to keep them for him and to love them just as he had. Over time we have framed the most striking of them and they have hung around us in all our homes all these years. I can look at them on the walls when I take a break from writing, and I often do. One year I managed to track down a copy of the original full size volume of 'Florentine Villas', still in a cardboard slipcase with tissue paper leaves, and wrapped it up for Peter and put it under the Christmas tree.

When Peter started telling me as much of Nelly's story as he had uncovered, and mentioned that the artist was buried in a place called Bagni di Lucca, a smile of recognition and anticipation came over my face which clearly puzzled him. It turned out that 'Italy' can mean very different things to different people. To me, Italy was the place where I had had the loveliest and best sunny holidays, and Tuscany in particular. I had first been to Venice and Rome when I was a teenager on a school cruise, but even the horrors of the SS Uganda had not spoilt the revelation of the glories of these cities. Early in my previous married life the rentable villas of Chiantishire had been a regular holiday destination. I was pretty sure I had even been to Bagni di Lucca, although I couldn't remember much about it. Florence was a city of beauty, Tuscany was a paradise of gardens with pools, olive trees, vineyards, churches and palaces, history, art, wine and pasta, where the waiters loved to make a fuss of my scampering children and where the sun always shone. Now we had an excuse to go back. However, to Peter, who had only ever been to Turin and Milan, and that as a motoring journalist in the 1970s, it was 'the land of the ghastly factory tour and the dead dog', a particularly colourful impression he had gained while driving round the industrial north of the country. Consequently, he had never felt inclined to follow Nelly to her final home. But just a few months later there we were in Tuscany, tracing Nelly's steps as best we could, through Florence and up into the hills, even as far as the graveyard.

British writers and artists had been visiting Florence for centuries, but the community expanded rapidly from the 1840s, when Robert and Elizabeth Barrett Browning and Fanny Trollope and her sons arrived. Over the next fifty years, the city and its surroundings would become a haven for intellectuals, and in particular, a refuge for those whose sexual preferences made them uncomfortable in their own land. There were additional advantages - the climate suited invalids, and one could manage to live well on very limited means. For Nelly, constantly struggling to make ends meet and prone to nervous ailments, these were important considerations. As Shelley wrote, Florence was the 'paradise of exiles'.

The city did not suit everyone - there was little attempt by the incomers to learn Italian or to mix with the locals, and the poet Walter Savage Landor described it as 'the filthiest capital in Europe.' But in the 1870s, it is estimated that some 30,000 of the population of 200,000 were British or American. By 1911, the British community living in and around Florence had reached 35,000, and of course there were just as many Americans, plus a smattering of Europeans, particularly Poles and Russians. There was an English bank, several English doctors, chemists and dentists. You could buy tea, tweeds, mackintoshes. For artists such as Nelly, Molini's stocked Reeves' colours, paintbrushes, pens and ink. There were several English language publications such as the

Florence Directory and the Florence Herald, to allow the expats to keep up to date with society's comings and goings. Living was cheap, servants were easier to find and more amenable than at home, and British and American spinsters and widows could swap dingy suburban rooms for top floor apartments with amazing views. Or you could sample the delights of Miss Godkin's pensione on the Lung'Arno, where Nelly and her friends the Noyes sisters stayed on more than occasion. I cannot find any written descriptions of Miss Godkin's pensione, but I assume that the Pensione Bertolini, where Lucy Honeychurch stays in 'A Room with a View', would be quite a good approximation of the original. *'It was pleasant to wake up in Florence, to open the eyes upon a bright bare room, with a floor of red tiles which look clean though they are not.'*

Pension Godkin, 1 Lung'Arno Guicciardini. Centrally located. Comfortable and homelike. Good table. Fine view, moderate terms, from 5 to 8frcs.
Regular advertisement in the Italian Gazette.

It was in 1888, seeking distraction after the death of his wife, that the publisher Joseph Dent journeyed abroad for the first time in his life, to Florence. He later wrote *"In 1888 the Toynbee Club, founded in the previous year, arranged its first journey to Florence to be carried out on co-operative principles. I was worn out physically with the reconstruction of my business...in desperation I took the opportunity to travel, and so began to widen my vision of the world... The cost of that three weeks of glorious life, including every expense (even tips and coach fares) was only some £13 or £14. And mind you we travelled in real comfort."*

Dent did not just find rest and relaxation, at a bargain price, in his foreign travels he found his next great publishing idea. *'I began to feel that these cities of the old times were small nations in themselves, especially in Italy...In producing [a]series of books on the old European cities it was one of my chief desires to help in the revelation of these different personalities and in arranging with the authors of the different volumes I urged that they should attempt to unveil in their stories as much as possible of the distinctive individuality to be found in those wonderful medieval towns'.* Over the next 25 years his 'Medieval Towns' series of guidebooks, predominantly focused on Italy, but also including other European towns on the British tourist circuit, was to be a major money spinner for his firm. Eventually the series would run to 39 volumes, many of them still in print in the 1930s. It was sufficently well-known for Forster to poke fun at in 'A Room with a View' when he jokes of one resident: 'Doubtless you know her monographs in the series of Medieval Byways?'. It also provided a new creative opportunity for his expanding circle of authors and illustrators, including Nelly Erichsen.

Dent's original choice for series author was the well-known writer Mrs Margaret Oliphant - he had read her works 'The Makers of Florence' and 'The Makers of Venice' and thought she would bring the tone he wanted. He commissioned her to go to Siena, but before she could make any progress she upset his plans by dying. Short of other ideas, he turned to his well-connected young publishing assistant, Gerald Duckworth. Among the Duckworth family's friends were the two daughters of the writer and critic John Addington Symonds. Duckworth suggested that they offer the commission for *'The Story of Perugia'* to the elder sister Margaret Symonds, known as Madge, who had already written a short travelogue, Days spent on a Doge's Farm. She agreed to take the commission jointly with her friend Lina Duff-Gordon. Dent describes meeting Lina and Madge for the first time in his memoirs: *'I was busy in my office one beautiful summer morning when two ladies were announced and shown into my room. I know I shall be accused of hyperbolic sentiment when I say that I was startled by a vision of beauty such as I have never beheld before nor since, heightened by the exquisite contrast of two faces. One was a dark brunette with a golden-olive complexion and the other fair with grey-blue eyes and mouse-coloured hair and as fair a face as I ever saw; each had features of perfect outline and distinction, and each lady was tall and graceful in figure. They were a perfect complement one to the other. No such vision of human beauty has ever come to me though I have travelled far and seen much of loveliness in women of many nations.'*

Naturally, after this introduction, Dent was unable to resist giving them the commission. The original plan was to illustrate the series with just a few photographs, as Dent could not afford line drawings within his 'popular books' budget, but in his autobiography he explains that he changed his mind when a professional illustrator, Helen James, wrote to him asking for work. Dent noted that Miss James, who was disabled, wished to base herself in Italy for the greater part of the year, and offered to produce the drawings for a nominal sum. *'...she showed me her drawings, which though somewhat weak in line were full of the right feeling for architecture: we soon arranged terms and she became the illustrator of the series until her death from an attack of measles in Italy.'*

Madge Symonds had first met Lina Duff-Gordon in the early 1890's, when she and her sister Katherine were taken to Tuscany by their father, during one of his bouts of ill-health, and had gone to stay with Symonds' great friend Janet Ross. She wrote many years later of her first visit to Mrs Ross' house : *'We had come through the crowded streets of Florence out into the open country and up through the carefully tended olives and vineyards of Poggio Gherardo, to the huge wooden door of the villa...the fire in Aunt Janet's hearth never goes out and it is made of olive boughs and the ash of the olive is very sweet to smell and very white to look at.'* There the sisters met Janet's niece, Lina, and became close companions. When Madge was asked by Dent to launch the 'Medieval Towns' series by writing a book on Perugia, it was natural that Madge, who lived in England, should turn to her friend Lina, resident in Florence, for help with the research. Lina's autobiography explains: *'I saw a great deal of Madge, and when in 1896 she was asked by Mr Dent to write the story of Perugia, she wanted me to join her in Perugia to help her with reading Italian books and studying the history of the place'.* At the time, Madge was 25, Lina just 22.

Janet Ross, Lina's aunt with whom she lived in Florence, was born Janet Duff-Gordon in London in 1842, the daughter of Alexander Cornewall Duff-Gordon, and his wife, Lucie. Her parents moved in prominent social and literary circles: her father, a Treasury clerk and later a commissioner for the Inland Revenue, was from a patrician family which had fallen on hard times. Her mother was the only daughter of the jurist John Austin and the German

Henry and Janet Ross with Lina Duff-Gordon at Poggio Gherado

translator Sarah Austin. As Lucie Duff-Gordon she travelled in North Africa and wrote of her adventures in *Letters from Egypt*, published to great acclaim in 1865. Janet's siblings, Maurice and Urania, were not born until some years later, and hence she spent her childhood as 'a spoiled and rather lonely child'. She did not seem to make friends of her own age, preferring the company of her parents' circle: Thackeray, Tom Taylor (playwright and Editor of Punch), the artist Richard Doyle and the historian Thomas Carlyle (whom she disliked, considering him to be rude to her mother).

Soon after moving from central London to Surrey in the early 1850s, the Duff-Gordons realized that they had neglected their daughter's education. They hired a German governess and later sent Janet to spend a year at a school in Dresden; but it was clearly too late for education to turn her into a model Victorian maiden. A daring enthusiast for outdoor sports, especially riding, hunting, and fishing, Janet Duff-Gordon had developed into a highly unconventional young woman, with a free and easy manner which offended more mature society ladies. She cultivated an extraordinarily diverse collection of men friends, addressed her father as 'dear old boy', and moved with a staggering lack of awe among a glittering circle of artistic, literary, and political celebrities. She picnicked on the River Mole with Millais and spent a winter with the Tennysons, becoming devotedly attached to the invalid Mrs Tennyson. She rode with the Duke of Beaufort's hounds and was sketched by G. F. Watts for the frescoes commissioned for Bowood House. The writer George Meredith (who, Janet later claimed, had fallen deeply in love with her) portrayed her as Rose Jocelyn in his semi-autobiographical novel *Evan Harrington* (1860).

At a dinner in 1860 Janet Duff-Gordon met Henry Ross, a friend of the explorer and archaeologist, Sir Austen Henry Layard. His tales of pig-sticking in Egypt proved to be irresistible, and she invited him to stay at Esher. Here they hunted together, and, *'impressed by his admirable riding, his pleasant conversations, and his kindly ways'*, she accepted his proposal of marriage, despite his twenty years' seniority. She was only 18. They were married at Ventnor on the Isle of Wight on 5 December 1860 and then departed to take up residence in Egypt. The marriage produced just one child, a boy called Alick, born in 1862, the same year as Nelly, but he spent very little time with his parents, being sent home to England to be educated.

The appeal of Eastern adventure, and the chance to follow in her mother's footsteps, may well explain Janet Ross's surprising marriage. After the couple landed in Alexandria in January 1861, she immediately began to learn Arabic from her house-boy and visited Cairo. She rode desert races against Egyptian pashas, travelled by camel to see the Suez Canal under construction, and acted as the Egyptian correspondent for *The Times*. However, by the mid 1860s the bank in which Henry Ross was a partner had hit financial difficulties; the couple decided to cut their losses, give up the house in Alexandria, sell the furniture and retire to England. Ross sent Janet on ahead to Florence to wait for him as it would be warmer than England and she had friends there, Sir Henry and Lady Elliot. Sir Henry was at that time the British Ambassador to Italy, so Janet was immediately launched into the centre of Anglo-Florentine society. The Rosses were never to leave, and Janet's nearly sixty years in the City would make her one of its celebrities.

By September 1869 the Rosses had settled into an apartment in Florence right on the banks of the Arno, where they mixed in Anglo-Florentine literary, artistic, and social circles; and in 1888 they bought their own property, near Settignano, some two miles south of Florence on a spur of the Fiesole hills. It was Poggio Gherardo, an old castle with a romantic history, and here Henry and Janet spent the rest of their lives. Legend has it that this was one of the two villas in which the tales that make up Boccaccio's Decameron were first told, by young nobility fleeing a plague in Florence. Nelly drew the house several times, setting it among its olive groves and gardens. It is an austere, plain building, with crenellated battlements and a lookout tower - more like a castle than a home. It is certainly not the most beautiful of the palazzos that Nelly would draw, although its setting is grand. It still survives, home to a slightly obscure Catholic monastic order. We found it on our travels, or at least we were able to get a glimpse of it through the trees - the entrance was impossible to find.

By the 1880s the Italians had taken control of the independent Rome, which became the newly-unified nation's capital, and Florence's political influence began to wane. A quieter country life suited Henry Ross, who wanted to cultivate orchids, and Janet also learnt to enjoy more peaceful pursuits. She studied the agricultural life of Tuscany, helping out with the olive and grape harvests and collecting Tuscan peasant songs, which she sang to visitors, accompanying herself on the guitar. It sounds rather trying.

One local resident, with whom Janet initially became friends, was the celebrated if slightly scandalous English novelist Ouida. This friendship was wrecked when the flamboyant writer fell ostentatiously in love with Janet's protector Della Stufa, and began to view Janet as a rival. The conflict reached its climax when Ouida wrote a novel portraying Janet quite viciously as an aristocratic adventuress (*Friendship* - 1878). This feud was to split Anglo-Tuscan society, but there is little doubt that Ross had the practical, if not the moral victory, as the row rolled on and Ouida left Florence for good in 1894. Although she continued to write and publish novels, she rapidly ran out of money and died alone and unloved in Viareggio in 1908. We saw her tomb in the cemetery in Bagni di Lucca.

During the last two decades of the 19th century, Mrs Ross established herself as a fashionable hostess in the Anglo-Florentine literary world. Her writings began to be published - these included *Italian Sketches* (1887), and *The Land of Manfred* (1889) - a historical-cum-travel narrative of a tour of south Italy. In 1888 she published *Three Generations of Englishwomen,* a triple biography of her mother, her grandmother (Sarah Austin), and her great-grandmother (Susannah Taylor of Norwich): based on and containing family papers, it remains the most important source for the lives of these three women of letters.

'Handsome ... [with] classical features and ... thickly marked eyebrows accentuating the earnestness of her gaze', Janet Ross was, according to her niece Lina, ceaselessly active, and practical. Despite an irresistible joie de vivre and an exceptional talent for friendship, she had no understanding of romantic passion, limited imagination, and curiously little appreciation for beauty (she was apparently unmoved by the beautiful views surrounding Poggio Gherardo). The art historian, Kenneth Clark, who knew her at the end of her life when he was working with the art expert Bernard Berenson, described her as *'the most completely extrovert human being I have ever known ... her passions had passed like water off a duck's back.'* Formidable yet approachable, cultured but not erudite, she was an unconventional and vital Victorian woman who used her privileged social standing, intellectual background, and attractive appearance to achieve the fullest life available to her. I think she may have taught Nelly a few lessons about self-promotion, especially when it came to negotiations with publishers.

After Janet's death, Madge Symonds wrote a memoir fondly recalling her visits with her father and later with Lina to Poggio Gherardo. She remembered that Janet was *'impatient of all social bores, and vehemently intolerant of fools…[but that] she showed the utmost tenderness for all sick and ailing persons. How often had she gone down from her roomy villa to some hot fever bed in lodgings or in a hotel in Florence and packed and brought back with her and herself nursed back to a new life some suffering creature...If one had once become the privileged guest of the villa, one must expect to see little or nothing of the society in the city. The city might come up to the villa, and it did come in very great crowds on Sunday afternoons, but down to the drawing rooms of the city one very rarely went except to visit its churches and its picture galleries and to hurry home with some rushed shopping done.'*

Lina and Madge began researching *'The Story of Perugia'*. They travelled together, Lina mostly doing the library digging, with advice from Janet, and Madge writing the text. By the end of 1897 the manuscript had been despatched to Dent for publication, and the girls waited eagerly to see their work in print. Lina wrote to Madge in February 1898: *'I've quite given up all hope of ever seeing the B [book] published and no doubt you have also. Dent must live in the clouds on the top of Mount Hymettus (sp.?) eating honey instead of studying whether Miss James' illustrations are printed on the proper paper….'* Later in the same letter Lina refers to their publisher, tongue in cheek, as 'the awe-inspiring Dent'.

On 2 March 1898 Lina wrote to Madge from Siena and Volterra. She dreaded returning to Florence, where she sometimes found the ex-pat community a little stifling: *'The misery of returning among those cackling Florentines who are always asking about 'Perugia' is intense'*. The book finally emerged later in 1898: *'Dent was pleased, the reviews were favourable, and we felt we had come through our first test, but we were disappointed that we did not get more than about £100 each which had also to cover our expenses'* But no sooner had the book been accepted for publication, than Dent had commissioned Lina to write another book - on Assisi. *'I've written pages and pages of history notes about Assisi and tomorrow am going to Bruschi in search of legends. As far as I can see the interest historically ends after you have traced Assisi's rise and growth. In 1400 she is already dull.'*

For the next eighteen months Lina tried to tempt Madge to take an interest in the Assisi project although she seems to have worked hard at the research and became entranced by the story of St Francis, she lacked either the self-confidence or the application to tackle the writing on her own. But meanwhile in England, Madge was being wooed by William Vaughan, a schoolmaster at Clifton College, Bristol, and would not commit to any further visits to Tuscany. Later that summer Lina went back to England, staying with family friends Mr and Mrs Rate, at Milton Court, their beautiful Elizabethan manor house near Dorking, Surrey. Lachlan Macintosh Rate was a wealthy banker and philanthropist. While she was with them, Joseph Dent came to call on his young author. *'Mr Dent's visit here was very amusing (at least to me). I chuckled as I saw him get down from his dogcart, swathed in a mustard coloured waistcoat....'* He was trying to get Lina to hurry up with her project - *'Couldn't I sit down at once and begin Assisi. I said I must have time and I must also have Mrs Vaughan'... 'Dent distinctly said that he was keeping Assisi for us so some day we shall meet there'.* Lina still hoped to tempt Madge back to Italy, but very shortly after her marriage Madge fell pregnant and as a young mother, her chances of being free to roam abroad and resume the life of a travel writer were bound to be sadly limited.

By December 1898, back at Poggio Gherardo, Lina had once more committed herself to her task. *'The later history can be told as Mr Dent expects it 'street by street', not that there are many streets in Assisi'.* But the following month she was again discouraged, pleading to Madge for help. *'The story of Assisi must have your magic pen to make it in any way worthy of the subject. I am only a humdrum creature and have but small literary capability. The little I know is learnt from you.'*

In February 1899 she left Tuscany to join the Rates in Cannes. Meanwhile Dent had been so impressed by the meals he had eaten on his travels in Tuscany, that he thought there would be a market for a genuine Tuscan cookbook. *'Now to make you laugh, for I know it will amuse you to hear that Mr Dent is to bring out a cookery book for me....the truth is I wanted to make a little money in order to be able to stay at Assisi in September. Dent was also asking who could do The Story of Florence?'* The commission for Florence was soon given to Edmund Gardner, who must have been a faster worker than Lina, as the book was published in 1900, with illustrations by Nelly.

In May Lina wrote that she had received *'a quaint unbusinesslike letter from Dent about the cookery book',* containing a promise to visit Florence himself. Lina was unhappy about this proposal, as she clearly though that Dent had the potential to be a very embarrassing guest. She said to Madge *'can you imagine me 'bear-leading him' through the streets of Florence.'* However Janet Ross was keen to encourage the visit. *'Aunt J is determined to get good terms from him for her villa book [Florentine Villas] as she has invited him here for two nights. I begged her not to do so but useless. We shall sit on the terrace under the stars, Mr Dent's mustard-coloured waistcoat gleaming in the moonlight.'*

Lina was already annoyed with Dent's commercial terms: he had offered only £10 to the authors for a second edition of the Perugia book. *'Dent writes most vague and affectionate letters to Aunt J and myself. He is anxious to come here at the end of June but is 'nervous' about the heat. I am sending him the degrees of fahrenheit we have to endure at that time and probably he'll deem it more prudent to stay in England. He calls for some copy of Assisi. He may whistle for it'.*

But Mr Dent was not so easily put off and did indeed arrive at Poggio Gherardo, with his wife, that summer of 1899. Lina said *'Aunt J has got him into her claws and she's going to make him 'pay up' for any work she does for him!'.* Clearly Janet thought that Lina and Madge had been outmanouvered in their own author's contracts and that she could do better. The cookery book project was rapidly abandoned by Lina who found the work of transcribing recipes from her Aunt Janet's Tuscan chef far too boring. But Janet, never one to miss an income generating opportunity, took the project on herself. Or, as Janet put it *'my niece very soon got tired of such dull work, so I took it up and was rather amused, and I confess puzzled, when I sent the last pages to London, by Mr Dent asking me to write a 'literary introduction' to the work.' Leaves From a Tuscan Kitchen,* published by Dent later that year, was a kitchen classic for many years. For some people, this is the only work by Janet Ross that they will ever see - several times updated by Lina's grandson Michael Waterfield, it is still in print. It was dedicated rather pretentiously by Janet to the wife of her old friend, the painter GF Watts. It is worth remembering that Janet never cooked herself - these are all transcriptions from the recipes of her cook of thirty years, Giuseppi Volpi. My copy dates from 1914, by which time it had already been reprinted half a dozen times, with additions of recipes which Janet claimed her friends had requested, for simpler ways of cooking vegetables and 'maigre' soups, to be eaten on non-meat days.

Nelly arrived in Florence in the May of 1899, signing in to temporary membership at the Vieusseux Library, and ready to start the next chapter of her professional career, as an illustrator of travel books. By this time, as poor Miss James had died of the measles, Lina had taken the opportunity to persuade Dent to hire a new illustrator - *'a Miss Nelly Erichsen that she had met earlier that year'.* There was a happy coincidence of influences at work here, Nelly was already known to Dent, having worked on the Pontoppidan translations as long ago as 1894. But when Lina wrote to Madge on 8 June 1899 she said *'I am anxious that a Miss Erichsen, whom I have lately got to know, should illustrate Assisi. I refuse to have Miss James' drawings....Gerald Duckworth knows Miss Erichsen, a young Danish lady who lives in London. Her sister is now translating Hans Andersen for Dent. If Dent agrees with my suggestion Miss Erichsen will return at once from Venice & join me at Assisi & together we can choose the subjects for her pen - I should be willing to give her £20 from my money to pay her for the illustrations, for I do want them to be nice to balance the defective letter-press.'* But around the same time, Lina was writing to another friend Bessie Trevelyan about Nelly, *'I believe we have you to thank for her acquaintance. She is very charming, I think.'*

Nelly was delighted with this new contract and with the friendships it opened up for her. She knew Duckworth well, she had worked for Dent before, and now she was travelling round Tuscany and Umbria with the favoured niece of one of the most well-known Englishwomen in Florence. The joy was mutual: Lina had at last found in Nelly an interesting companion for her travels to Assisi, a reasonable substitute for Madge, and the book project seemed to take on a new lease of life. By the end of June 1899 she and Nelly were ensconced at the Hotel Subasio in Assisi where she and Madge had stayed together in previous years, as she writes to Madge mentioning names of hotel staff and town curators in a very familiar way. *'[Nelly] and I are sole inmates of Hotel Subasio, with Signor Rossi looking after us like prodigal daughters'.*

The Hotel Subasio is still thriving today. In fact, it looms large in Harkness family legend. Just a few years ago, while researching Nelly's life, I booked to take all my family to Assisi for a night on our way to Tuscany. We left our car in the unpleasant concrete municipal parking area at the bottom of the hill and lugged our bags up through the hot and dusty streets, crowded with coach party tourists, and into the cool shady lobby of the very inviting Hotel Subasio. My children immediately flopped all over the soft furnishings and started checking their phones. The receptionist looked extremely surprised when I produced our passports and demanded our room keys, but did her best to look obliging. It took more than a few minutes for me to check my paperwork and discover that I was in the wrong hotel. Subasio was such a memorable name for a hotel, and staying where Nelly and Lina had stayed would have been wonderful. Sadly, though, I had booked somewhere cheaper. It may have been about this time that my children realised the Nelly obsession was getting out of hand.

On leaving Assisi, Nelly drove Lina to revisit Perugia –and according to Lina, *'lost her heart to Bellucci, wonderful person that he is, he could discourse to her of her native land having visited Copenhagen for the pre-historic museum there.'* Their excursions also included a visit to Spello. They then both returned to England, and visited Dent in his office together. Lina writes that they were *'ushered into his den with a trembling gait but the sight of his well-remembered mustard-coloured waistcoat soon restored me to a feeling of self-possession. He is horribly frightened of women ...And if only you are tall and speak in a firm decided manner you get him to do anything. I am not successful in the management of the great Dent but Miss Erichsen is splendid and Aunt J will fairly double him up and put him in her pocket.'* Nelly would continue to cross swords with Dent over the next two decades, never afraid to take him on over contractual matters, until he quite lost patience with her.

Nelly spent much of the winter of 1899/1900 in Rome, staying at the Hotel Victoria. The almost daily letters and postcards sent home to her mother suggest a whirl of work and socialising, mixing with a jolly group of other English and American tourists, many of them young women of her own age, who were travelling alone. At first her work was delayed by the need to obtain a permit to sketch from the Italian government, but she filled her time with visits to the opera and to other local attractions. The main concern of all the Brits was progress (or lack of it) in the Boer War; she wrote that it was all anyone talked about and that most people spent their time at Miss Wilson's English Library waiting for telegrams from home. But she was really enjoying life, she wrote *"Happy I always am in Rome as you know – there is something in the mere fact of drawing breath here that suits me perfectly."* When she was not dining out, she took meals in her room: soup and roast pigeon, a nice dish of oranges to help get over a cold. A cup of Bovril mid morning, and a Horlicks before bed. She had given up drinking 'sour Italian wine' as it upset her digestion and gave her gout. The letters suggest she was torn, knowing that now that Herman had married, her elderly mother was alone when Frederick was travelling with work, and perhaps feeling that she was expected to drop her own career and return home. To avoid the issue she wrote about how busy she was and how Miss James' death had given her yet more opportunities to work for Dent.

She stayed in Rome until the end of March, sometimes lamenting the difficulty of the work, how complicated and intricate everything was to draw, how annoying the tourists were with their insistence on looking at her work in progress (if she got really angry she would turn her drawing wrong side up and sit in silence until they had passed on). She tried laughing at their stupidity: one

American woman had tried to point out to Nelly the cloister where 'The Last Supper had taken place'. The final straw was the rudeness of the local boys, who shouted abuse at her while she sat trying to draw the Arch of Constantine. But generally she wrote *"I really think few people are more to be envied than I, in this peaceful delightful existence, doing the work I love and with beautiful things to look at everyday – out everyday from half past eight in the morning until six in the evening. I am sunburnt and healthy and stupid and sleepy in consequence. Next week I hope to get out by eight…by the time I get to Florence I will be up at six like last year in Assisi."*

The other major topic of her letters home were her clothes: packing winter clothes into a specially-made wooden box to send back to mother, to be put away with her brother Fred's famous moth tablets; asking Alice to shop for new cotton shirts (one white and one pale blue or green or any colour but pink. Collar size 14). She was concerned that she would not have enough smart clothes for visiting the wealthy villa owners in Florence, but on the whole thought that her smartest outfit, a white woollen dress and a new summer hat, black chip trimmed with black chiffon and white lilac, made a very nice effect. She also invested in a new skirt and short jacket of pale grey flannel with glass buttons, and a readymade pale blue linen skirt and two blouses in pale blue.

In March 1900 Lina invited Nelly to stay at Poggio Gherardo. Janet had previously embarked on a major historical work which she now persuaded Dent to publish, to be called 'Florentine Villas', and it was decided that it should be lavishly embellished with illustrations by Nelly, who was already completing her drawings of Florence for the "Medieval Towns" volume. Nelly travelled around Florence, sometimes on a borrowed bicycle, drawing and sketching the villas that Janet wrote about, often with Lina and a chaperon called Herbert Horne (a Florentine based art historian and collector, the founder of the Museum Horne). Lina wrote: '*Beneath the shadow of a huge umbrella ..I have gone on a voyage of inspection of Florentine Villas for the Zia [Lina's name for her aunt]. Yesterday was a typical excursion...we started by tram to Bagni a Ripoli ...and with some difficulty procured an animal, I can hardly give it the dignified name of horse, and we shambled along...then began the drenching rain and the horse refused to drag us up the hills so bidding sad farewell to our sheltering though inelegant vehicle we trudged bravely over hill and dale and across numerous ploughed fields until after much weariness we reached a deserted and battered looking villa, the former royal Medicean villa of Lappeggi, ye Gods what a scene of havoc and squalid poverty to be viewed on such a day. You may imagine with what suspicion we were looked upon by the fattore as he saw three drenched individuals laden with sketch books, Kodaks, umbrellas, rugs and luncheon baskets claiming admittance to his villa.'*

Eventually they were allowed in, where they caught glimpses of what must have been once a sumptuous interior, but with visible evidence of the destruction wrought by centuries of neglect, compounded by the effects of a terrible earthquake which had struck much of the area in 1895. After they had finished peering round the interior, presumably full of polite compliment, the fattore relaxed enough to let them spread their picnic out to eat, whereafter they *'wandered about the garden in the drenching rain taking photographs beneath an umbrella.'* It is no great surprise that Nelly used a camera, borrowed from Lina, to help her with her illustrations - so much of her work has a photographic quality that it is an obvious assumption. The first box camera which made amateur photography accessible and portable had come to market in 1888. The film was on a roll, not plates, and would be returned to Kodak agents for development. 'You press the button and we'll do the rest' went the strapline.

Photography: -Developing, printing, enlarging etc under the superintendence of English experts; full line of Kodak films, plates, papers, etc; moderate charges. H. Roberts & Co's Pharmacy, 17 Via Tornabuoni, Florence.
Advert in The Italian Gazette October 1910

In the summer of 1900 Dent visited Janet Ross again and fell further under her spell. He was later to write: *'Mrs Ross was quite the Grande Dame, yet democratic in her choice of friends. To have done anything of note was sufficient for an entrée to her circle. Cleverness, talent or capability were the qualities that made her your friend'.* He enjoyed the social life on offer at Poggio Gherado *'Here I met many notabilities, for Mrs Ross's Sunday afternoons were a marked feature in Florence and people of all nationalities resorted to these conversaziones.....Professor and Madame Villari...Lady Paget...Mr Bernard Berenson and his wife, Sir William and Lady Markby and many others.*

'I went year after year to Italy up to the year 1908, and had generally some enterprise that drew me there a book on the Florentine villas, one on the Casentino, books on Rome and one on the Venetian palaces.' Twice, but only twice, his wife went with him. *'Some of the books gave me infinite pleasure in the making, such as Mrs Ross's great book on the Florentine Villas.'*

He tells a charming story of the perils of being one of a party led by Mrs Ross. *'On my last visit to Florence, while staying at Poggio Gherardo, together with Miss*

Nelly Erichsen (the artist who took up Miss James's task after her death) and Dr Lindsay, we decided with Mrs Ross to take a carriage and drive to Siena and stay at San Gimignano by the way. The four of us were packed comfortably into an open carriage…' but when they got to Poggibonsi the heavens opened and the party were soaked. Lindsay and Nelly turned back, but Dent had a business appointment to keep and so he and Mrs Ross went on to Siena, with Ross insisting that Dent, who spoke no Italian, could not manage alone…Arriving in Siena, they had terrible trouble getting rooms. When they eventually found lodgings, Dent was enchanted by the view from his window: But Janet was less enchanted: *'When we met in the morning Mrs R was very cross…had never slept a wink…had lain in her rug on the sofa all night. When breakfast appeared, the bread was unleavened and sour …and she could eat nothing. I was crushed! She suggested that people who were unable to take care of themselves should not go travelling about to other people's annoyance, and I, a poor boy of only some 50 odd summers, followed her down to the carriage with my tail well between my legs.'*

Although Nelly had presumably completed the illustrations for Assisi in the previous year, it was not until October 1900 that Lina finally finished writing the text. There are nearly fifty line drawings illustrating the text, of which about half appear to be the work of Nelly, and have a much more solid and precise line to them than the faint sketches of Miss James. It was a wise move of Dent's to go with line drawings rather than photographs these illustrations have far more immediacy and charm than the poor black and white reproductions in other travel books of the period.

The commissions from Dent marked the beginning of an extremely fruitful decade for Nelly. By 1900 she had completed not just The Story of Assisi, but also produced nearly 40 drawings for Edmund Gardner's *The Story of Florence*, many carrying the date of May 1900. Her work rate was remarkable. The following year Dent published her illustrations for *The Story of Rome*, with some 36 drawings dated 1899 and 1900, and the year after that she worked again for Dent in books on Prague (written by Count Lutzow 33 illustrations), Verona (written by Alethea Wiel), where some of the work had been done by Miss James but with at least a dozen completed by Nelly in February 1902, and Venice (Thomas Okey) with over 50 beautiful drawings.

Janet Ross's *Florentine Villas* was a very different proposition. It was a highly unusual project for Dent, a limited edition (200 copies in England, 100 in the US) of what we would now call a 'coffee table' book, much larger than the guidebooks. Janet dedicated it to her cousin Margaret, Countess of Crawford, who owned one of the villas featured, the Villa Palmieri. In all the book featured some 23 villas, and was illustrated with more than 50 beautifully detailed line drawings by Nelly. With only 300 copies printed, the target audience must have been the owners of the villas and those who aspired to own them or to be invited to stay in one of them. Not Dent's usual target audience at all, and it is hard to think how he was persuaded by Janet and Nelly to undertake the project. Lina was right to say that he was incapable of resisting forceful women. But Janet was particularly proud of the work, her scrapbooks in the British Institute in Florence contain carefully clipped reviews from the New York Daily Tribune, the Daily Telegraph and The Spectator among others. The book has little in the way of architectural or aesthetic description, Janet's preference was always to revel in the historic scandals of the Medici and their contemporaries, occasionally brought slightly up to date with references to the Brownings or Victor Emanuel. If the reader wanted to know what the villas actually looked like, they would have turned to Nelly's illustrations. As Janet wrote in her introduction, Nelly's *'charming drawings of the villas and gardens as they now appear add so much to the beauty and interest of the book.'* Nelly and Janet were to collaborate on two other works over the next dozen years, but never entirely happily. Janet was clearly jealous of Nelly's creative talents, as it has to be said that her own writings are unoriginal, although notable for the linguistic scholarship they demonstrate.

Meanwhile Lina was constantly planning new works with Dent, none of which came to fruition. In May she travelled to Ravenna to scope out a possible book for Dent, but when she returned to Poggio Gherardo she found Dent *'enthroned and delighted, upon my return, and the descent from the steps of Gothic and Roman thrones to the publisher's arena was swift and painful. So like him. He had scoffed at my idea of doing Orvieto and offered me Ravenna. I come back in the seventh heaven about the place to find Mr D anxious for a book on Umbria and scoffing at the town he had offered me.'*

Over the next three years, Nelly stayed regularly with Janet, particularly over the winter period, but soon the harmony of Poggio Gherardo was to be shattered. Lina became more than a little side-tracked from literary pursuits, first by her falling in love with a young artist Aubrey Waterfield, and then much more distractingly by the huge and vicious row that this engangement precipitated with her Aunt Janet. Waterfield had trained at the Slade under

Henry Tonks, but had no fortune and in Janet's view, no prospects. The row was deeply unpleasant for both aunt and niece, and Nelly had to try to keep the peace. In December 1902, Mary Berenson wrote in her diary: *'Miss Erichsen said Mrs Ross was in such a desperate state that she was almost ready to marry her butler Davide. She takes her head in her hands and rocks backwards and forwards crying out "oh what am I to do with my life?"*

Bernard and Mary Berenson also lived in Bellosguardo, just a fifteen minute walk from Poggio Gherardo at a villa called I Tatti, and formed the nucleus of a small group of British and American intellectuals and writers who spent their time talking about art and going off on expeditions to look at art. Their friends included JM Keynes, Lytton Strachey and Edith Wharton. Virginia Woolf, who visited in 1904, said of them that their circle consisted of 'numbers of weak young men and old ladies arriving in four-wheelers.'

After Lina married, the relationship between Lina and Janet was never again as close as it had been. Lina and Aubrey were wed at ChristChurch, Mayfair in July 1902, and their first child, a boy called Gordon, was born in 1903. But Aubrey was struggling to make a living and when Dent offered them the opportunity to write and illustrate a history of Rome they jumped at the chance and returned to Italy. However, following a second, deeply unpleasant row between Lina and Janet, who had accused her niece of meddling with the provisions of Henry's will, (which Lina vehemently denied), living permanently with Janet was not an option. Instead the couple looked for a place of their own, where they could live cheaply and at a reasonable distance from the gossipy Anglo-Italian set in Florence. They found and bought an old ruined castle further north on the Tuscan coast at Aulla, where they lived and brought up their children until the First World War intervened. Nelly loved visiting them in this cliff-bound hideaway.

Meanwhile Janet had got her claws firmly into Mr Dent to mutual commercial satisfaction presumably, as in 1902 Dent published '*Letters from the East*'. These were the edited recollections of Janet's husband Henry Ross who had died that year, worn down, one can imagine, by the constant rowing in his household occasioned by Lina's marriage. The same year saw Nelly's friend Reginald Brimley Johnson publishing a new edition of Lady Duff-Gordon's Letters from Egypt, under his own imprint, with an introduction by Meredith and revisions by Janet. Maybe Nelly had helped to engineer this project, as a way of distracting Janet from her misery over Lina, and also as a helpful bit of work for Rex.

In October 1902, Nelly had a much more pleasant family interlude. Her nephew Frank (Francis Herman Lucas, the second child and only son of Alice and Edgar) was engaged to be married to a young Anglo-Scottish girl, Helen Mary Smith, and they wanted to take a holiday in Venice. Helen had just completed a degree at Oxford University and as a reward her aunts had given her the money to make a trip. It was, of course, out of the question that they should travel alone before they were married, so Aunt Nelly was drafted in as chaperone. Frank was to have a distinguished career in the Indian Office of the Civil Service, rising to be Principal Private Secretary to Lord Morley and Austen Chamberlain. Educated at Winchester, he had followed in his father's footsteps to Trinity College, Cambridge where he was awarded a First. They stayed on the Fondamenta Venier, the Murano canalside, and hired a gondolier for the week called Pietro, who would row Helen and Frank around sightseeing in the mornings, while Nelly worked, and in the afternoons would take them all across to the islands with a spirit kettle to make tea. Frank and Nelly would sit and draw while Helen read Italian novels. Frank's notebook from the journey has been preserved by his descendants Nicholas and Serge, detailing expenditure (3 lire for tobacco, 2 lire for a new Meerschaum pipe, tips for the gondoliere), and a sketch, done by Frank, of a lady sitting in the prow of a gondola next to the tea set. This must surely be Nelly.

Gnocchi 'alla Romana'

Mix five and a half ounces of flour and two eggs in a saucepan, add one pint of milk by degrees, and three quarters of an ounce of Gruyere cheese cut into bits. When the paste is cooked put in salt to taste, and three quarters of an ounce of good butter, spread it in a dish to the thickness of three-quarters of an inch and let it cool. Then cut it into small square pieces and pile it in layers in a baking dish with three-quarters of an ounce of good butter in bits, and three-quarters of an ounce of grated Parmesan cheese between the layers (but not on the outside). Brown with the salamander or in a hot oven and serve at once.

Note: Eggs must be quite fresh, if they taste of straw the sauce will be spoiled.

Extract from "Leaves from our Tuscan Kitchen" by Janet Ross, 1899

A drive out in carriages

"Now, the English colony at Florence, Miss Honeychurch, - and it is of quite considerable size, though of course not all equally a few are here for trade, for example. But the greater part are students. Lady Helen Laverstoke is at present busy over Fra Angelico. I mention her name because we are passing her villa on the left. No, you can only see it if you stand no do not stand; you will fall. She is very proud of the thick hedge. Inside, perfect seclusion. One might have gone back six hundred years. Some critics believe that her garden was the scene of The Decameron, which lends it an additional interest, does it not?"

"It does indeed!" cried Miss Lavish. "Tell me, where do they place the scene of that wonderful seventh day?"

But Mr Eager proceeded to tell Miss Honeychurch that on the right lived Mr Something Something, an American of the best type so rare! and that the Somebody Elses were farther down the hill. "Doubtless you know her monographs in the series of "Medieval Byways'? He is working at Gemistus Pletho. Sometimes as I take tea in their beautiful grounds I hear over the wall the electric tram squealing up the new road with its load of hot, dusty, unintelligent tourists who are going to 'do' Fiesole in an hour in order that they may say they have been there, and I think - I think - I think how little they think what lies so near them."

A Room with a View, EM Forster.

Poggio Gherardo

Miss Nelly Erichsen

requests the pleasure of

Company

at an Exhibition of some of her

Italian Drawings to be held at

The Ryder Gallery,

10, Ryder Street.

from March 14th to the 21st inclusive.

Private View 14th March. 10 to 6.

Chapter Eight: Highways and Byways

In 1903, after four years of constant work in Italy and elsewhere on the continent, Nelly returned to England and took studios at 136a Grosvenor Road, right on the Thames Embankment in London. Her younger brother Frederick had finally announced his intention to marry and as his fiancee, a widow, had two young daughters already, he needed to establish his own household. This would leave Nelly's increasingly frail and poorly-sighted mother living alone in Tooting, and Nelly, the youngest daughter, had to come home and lend a hand. But she was not proposing to give up her independence or her career. Her work had been well-received in England, and had recently received very honorable mention in a book called "English Book Illustration of Today' by Rose Sketchley. *'She works with graceful distinctness and many of the drawings in The Story of Rome...show what she can do.'* She had some success showing her work at an exhibition at The Ryder Street Gallery, and now looked around for other opportunities. She wrote to Frederick Macmillan, Alexander's eldest nephew and now the head of the Macmillan publishing empire:

'Dear Mr Macmillan
George [Macmillan, his cousin] may possibly have mentioned to you that I am anxious to submit some of my recent pen drawings to you. I have been working in Italy with Mr Dent for the last four years, and since my return have had an exhibition of some of my drawings at the Ryder St Gallery.

'You did not, I think, see this, & if it did not trouble you I should like to ask you to look at a few of the drawings. I could either send them to you at St Martins Street, or I should be very glad to see you here.

'I am anxious to arrange for work in England & should be glad if you had anything in my line that you cared to trust to me.
Yours sincerely
Nelly Erichsen

It would take me a day or two to gather together the drawings I want you to see as they were nearly all sold.'

The Ryder Street Gallery exhibition was a very small affair, just twelve of her drawings from Assisi and Venice, selling at 3 or 4 guineas each. It was well-reviewed in The Illustrated London News: *'very intelligent and appreciative studies of the best things in Italy in sound pen drawing.'* But even if she had sold as many as ten, it would have made her no more than thirty or forty pounds before commissions to the gallery. Life must have been financially very precarious. However her pitch to Macmillan must have been successful, for in early September she was writing to Frederick Macmillan from her sister Dora's home in Hillerod, Denmark to say:

'Olive [Maclehose, cousin of Frederick and friend of Nelly] has forwarded me a note from you to her containing an offer to me of the illustrating of a volume of your [Highways and Byways] series, and asks me to answer it directly to you.

'I am very grateful to you for remembering me & accept your offer with great pleasure. It's exactly the work I had wished for now that my mother's advancing years prevent my going so far afield as I have done of late years.

'As to the choice of subject you give me perhaps I may postpone my decision till I return to London in about 10 days when, if you will allow me, I will come and see you at St Martins Street.

'I am just now with Dora whose husband's health has broken down and we have been selling their place in the country and settling them in this little town.
'Again thanking you
I am yours sincerely
Nelly Erichsen
'Quote your proposed terms'

Poor Nelly, burdened as ever with the lot of the spinster, to be worrying about her mother's health and helping her sister whose husband was dying.

By March 1904 she was back in London at the Riviera Studios, writing again to Frederick Macmillan:

'Dear Mr Macmillan
I am hoping to start for Derbyshire in about a fortnight to make the drawings for the Highways and Byways Vol. of that county and before going I thought it wiser to ask you if you have any further instructions to give me. I have Mr Firth's itinerary, but as it is some time since I spoke to you it occurred to me as possible that he might have made some changes in his plan.

'If this is so, or if you have any remarks to make perhaps you will kindly let me know'

In June she wrote from lodgings in Ashbourne, Derbyshire asking for further instructions on whether all drawings had to be full page, or whether smaller sketches could be inserted into the text. She was working directly with Firth the author and enjoying her work, she said. The two of them had conferred and had decided to widen the scope of the drawings to include the more minor but equally charming smaller manor houses and village churches. There is a pencil note on the letter from Macmillan which seems to suggest the fee was £3 each for 50 drawings. The 70 or so drawings were to be completed over Christmas 1904 and sent to George Macmillan. Her work was slightly delayed by an attack of influenza. Nelly then sublet her studio and planned to moved back to her sister Alice's house in Tooting, after a stay with old Fabian Socialist friends, Aneurin and Helen Williams, in Hindhead on the Surrey Downs. *'Hindhead air is the best specific I know for all the ills of the flesh'* she wrote to George, who had praised her drawings very kindly. But the project did not finish without a hitch. Just a few weeks later she wrote from Meadowside, in Grantchester, home of Harriet, Fanny Johnson's sister, who had recently married an academic named Arthur Berry.

'Dear George
I apologise sincerely for having been so careless in my last communication as to omit telling you I should be unable to furnish the two drawings of which you speak. Wootton Lodge, Ellerton, proved to be off Mr Firth's route, and I have unfortunately lost my sketch of Bakewell. Pray forgive me.

'It was a real pleasure to me to have this glimpse of Will [George's son]. I have had few opportunities of meeting him since he was a boy and am greatly charmed with the beauty of his expression and his mind.'

Nelly had needed to develop a good working relationship with the author, John Benjamin Firth, because he had decided that the best way of tackling his book on Derbyshire was by means of a walking tour. He wrote: *'The truth is that you cannot see Derbyshire by rail; you cannot this is a matter for deep thanksgiving see it by motor; nor yet can you see it by cycle....to see Derbyshire you must walk.'* All very well, but hard work for his illustrator, who seems to have followed pretty faithfully in his footsteps, as there are drawings of river banks and Peak District hills which suggest she often had to carry her equipment a long way off the beaten track. But her contribution was appreciated: Firth wrote in his preface that he was grateful to Nelly not just for her charming illustrations, *'but for numerous interesting details relating to persons and places.'*

Netherfield, Upper Tooting
Feb 28th 1905

Dear George
Will you do me a great kindness? I am starting for Italy on 7 March & I am now obliged to manage all my small affairs myself. If, therefore, it were not asking too much it would be doing me a great service if you would kindly let me have a cheque before I start.

Not only should I be able to arrange for its disposal, but should avoid the difficulty that might arise from my having no fixed abode, as will be the case for the present.....It is a very ungracious action, I am only too conscious, to trouble you on the eve of your departure, but I feel sure you will forgive me.

I am to see Sir Frederick Treves tomorrow....

A cheque for £150, a considerable sum, was received by return of post. The meeting with Treves, an eminent surgeon who had been knighted for his success in performing an appendectomy on King Edward VII in 1902, was to plan a volume of the Highways and Byways Series on Dorset, Treves' home county. By May Day 1905 the Derbyshire book was published and Nelly was back from Italy and off to Dorset, where she started her next set of drawings. However, all this rushing about proved too much and Nelly fell ill. On 7 August she wrote to George from lodgings in Shaftesbury, Dorset, requesting a meeting before she left for Switzerland. She met him to explain that although she had started the project, ill-health would prevent her from completing it. Her family had persuaded her to take a complete break, and she was setting off for a hotel in Adelboden, acknowledging that she would not be able to finish the work due to the breakdown she had suffered, and asking for her regrets to be conveyed to Treves for the trouble she had caused him. At the meeting, George had tried to persuade her to finish the project, or at least to submit what she had completed for payment, but she was too ill. '*With regard to your kind offer to pay for the work already done, while thanking you, I prefer to abide by the decision I expressed to you when I saw you at St Martins Street. It only remains for me to express my extreme regret that the matter should have turned out so, & to thank you for your offer of future work, of which I shall venture to remind you as soon as my health is sufficiently established.*'

From Switzerland, Nelly travelled on to spend the winter in Tuscany. She was by now a regular guest at Poggio Gherardo, although this had the disadvantage that she had to cope with Mrs Ross's increasingly 'formidable' behaviour, as noted by her neighbours the Berensons. She was at Poggio for New Year's Eve 1905/6, when Janet invited Berenson to join them for dinner. He wrote to his wife Mary who was back in England '*Dined with Mrs Ross, She is frightfully bored directly the conversation rises above "dear so-and-so" and "horrid such-one" as it did repeatedly last night thanks to Miss Erichsen [who] is a person with some abstract interests and that, after all, is what I want out of people in the long run*'. This is a very comforting note for a biographer to find - Berenson was a well-known intellectual snob, and for Nelly to have kept his interest paid her a great compliment. In fact Berenson took quite a shine to Nelly - just a few days later he wrote again to his wife describing a lunch party he had given for the some German friends, the Davidsohns, with Janet and Nelly, where the conversation had been conducted largely in German, although, as he said, '*I find mine is clean gone. I was surprised at the excellence of Miss E's. D is a very sweet-seeming man, so well informed and very reasonable and thoughtful, that he leaves you nothing to say except "of course" or Miss E's "obviously". They took to one another greatly.*'

One more glimpse of Nelly's complicated relationship with Janet is given in a letter from Lina to Bessie Trevelyan in early 1907, when Lina and Janet were still at daggers drawn over Henry Ross's will. She talked to Bessie about the attitude of Nelly and of Mary Berenson '*they are not in the least horrified at her conduct... they are both dependent on Aunt J for much and have to shut their eyes and pretend to find endless excuses.*'

Madge Vaughan never did visit Lina in Italy again, although they met in England. In 1904 Virginia Stephens, later Woolf, recovering from her first serious bout of mental illness, went to stay with Madge and her husband Will at Giggleswick School. Virginia recorded her pity for Madge: *'a woman of stature and literary ambition, now condemned to intellectual penury.'* [9] At the time, Madge was keeping her literary interests alive submitting occasional book reviews, and she encouraged Virginia to keep writing, and to submit some of her pieces to The Guardian for publication. Before long, Virginia would summon the courage to complete her first novel. Madge's relationship with Virginia was of longstanding when she was seven she had stayed with the Stephens family in Hyde Park Gate, and her husband Will Vaughan was a cousin. Virginia seems to have had an adolescent crush on Madge. But later this friendship withered - Leonard Woolf found Madge's 'flightiness' unbearable, and neither he nor Virginia liked Will Vaughan, whom they considered priggish. The situation was not improved when Madge 'cut' Virginia's sister Vanessa because she disapproved of her extra-marital relationships. But many think that the character of Sally Seaton in Woolf's Mrs Dalloway was based on Madge.

In 1912, Vaughan took up the post of Headmaster of Wellington School, and bought his wife, as a surprise, a first class return ticket to Florence, to stay with Janet. *'When the time to pack came round, Aunt J said she would come a bit of the way with me so we all motored off to Collodi. It was the end of October: the woods up behind the splendid palace felt very still, and under the mighty ilex trees there was a carpet of wild pink cyclamens. We lunched on the long stone table up on the terrace above the ilex groves, and we said goodbye. Late in the afternoon Nellie [sic] Erichsen fetched me and drove me on to her home in the Bagni di Lucca, then she and I drove over the Appennines to Bologna in the splendid autumn weather with the cherry trees ablaze and the gentians blue beneath them. Another two days and I was home at Wellington.'*

When Lina found out that Madge had been so near, but that neither she nor Nelly had been brave enough to challenge Janet by arranging a meeting between the old friends, she was livid. She wrote to Bessie Trevelyan to say that Nelly had offered to bring Madge to see Lina, but then had changed her mind thinking it would be disloyal to Janet, to whom she had given her word. So instead, according to Lina, Nelly and Madge spent three days at Bagna. Poor Nelly, still stuck in the middle of this ridiculous feud, especially as by this time Lina and her aunt were supposed to be reconciled. But by then, Nelly had found new friends to live with in Italy, and her ties to Janet began to loosen.

---

[9] *Nigel Nicholson: 'Virginia Woolf' 2000*

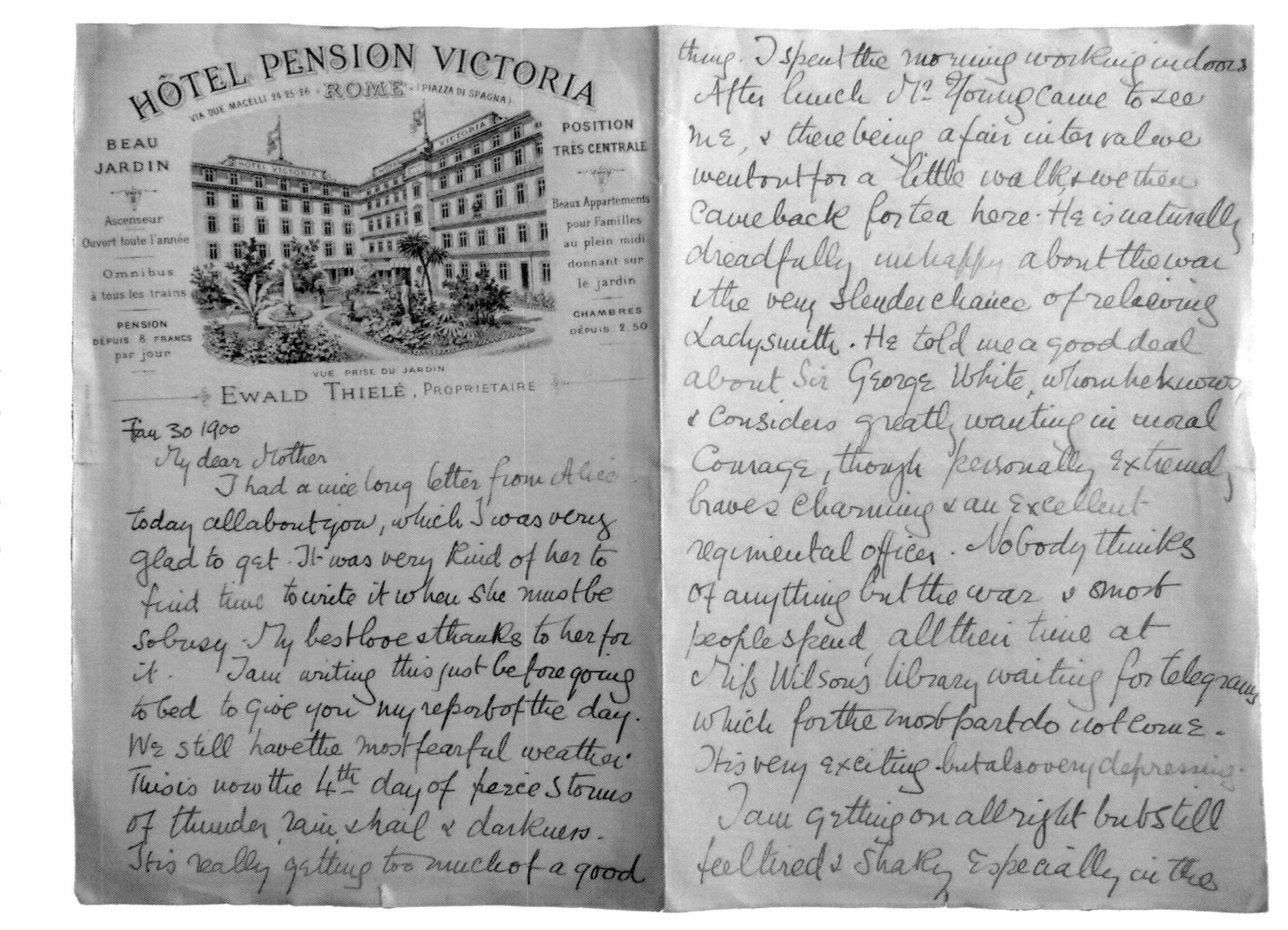

HÔTEL PENSION VICTORIA
VIA DUE MACELLI 24·25·26 · ROME · (PIAZZA DI SPAGNA)
BEAU JARDIN
Ascenseur
Ouvert toute l'année
Omnibus
à tous les trains
PENSION
DEPUIS 8 FRANCS
par jour
POSITION TRÈS CENTRALE
Beaux Appartements pour Familles au plein midi donnant sur le jardin
CHAMBRES
DEPUIS 2.50
VUE PRISE DU JARDIN
EWALD THIELÉ, PROPRIETAIRE

Jan 30 1900

My dear Mother

I had a nice long letter from Alice today all about you, which I was very glad to get. It was very kind of her to find time to write it when she must be so busy. My best love & thanks to her for it. I am writing this just before going to bed to give you my report of the day. We still have the most fearful weather. This is now the 4th day of fierce storms of thunder, rain, & hail & darkness. It is really getting too much of a good thing. I spent the morning working indoors. After lunch Mr Young came to see me, & there being a fair interval we went out for a little walk, & we then came back for tea here. He is naturally dreadfully unhappy about the war & the very slender chance of relieving Ladysmith. He told me a good deal about Sir George White, whom he knows & considers greatly wanting in moral courage, though personally extremely brave & charming & an excellent regimental officer. Nobody thinks of anything but the war & most people spend all their time at Miss Wilson's library waiting for telegrams which for the most part do not come. It is very exciting but also very depressing.

I am getting on all right but still feel tired & shaky especially in the

Letter from Nelly to her mother, January 1900

Portrait of Thomas Martin Lindsay

Chapter Nine: Thomas Lindsay

In the summer of 1906, a new character arrived in Nelly's world who was to play a major role in her life for nearly a decade, offering practical and emotional support with a light-hearted touch. Dr Thomas Lindsay was a Glasgow academic and a minister of the Scottish Free Church. Recently widowed, he had five grown children and was twenty years Nelly's senior. With a twinkle in his eye and a wicked sense of humour, he seems to have brought some much needed happiness and friendship into her life. His wife Anna, a keen campaigner for women's rights, had died in 1903. He was visiting an old friend, Isabel MacDougall, who was living in Florence when he first made the acquaintance of Janet Ross. It was a source of a long-lived joke between them that Janet did not immediately grasp that Lindsay was a minister of the Church, as he wore no dog collar on holiday, and that they might never have become such firm friends had Janet known - there was very little room for the religious in Janet's life.

Loneliness and the difficulties of the single life were problems that caused both Nelly and Lindsay some unhappiness. But they had many other enthusiasms in common - a mutual love of the Florentine countryside, an interest in historical research, a passion for writing, and a slightly morbid interest in each other's health. At various times over the next eight years, until Lindsay's chronic asthma finally led to his death, Nelly, Janet and Lindsay were writing several times a week, and much of this correspondence is preserved: many of Janet and Nelly's letters to him have survived in the Lindsay family archive at Keele University, and after the Great War Janet published an edited selection of Lindsay's letters to her. Nelly also carefully preserved many of Lindsay's letters - it is not known when these were returned to the Lindsay family, whether it was after his death by Nelly herself, or perhaps after her own death by her family.

[Thomas Lindsay]

My copy of Janet's collected letters from Lindsay, published in 1923, has a fascinating pencil note written on the flyleaf. The writing is indistinct, but I think it says 'I came on this book in Matthews bookshop, Eglinton Street, Glasgow on Thursday 30 March 1939. I used to see this ugly-looking man walking up Woodside Crescent Glasgow going to the Free Church College in the Nineties. He must not have been living in Westbourne Gardens then. He had a turned up nose but seemed to have a [pretty] good idea of himself. He was undoubtedly a man of some ability but common.' It seems a rather mean-minded summing up of a stranger who I have come to know through his letters and feel very fondly towards. The photograph that Janet chose to include in her book certainly does not make him look ugly his trim white beard, snub nose and kindly, twinkling eyes suggest an attractive and amusing companion. Janet wrote that his eyes were very blue.

Although resolutely formal in address: 'Dear Mrs Ross, Yours ever, Thomas Lindsay', 'Dear Dr Lindsay, yours very sincerely Nelly Erichsen', ' Dear Miss Erichsen, Yours ever, Thomas M Lindsay' 'Yours ever, Janet Ross', some of the letters contain an element of flirtaciousness, and certainly a great deal of affection. Lindsay laughs gently with Janet about Nelly's passion for fresh air and drafts, and teases Nelly with gentle sideswipes at Janet's bossiness and nosiness. But for both ladies, he seems to have a been a treasured correspondent, with perhaps a trace of jealousy visible in their words when either seems to have been preferred. Janet certainly loved to patronise Nelly. But Nelly's letters seem more amusing, and are much more interesting than Janet's, which often seem to be a litany of complaints and bitchy remarks.

When they first met, Janet invited Lindsay to stay with her at Poggio Gherardo - which he then did most months of May until his death in 1914, and sometimes in early September as well. One year, when he could not get to Italy, Janet visited him in Glasgow, although appalling weather made it a rather frustrating and unsuccessful trip. Janet was not an easy guest. And as Dent had learnt, Janet was not one to pretend she was happy if she did not have her creature comforts. Nelly was more often staying with Janet over the New Year, but there were several occasions when Nelly and Lindsay met at the houses of mutual friends in Scotland or sometimes, daringly, in Italy without Janet to chaperone them.

When Janet introduced them, Lindsay and Nelly discovered they had good, longstanding friends in common - the MacLehose family, publishers to the University of Glasgow, were closely related to Nelly's great friends, the Macmillans, and were also friends of Lindsay. In 1886 Olive, one of the older daughters of Alexander Macmillan and a great friend of Nelly, married Norman MacLehose, the same age as her and a distinguished opthalmic surgeon. Ten years later Olive's younger half-sister, Mary, aged just 21, married Norman's older brother James, by that time nearly 40 and a successful publisher in his own right. James and Mary set up home at The Old Parsonage in Lamington, where both Nelly and Lindsay were invited to spend time. Lindsay also knew Joseph Dent and had worked with him.

Janet also had mutual friends with Lindsay - in particular, two fascinating sisters, Lady Lucy Duff-Gordon and Mrs Glyn. Lucy Duff-Gordon was married to Janet's cousin, Sir Cosmo Duff-Gordon, and had become famous as a couturier and fashion designer, working in London and New York under the name of Lucille. Mrs Glyn, better known by her professional name of Elinor Glyn, worked to support her family by writing sensational, sometimes racy novels. Both of these ladies were a source of fascination to Lindsay - he was, he claimed, cajoled by them into reading (twice!) Mrs Glyn's most infamous work, *Three Weeks,* (published by Duckworth) about an affair between a Balkan princess and an aristocratic Englishman. Sir Cosmo and Lady Duff-Gordon were later, notoriously, survivors of the Titanic - having managed to get into the first lifeboat to leave the ship (capacity 40, occupants 12).

In the summer of 1906, when Lindsay met Janet and Nelly, the two women were collaborating for the first time as authors for Dent on *The Story of Pisa.* This was to be a long and painful process which would nearly ruin their friendship on many occasions as it took them three years to finish writing and get the book published. Many of Nelly and Janet's letters to Lindsay had, as a pretext at least, the desire to pick his brains for these personal literary endeavours. At first the only correspondence was between Lindsay and Janet. But in the middle of November 1906, Janet wrote to Lindsay to say that Nelly, who was staying with her, was very ill. It may have been a recurrence of the nervous breakdown that had so affected her in the summer of 1905, but it is hard to tell the extent to which it was physical or mental. There certainly seems to have been an element of nerves or depression. Janet was quite worried about her, but, on Nelly's instructions, her illness was to be kept secret and in particular, the publisher Dent was not to be told. *'We both wish you were here, very much indeed.'* Furthermore, Mrs MacLehose was to be told not to write with good wishes for Nelly, *'My orders are that she is to be encouraged in every way, so I tell a lie every morning and say she looks better. Her nerves have entirely broken down.* She trembles all over, and is so weak she can hardly stand.' This sounds terrible, but one must remember that Janet was quite a drama queen and only too happy to put other people down.

The news seems to have prompted Lindsay to pick up his pen to start to write to Nelly, much to her delight and obvious gratitude. She wrote to him, while staying with Janet, in December 1906 *'Dear Dr Lindsay, I hadn't yet got over the pleasure your first letter gave me, and was still chuckling at intervals at the thought of you sitting, sleepy but steadfast, on your hatbox, soothing the terrors of your poor fellow travellers, when your second arrived yesterday. This was even better than the first as its gossip was about people I know, which is always better than general gossip, though that is next-best.*

'Your dinner party must have been one of the very nicest on record, though when I told Mrs Ross that you had consumed a bottle and a half of vermouth she was horrified. I wish very much I'd been there.' Then comes one of those paragraphs that really makes me wish I had the other half of the correspondence: *'With regard to chaperones. My only objection to the system you so be-laud is that the poor chaperones do suffer so dreadfully. It was always a shadow cast on my pleasure, in the days when I used to go to dances, to see their poor patient faces planted round the walls, and their heroic efforts to keep awake - so let's have none of them (perhaps it will be necessary to start a society to protect them from you.).'* If Nelly's illness had truly been depression rather than physical, then it is clear from the tone of this letter that hearing from Lindsay was a huge tonic. I love the way Nelly has managed subtly to introduce a picture of herself as a young girl being whirled round the dancefloor. It is pretty clear that she likes this image and does not want to be thought of as the maiden aunt chaperone, even though we know that, by this stage in her life, her early forties, she often was.

The other guest at Poggio Gherardo that winter was Lina Duff Gordon's aged relative, Canon George Waterton: *'You asked how I treat the Canon. I didn't know, & so I asked him....he said that I treated him with great condescension. This was a fearful shock, for I had imagined myself humbly sitting at his feet, but one never knows.'*

Nelly was by this time convalescing at Poggio, and playing patience rather than working; but Janet was in bed with bronchitis, and getting worse, worn out, she said, by looking after the Canon and keeping Miss Erichsen's spirits up.

Nelly's letters to Lindsay sound playful and cheerful, but that does not seem to be the effect she had on those who met her. Indeed, in November 1906 Isabel MacDougall had written to Lindsay *'Mrs Ross has been ill and looked very old and pulled down. Entre-nous, I don't think Miss Erichsen is a healthy influence. Everybody seems to get ill where she is, and the way in which she talks perpetually about her health and symptoms is very terrible and unedifying in the real sense of the word.' Janet wrote in late December that 'Miss E is a little better, but she is in a terribly nervous excited state, which sometimes makes her difficult to live with.'*

Nelly and Janet seemed to have two principal bones of contention, apart from squabbles about the book they were writing: women's rights, a cause of which Janet was very suspicious but which Nelly supported; and fresh air. Back in England, the Pankhursts and their organisation, the Women's Social and Political Union, with its far more militaristic strategy than Mrs Fawcett's earlier group, were beginning to have an impact of a kind which would make headlines on a regular basis, and headlines which would reach Italy. In October 1906 around 100 suffragettes attempted to invade the House of Commons at the opening of Parliament and in the ensuing scuffle ten women were arrested and sent to prison. In December 1906 Janet wrote to Lindsay *'I read with disgust the spectacle women (females I would almost call them) made of themselves in London! Wallowing on the ground and kicking and embracing policemen! Why will not women be content with being women and not try to ape men! If they reflected they would know that women always get all they want if they remain women. Fancy a parliament of women's rights women!!! But I think that spinsters and widows with property, and therefore a stake in the country ought to have votes: not married women. They would either vote with their husbands or with their possible lovers, and then there'd be a row!'*

The second difference between them was fresh air: Nelly was a fan of open windows, Janet believed they caused illness. *'To a person who abhors cold, it is rather sickening to be told how nice an open window would be, and how I am sure not to be well because I don't sleep in mid-winter with both my windows open! Why are open-air people so cock-sure they are right? Both my maids have caught very bad colds by Miss Erichsen's wanting tea at 7am in bed with wide open windows. Brr! Brr! However I am glad to say she is really on the mend, and goes on Tuesday to Aulla.* [Lina's home in Northern Tuscany].'

Lina was staying at Poggio, still trying to mend fences with her aunt. Nelly spoke of *'Mrs Ross's beautiful niece…she is as sweet as she is lovely and so is good for both soul and eye.'* On 3rd January 1907 Aubrey Waterfield wrote to his mother from Aulla: *'Lina is still at Poggio. Returns today. I pressed her to stay if it was any good - very self-denying of both of us. Her old uncle Waterton is at PG and failing; Miss Erichsen has some incurable illness and Mrs Ross is a martyr to all the ills in the Pharmaecopea....thank goodness she comes back tonight.'* However on the same day, Mary Berenson wrote to her mother: *'I went to Mrs Ross this afternoon. When I was leaving, Nelly Erichsen took me into her room to tell me that Lina (who left today) and her aunt have really begun to make it up. Lina is not very well and she let Aunt Janet have her own doctor to see her and he worked on Aunt J's feelings that Lina needed her care. This touches her heart'.*

Four days later, Mary went to Poggio to say goodbye to Nelly *"whom Lina is taking off Mrs Ross's hands for a while"* - presumably to stay with her at Aulla. A month later, Lina wrote to her friend Bessie Trevelyan *'I quite forgot to tell you about the Poggio visit. It was successful as far as it went but very trying as I found the effort to dissolve the iceberg very difficult. The first days my aunt never looked at me or addressed a single word to me. My uncle (Waterton)'s presence and Miss Erichsen's made the position just tolerable.'* So Nelly cannot always have been moaning about her health.

After all, Nelly had a new occupation to keep her busy and in limited funds. This is an extract from the Annual Report of the British School in Rome, Session 1905-1906:

"Miss N. Erichsen spent four months of the spring in Rome in the study of villas and gardens both of the classical and the Renaissance period, in preparation for a comprehensive work on the subject, which will be illustrated by her own drawings. Her work will be continued in the coming session."

The British School at Rome had been established only in 1901 and was to receive a Royal Charter in 1911 and splendid new buildings designed by Lutyens. Its aims were *"to promote knowledge of and deep engagement with all aspects of the art, history and culture of Italy by scholars and fine artists from Britain and the Commonwealth, and to foster international and interdisciplinary exchange."* It is clear from this report how well Nelly held her own in an academic environment still dominated by males she is one of only two women listed out of fifteen scholars. The expenditure of the Society amounted to just over £1000 that year, suggesting that Nelly's grant cannot have been more than £60 or £70.

By February 1907, Nelly was stationed in the Hotel Victoria, Rome, continuing her researches, and wrote to Lindsay, explaining that she had been

ill again, but had enjoyed her stay at Aulla, a place of enchanting beauty, she wrote, where Lina and Aubrey had, *'like the coneys, built their nest among the rocks...the mountain air is very ardent, and the sense of being raised above the weaknesses of humanity by its mere rarity is very strong...'*. Her doctor had advised her that she was indeed well enough to resume work, but that she should be taking it easy for two or three more years to come. She wrote to Lindsay *'I shall now have to learn how to go at a low speed without letting the fire go out in the furnace, and if taken as a fine art no doubt that will be interesting too. I think it is very unegotistical of me to tell you of this improvement, for I fear you will no longer think me in need of letters.'*

Later that month, Janet wrote to Lindsay *'I'm afraid poor Miss Erichsen feels the change from here to an hotel in Rome badly...I am so sorry for her, and I do feel such a beast at having let her nerves get upon mine, but she I'm sure did not know it, as she wants to come back here when my cousins the Markbys are gone in April.'*

Introspection brought on by the prolonged bout of influenza and by the prospect of an indefinite period of ill-health seems to be the order of the day, and Nelly's letters to Lindsay suggest that she was open about her problems and found him supportive. She spoke of her struggles to keep her spirits up, but wrote cheerfully enough to her new friend on many topics, for instance discussing the life of Shakespeare (a particular interest, she says, since she was a 'backfisch', her word for a teenage girl).

Lindsay had asked her to look after his sister-in-law, Mrs Molly Murray-Dunlop, who was shortly to visit Rome, and Nelly was only too happy to oblige although she warned that she would be heading northward back to Tuscany at Eastertime. She also discussed with him her love of books, her current treasure being a novella by Sachetti, a 14th century Italian writer. She was obviously an accomplished reader of the medieval Italian language, as well as an increasingly competent classical scholar, 'grubbing at' Roman villas. But she mentioned that, whatever Bernard Berenson had thought, she didn't feel her conversational German was strong enough to engage the professors in Rome.

In early March she wrote to him again, delighted with the acquaintance she had made of his sister-in-law. Then she continued *'I'm glad you have a warm corner in your heart for Maiden Aunts. I've been one since I was ten years old, I love the part. Nieces and nephews are dear things, & great-nieces, of whom I've two, exquisite. If one keeps away from the rocks of didactic superiority one can get as near them as if they were brothers and sisters. Two of my nieces, however, are little Danish girls of 12 and 13. So of course they are too far away from me in age to feel that, but they have invented a charming part for me to play that of fairy godmother - & of course one has to try to live up to it.'*

The young Danish girls in question, Xenia and Sylvia, were the daughters of Nelly's sister Dora. They would have been in Nelly's thoughts as their father was dying. He died in November 1907 and Dora chose to return to England, and move in with Alice and Edgar in Elm Park Gardens, Chelsea, where they had relocated in the early 1900s.

Nelly was planning to head north to Pisa and Lucca, via Florence and her doctor's consulting room, until the end of May, to make the drawings for the books she and Janet had planned. She explains that she has just begun to draw again. *'This little fact means a very great deal for me because, since my breakdown two years ago, the mere thought of touching a pencil or brush has been a nightmare. So now in essentials, 'Richard is himself again'* [a paraphrase of Shakespeare, just meaning 'back to normal'] *and a very thankful woman. The humour of the situation too is charming. Here is a woman.... solemnly making up her mind not to be able to work, and while she writes the benign influences above are healing her and filling her with both power and desire. Of course the mere body is still tiresome and has to be humoured, but that doesn't matter really.'* Janet Ross also noted that this was a good recovery by Nelly: *'when she left [here] she could not draw a straight line'.*

Lindsay and Nelly took pleasure in each others' intellect, and Lindsay in particular had become interested in her musings on Shakespeare. He wrote asking to see the notes she had made on the subject, but she told him they were at the bottom of a chest in a London warehouse. She then asked him for help with her project on ancient Roman villas and gardens, discussing the conversations she had been having with the professors in Rome, and encouraging him to visit both Pisa and Lucca next time he is Florence as they are 'so important and beautiful'. She had engaged his attention, or appealed to his intellectual vanity, for her next correspondence with him is full of gratitude for books sent and references suggested. She was heading back from Rome to stay at her favourite Florence boarding house, Miss Godkin's, but arranged to meet him in Pisa to show him round later in May.

At this time Lindsay's letters to Janet are also full of helpful notes for her researches into Pisa and Lucca, and this led Janet to say that she would acknowledge him in the introduction, but Lindsay objected: *'I always thought of myself as one of those rotary book-cases and you as turning it round every now and then for a book of reference. Let me be your rotary book-case. You would never mention a book-case in your preface!'* Lindsay said that keeping Tuscany ever in his mind that winter had kept his doctor's bills down.

In May 1907, Lindsay returned to Tuscany, taking his daughter Susie with him to Poggio Gherardo and meeting Nelly in Pisa. Together he and Nelly visited the Archives at Pisa: Lindsay later wrote to Janet that Nelly had 'made a conquest' of the Professore there. Is it significant that it is after this shared adventure, without Janet's interference, that Nelly started to keep Lindsay's letters? Until that date we only have the letters that Lindsay preserved from her. For Lindsay to tease Nelly about her conquests is in itself an admission of admiration, surely. Thomas Lindsay was an attractive and interesting man, and a widower. Several of his friends had urged him to think of marrying again. If Nelly had ever wondered about marriage, could she have begun to feel that it was never too late? After all, she was only in her early 40s.

The first letter from Lindsay which Nelly kept is dated 27 July 1907, when he wrote offering to lend her a book about Pisa when they met at Lamington in early August (the home of James MacLehose) which she could keep until they met again at Newton Stewart (the home of his sister-in-law Molly). A succession of coincidental meetings, or a plan? Nelly had also asked to borrow his Latin dictionary, but he explained that as it runs to 12 volumes, she would do better to come to Glasgow and *'work your difficulties out here…Susie will be here.'* Yet again, the question of a chaperone, but this time the suggestion is that it may be Nelly who needs one, staying with Lindsay.

In late summer 1907, Lindsay returned to Tuscany to visit Lucca, taking Susie with him. He had spent a lot of time researching the best possible route and had discovered one that could get him to Poggio Gherardo in less than 60 hours, including only one night on a train. Arriving at the station in Florence, they were met by Janet's servant David, who transported them and their luggage up the hill to Settignano in a 'dainty little red cart'. Lindsay had bought Janet a supply of carbon paper and was going to teach her to duplicate her manuscripts. He wrote to Nelly *'The selfish wish sometimes comes that you were here but it is purely selfish. I am sure you would be in a semi-fluid state [a reference to her dislike of the heat]. Midlothian would suit you….frost appeared there three days ago'.*

By the end of December 1907, Nelly was once again convalescing at Poggio Gherardo, presumably her burst of enthusiasm for work that summer had prompted a relapse, and Lindsay wrote to her there, teasing her because he had not heard from her *'I remember something about letters. If I wrote more to you, you were to write many to me. That was the sworn statement. I write more obedient as I always am: what of the letters? One only.'* The voice is flirtatious and fond, and Nelly must have found him hard to resist. The letter goes on with more teasing, this time about her preference for fresh air: *'I fear that Mrs Ross has not screwed up your windows, at least she has not said she has done so. Wait til you come to see Susie and me. The hottest part of the summer would suit the experiment best. I'd lodge you in a small bedroom, with a large fire, windows screwed up, wire screens in front to protect the gas and the door locked on the outside. I'm sure that a week of this treatment would restore you to perfect health.'*

We don't have Nelly's reply, but she had obviously joined in the joke with great relish, inviting him to stay in her imaginary 'ice palace', as on 6 January Lindsay wrote a brief postcard *'Many many thanks for your kind invitation which I accept with all the torpid feelings which its picture of exquisite cold already produces. To spend even a limited time in your mansion would be delightful. My only fear is that the warmth of your invitation and the greater warmth of your welcome when I arrive might somewhat modify the physical surroundings.*

'Hindu sages say that love has eight stages. My affection for ice, glaciers, cold damp mist,

blasts of north-east wind and in general what awaits me in your hospitable house is such that it has already gone through the first seven. There remains only, what would certainly come, the eighth and last which is death.

'But while places charm, your society amid such surroundings is more precious still. It cannot be one without. So I only wait the word that you yourself are in the abode you so graphically describe to fly there with all the speed the abounding ice-floes admit'

What a flirt! This card was accompanied by a longer letter, sent from 'The City of Dreadful Night', as Glasgow was fogbound. There is no doubt that Lindsay was both a wise and a witty man. When they weren't flirting and teasing, Lindsay and Nelly had begun to discuss the suffrage issue. Nelly has described herself as a 'permeator', a term she had picked up from Fabian Socialism, which described a method of achieving a political aim by effectively infiltrating other organisations and persuading the membership of a particular point of view.

He wrote '*When I married, my dear wife and I differed on many things the age of the Book of Daniel, whether space had three or x dimensions, women's suffrage, whether one ought to vote Tory or Radical. In a few years, continuous, soft feminine pressure judiciously applied (the constant dripping of water on stone, the disruptive force of an ivy on a wall, are feeble in comparison) made me a Radical (a somewhat jesuitical masculine self-respect suggested other reasons), so my first married argument for women's suffrage was that if women had votes men might have a chance of voting in their own way and in peace. That was tossed aside contemptuously by the statement that if women had one vote there was no reason why they should not have two.'*

Lindsay then describes how he once took his wife, who initially was not particularly interested in the suffrage issue, to hear him address a meeting of working women, where he focused his argument on the wrongs inflicted on working women, often, as he pointed out, the family breadwinners, *'by crude legislation which they had no means of preventing'*. And his wife became a convert to the suffrage cause, impressed she said, by the curious silent movement of the working women around her as they heard her husband speak.

Later that week Lindsay sent Nelly a humorous postcard and a pamphlet whose cover illustration reminded him of the 'Arctic House' as Nelly's joke invitation had suggested. And on 16 January 1908 he wrote to her in Italy again, a longer letter, saying that her last three letters to him showed her to be recovering well and in good spirits. He had been hearing from Janet that

Nelly was quoting him for support in arguments about their manuscript. *'How you have been heaving my name at Mrs Ross's head! I'll be even with you some day, my dear lady. Remember that.'* Within a few days he was very tactfully trying to dampen Nelly's enthusiasm for completely re-writing her chapters on Pisa, as she had just visited the city again and was bursting with new information. This would surely have driven Janet to distraction. So Lindsay told Nelly the story of when he was a curate and asked one of his parishioners for feedback on his sermon. *"Do you know how to make a sausage? ...if you stuff it too full of meat, you cannot get your teeth through it comfortably."* We can assume that Nelly took the hint. He recommended her to find a copy of the Contemporary Review, as he thought she might like to see a *'fervid socialist article 'Revolution' by Jack London, whoever he may be...'*

Lindsay obviously loved Nelly's letters and her style of writing: *'I do not quite know how it could be done but I'd like to see two pages of your letter to me in the book on Pisa. I wonder whether you could not get in somewhere your flirtations they evidently were flirtations - with "nice freshfaced" archepiscopal secretaries; with canons, portly and stern, of the Cathedral, with directors of charitable organisations, whose eyes you seem to have drawn (sad to say it) from the deserving poor. The little touch "Signora per l'amore del Dio" ought to find a place somewhere...when you write on the Roman Palaces in your great work on gardens let it take the form of letters. There is such swing and life in your descriptions when they are enclosed in epistles.'*

By February 1908, Nelly's enthusiasm for letting the fresh air blow through Poggio Gherardo had led, according to Janet, to both of them catching colds. Nelly blamed it on the stuffiness of the house. Lindsay must have been roaring with laughter. He wrote to Janet: *'So Miss Erichsen has caught cold. ...the fact fills me with a sad contentment...of course the cold must have come from the stuffiness of the rooms in Poggio Gherardo! The morning headache of the man who drinks too much is always due to the cucumber, or the salmon, or to the rice pudding to anything or everything but his pet failing. Your aeromaniacs are very like dipsomaniacs......I've no objection to a moderate and temperate use of fresh air; but I do object to drunken reveling in it, to windows open day and night, to artificial draughts, and carefully manufactured hurricanes within peaceful houses. It is sad, sad!'* the next letter brought the news that Janet now also had a cold. This was obviously Nelly's fault, and Lindsay again sent his sympathies: *'Oh, these aeromaniacs. Why do they not live, work, and sleep in small canvas tents with all the flaps up."*

By mid-March 1908 Nelly had left Florence for Rome and was staying in the Hotel Victoria, complaining of the weather and the fleas. Meanwhile in England her mother, now in her eighties, was dying and Lindsay sympathised *'I do hope that you will be able to be with your mother: for your sake as for hers. There is nothing I can sympathise with you more than your not having one place settled, fixed, stable which you can call your home and no-one else's.'* However Nelly was still in Italy when her mother passed away. Alice came out to visit her and they travelled to Orvieto, where Nelly fell ill again. When she was stronger she returned to England to look for a place of her own to live. Her mother had clearly been only too aware of the difficulties of Nelly's life living out of suitcases. In Anna's will, among the long dispositions of cutlery and jewellery, she specified that Nelly should have the first pick of furniture, sufficient to furnish one sitting room and one bedroom. It is a touching illustration of a mother's wish to see her spinster daughter at least comfortable in her solitude. The moneys, such as they were, would be evenly divided between Nelly and Dora. The total effects in probate were valued at around £1300 - could Nelly's share of the cash have been as much as £500? It was not more.

A month later, in May, Lindsay travelled to Poggio Gherardo where he spent six weeks. Nelly, back in England, had thrown herself into her work in her researches into Pisa, and she and Lindsay were deep in correspondence over the course of the ancient City walls. Lindsay wrote teasingly to Janet *'these walls of Pisa are much worse than the walls of Jericho. [Miss Erichsen] has built them up solid and safe. Then she takes three books, written by three infallible archaeological specialists and a thirteenth-century map. She twists books and map into a trumpet, and like the children of Israel marches majestically round the walls, and they fall down flat. Then they are built up again. The trumpets blare again: and down go the walls. The children of Israel did it once; but Miss Erichsen has done it three times..... '*

If Nelly and Janet had got on each other's nerves sharing a house when they were both unwell in 1906/7, the difficulties they faced trying to agree page proofs and corrections for The Story of Pisa during the summer of 1908, when they were a thousand miles apart, were monumental. When he returned to Glasgow from Italy in July Lindsay began ploughing through the proofs of The Story of Pisa, which Janet had asked Dent to send directly to him. He wrote to Nelly *'I have read all Mrs Ross's part and yours to the end of slip 50. I think it reads well.'*

But Janet wrote streams of letters to Lindsay, often on a daily basis, in which she complained about Nelly's insistence on making corrections for which Dent was threatening to make the authors pay. For example, on 15 July 1908 *'Miss Erichsen has sent me her first revise of 2 half slips and in spite of my preaching has put in a new para. Of course that means altering many pages. She really is pig-headed.'* And a week later: *'My fingers itch to turn some of Miss Erichsen's sentences, full of whichs, inside out. She never comes to an end. Just as I am too curt, she is far too lengthy....'*

Nelly was in London sorting out her mother's possessions and looking for a more permanent place to stay. Lindsay was more sympathetic to her than Janet was, he wrote that she was *'a bit of a nomad at present, [longing] for a fixed place of abode'. But Janet wrote to Lindsay 'How unfortunate poor Miss Erichsen is. She has had to turn out of Middlerow [a cottage in Chipping Campden] and go to another friend, a Miss Dodge*[10]*, whom I saw here some seven years ago and who is simply a bundle of nerves. How those two will get on together, I can't imagine. It would only need [Edward] Hutton to make a trio and then there would be a row!'*

The very next day she wrote again: *'I just heard from Mrs Berenson. Poor Miss Dodge is already at her wits' end. She went to stay 3 days with the Berensons to breathe. She is by profession a musician, and a good one, and Miss Erichsen cannot stand her practising. She says it drives her crazy. So poor Miss Dodge, who took her in out of kindness, as the other people could not keep her any longer, does not know what to do. I am only thankful she is not here (Miss E I mean) With this heat I think it would have ended with me drowning myself among the water lilies and the goldfish.'*

'...Miss E's proofs come in fast. She evidently after leaving [here] put commas in wholesale. I find them in ink all over the MS. I've struck out a lot but I doubt her accepting the corrections: and she does love that horrid word which. In one place there are 3 in 4 lines! I don't think anyone will wade through her interminable description of the Duomo. The intarsia work is very fine, I grant, but one does [not?] want a description of every panel. 'Troppa grazia sant'Antonio' as they say here if one has too much of anything. I told Miss E she must [give the] name of Benjamin da [Tudela's] book and she said you had given her his name like that, so it was enough. That silenced me. You must be careful dear Dr you see!!! How kind of you to go and search in the library for the old boy, whose name at first I thought was Toledo ill-spelt! Shows my crass ignorance.'

At the time, Janet was reading Gilbert Murray's translations of the Classics, sent to her by Lindsay: '*When I was reading the Bacchae, I was somehow irresistibly reminded of Miss Erichsen and her suffragist sisters. "wild white women...they work strange deeds and passing marvel." Heavens! How angry she'd be if she knew this. I had a postcard*

---

[10] Janet Dodge, musician and author, at one point lived in Fridays Hill, near Haslemere, Surrey but was now resident in Chipping Campden. Friend of Mary Berenson and of the artist Roger Fry

from her saying she would accept 'some of my corrections of commas, as she had not had time to master that art yet'. I know nothing about it, save my ear and common sense.' It does sound very much as if Nelly had had enough of Janet's comments.

Within a week, Lindsay had read Janet's first proofs of Pisa and sent her his thoughts. He must have commented on her lack of enthusiasm for her subject, for she replied: *'Perhaps some of the rubbing up the wrong way I had from Miss E comes out in Pisa. I've come to the conclusion that she is extremely conceited. I know she is about her drawings.'* Poor Nelly.

By the beginning of August 1908, Nelly had found herself at least semi-permanent lodgings, a house called The Martins in Chipping Campden: *'I am glad Miss Erichsen has her house, I did not know of it. But I pity Miss Dodge who thought she was giving her hospitality for a fortnight! And who is a struggling musician who lives by her music, and now can't practise without tears and scenes....I'm beginning to wonder whether Miss Erichsen has stopped her proofs coming to me, I've had none for days. 'Elle en est capable'.* Within a few days Janet wrote again *'Miss Dodge has fled for a month and left Miss E in possession! So I hear from Mrs Berenson...At last today I got another set of proofs from Miss E. Dent never sent them to me. In spite of my preachments she has re-written about half a page! And altered things I told her to alter in the typed sheets and which she said she would. It is most awfully long - the Campo Santo seems about 5 miles in length and 3 in breadth'.*

Janet became more and more furious with Nelly's amendments and prose style. *'I've just had from Miss E three proofs running...it is awfully long-winded and I think very dull. She tells about things that were and are no longer. Frescos etc. I got another proof yesterday evening. No-one will ever get through the churches. I do hope some critic will say her part is too long, or Lucca will be longer. She won't listen to me. We shall have to pay heavily for corrections. She would not let me go over the typed copy I did of her MS and said she would do it and knew perfectly all about [and] would correct anything she wanted to alter. Of course she has not done so....I expect she'll be very angry at my remarks about this lot.'*

Two weeks later Janet was still complaining about Nelly's drafting: *'I do hope some kind critic will say that he wonders she has not counted the paving stones in Pisa.'* But Nelly stood her ground, and she and Janet swapped icy notes: Janet wrote to Lindsay *'She sends me back my remarks "Thank you but I prefer my last"'*. Janet must have warned Nelly about the likely cost of the corrections she was making: *'Yesterday I had another proof. If we get off with £20 for alterations, I think we shall be lucky...she said she had understood that on slips one could correct as much as one likes in answer to a former remark of mine.'*

Meanwhile Nelly was sorting out the renting of The Martins and Lindsay was happy to discuss repairs and redecoration with her. *'I'm going down to Newton Stewart for a few days in September to meet the Findlaters - two women novelists. It seems my fate to meet women novelists. But after Mrs Glyn and Ray Devereux the Findlaters will be tame...I suspect I was near you when I was at Oxford, but my knowledge of the geography of England is limited in the extreme. I could not have come to see you however as all the little time at my disposal was thoroughly occupied. But if you do get the house, and if your offer is accepted, I hope to have the pleasure of entering that charming abode. By the way, there was nothing 'forward' in your offer. Is it not Leap-Year? Yours....Thomas Lindsay'.*

Leap year? Which includes 29 February, the one day in every four years when woman do not have to wait for men to do the proposing? A new chapter of Nelly's life seemed to be about to start as an independent householder, and a published author, with a flirtaceous widower, if not actually a romantic interest, in her life.

Chapter Ten: Chipping Campden – The Simple Life

On Campden Wold the skylark sings
In Campden Town the traveller finds
The inward peace which beauty brings
To bless and heal tormented minds

And there is beauty everywhere,
In that grey curving English Street
The man who goes a wandering there
I think his blood doth quicker beat

And no man walks her lovely ways,
And marks the shifty wind-vanes gleam
But thinks of noble deeds and days,
And builds a town of Troy in dream

For there those elemental fires,
Set hearts aflame like glowing coal,
To build and gild the carven spires
To crown the city of the soul.

John Masefield, written for Mrs Janet Ashbee, 1904

On 10 August 1908 Lindsay wrote to congratulate Nelly on securing The Martins *'So you are at last a householder - without a vote. How does it feel?'* Nelly had driven a hard bargain in negotiating her lease. The house had been fitted out by

The Martins, Chipping Campden

the landlord with a new window, a new chimney, a fireplace and a kitchen range, had been re-papered 'from garret to cellar', and Nelly had got £10 knocked off the rent. Lindsay was teasing her that despite all this she still called the landlord hard-hearted. He wrote that he hoped to visit her in her new abode, but did not expect it to be very soon.

The house stands today looking just as it did at the turn of the last century, in a prime position on the north side of Chipping Campden High Street, opposite the Market Hall. Although the house is thought to date from the 17th century, the frontage had been remodeled in 1714. Constructed of large cut stone, with a Cotswold stone roof, it is an unusual and striking L-shaped block with its entrance doorway sheltered under an attractive porch constructed in the angle between the two wings. The house has two storeys and attics, topped with a steeply pitched roof with three gabled dormers. Inside there were Queen Anne fireplaces on the ground and first floors, and a staircase of the same date. Nelly had rented a gem of a house, right in the middle of the town.

Chipping Campden is a small Gloucestershire market town, in the heart of the Cotswolds and one of its most picturesque spots. In 1902 Charles Ashbee, a leading light of the Arts and Crafts movement, relocated his London workshop to Chipping Campden and for the next decade the little town became a gathering point for craftsmen, writers and painters celebrating the values of the Arts and Crafts movement. She was drawn here by knowledge of Ashbee's vision, but also the presence of fellow artists such as Frederick Landseer Griggs, who like Nelly, was working on the popular Highways and Byways series for Macmillan. Griggs had arrived in the village in 1903 and lived there until his death.

Charles Ashbee was an architect and designer, and a disciple of Ruskin and Morris. Like them, he believed that social change, meaning specifically resistance to the worst effects of the Industrial Revolution, could best be achieved by local and practical solutions. In 1888 he set up a Guild of Handicraft and by 1891 he and his fellow craftsmen had moved into workshops on the Mile End Road, in London's East End. Ashbee created a thriving community of talented and committed artisans across a wide range of crafts, including furniture, woodcarving, metalwork, jewellery and printing. He combined the output of the working class artisans with a strong emphasis on training and education for all, and the Guild ran lectures and evening classes, organised sports and plays, and took the members and their families on holidays into the country. Indeed, he began to feel that the Guild belonged more in the countryside than the town, and in 1901, when the lease on the Mile End premises fell due, his friend and supporter Robert Martin-Holland suggested a move to Chipping Campden, with its old silk mill and many small cottages lying empty. A vote was taken among Guild members and early in 1902 the craftsmen and their machinery began to arrive in the small Cotswold town. *'For the romantic medievalist in Ashbee, Campden was Camelot, his dream of unspoilt rural peace and beauty come true, a small moribund town waiting to be caught up in his great social experiment.'* [11]

For a while the Guild flourished, and certainly its members had a major impact on the little town by rebuilding and renovating houses, digging out a public swimming pool, putting on plays and lecture evenings. But the move was never a financial success and over the next few years some of the leading craftsmen drifted away in search of better incomes. Campden was just too far from their suppliers and, more importantly, their wealthy London customers. If it had been established a hundred years later it may have thrived, selling its distinctive hand-crafted articles to the tourists and wealthy holiday-homers who now throng Campden at the weekends, but it was ahead of its time. The Guild was formally liquidated in 1908, just as Nelly arrived, although Ashbee and others, such as the sculptor Alec Miller, and the artist Frederick Griggs, stayed on.

We do not know if Nelly knew Ashbee before she arrived in Chipping Campden, but they certainly had mutual acquaintances. George Bernard Shaw was an early visitor to Chipping Campden. Furthermore, one of the principal influences on Ashbee when he was studying at Cambridge in the 1880s had been the philosopher and writer Edward Carpenter, the best man at Alice Erichsen's wedding, who was still in correspondence with Nelly's brother-in-law

---

[11] *Campden: a new history, published by CADHAS*

Edgar Lucas. Another friend of Ashbee's from student days was Arthur Berry, an academic mathematician, later Provost of Kings College, Cambridge, who was married to Harriet Johnson, sister of Fanny and Reginald, and well-known to Nelly. In fact, Nelly had stayed with the Berrys in Cambridge in 1905 when recovering from her breakdown. It may be that they had planted the seed in Nelly's mind that the Ashbee community would be a refuge for her.

She also knew a more recent disciple of Ashbee, Frederick Griggs. Griggs was younger than Nelly, born in 1876 in Hitchin, Hertfordshire, and had early training as an architectural draughtsman. In 1900 he was commissioned by Sir Frederick Macmillan, who lived near Hitchin at Temple Disley, to provide the artwork for the Hertfordshire edition of the Highways and Byways series, and this type of commission became a principal source of income for him, as he went on to illustrate 15 separate volumes for Macmillan, travelling the country loaded with equipment on a three wheeled motorcycle. In 1903, while working on the Oxford and the Cotswolds edition, he stayed in Chipping Campden, met Ashbee and his followers, and the following year moved there permanently, living in Dover House on the High Street until 1930.

In September 1908, Lindsay wrote to Nelly '*I know nothing of Chipping Campden save the scanty information to be gleaned from the top of your letters and have drawn the inference - probably unwarrantable - that it is a somewhat pretentious place. It seems to affect a simplicity, like that of a Quaker dress, which at once draws attention and remark. 'Middlerow' was bad enough, savouring of the pride that apes humility, but 'The Thatched Cottage', 'The Martins' are worse. 'Behold our sweet rural simplicity which can be found nowhere else' they seem to say: - 'Come and look at the England surviving here and here alone.' As if thatched cottages did not abound and swallows twitter under innumerable eves all over this and all other lands! How insistent is that definite article! Yet with all that pride of old-worldliness you cannot help rejoicing in modern dairies and sanitary plumbers' traps, and they are anything but simple.*'

From his replies, it seems that Nelly wrote regularly to Lindsay about her difficulties with cleaners and house decorating, and he had discussed her choice of residence with his daughter and her friends, who told him how attractive the Cotswold villages were. But he continued to tease her: *'I told my sister-in-law that you had invited me to visit you (presumably when you were fairly sorted with a good servant). Guess what she wrote: "if I were you I would not visit Miss Erichsen tho' she had fifty servants until the warmest days of summer. Her zeal for fresh air is overwhelming!" There is a blow delivered by one whom, in my secret heart, I am inclined to suppose to be herself an aero-maniac!'*

Nelly was toying with the idea of withdrawing from her collaborations with Mrs Ross - with Pisa nearly put to bed, work was due to start on the second volume, Lucca. Lindsay wrote that he was relieved that she was considering giving up the project. Reading between the lines it sounds as if he was mostly hopeful that he would no longer have to keep the peace between the two warring authors, Nelly and Janet. He says firmly *'I do not believe in double authorship. Save in the very rarest of cases it does injustice to both persons and is unsuccessful. In the rare cases in which it has succeeded, the success has come from one of the partners being subordinate to the other in almost all things: and I doubt whether that rule would do justice either to Mrs Ross or to yourself. So I am very glad that you and she are not to write another book together.'* What a tactful man, you can almost hear him chuckling to his other friends about the difficulties these two women have caused him. He went on to encourage Nelly to concentrate on her book on Roman gardens. He thought there was plenty of interest in the subject, but no-one else was trying to write a complete history, which obviously would make it more likely to succeed commercially.

In early September 1908, Janet Ross wrote to Lindsay with news that she had joined Mrs Humphrey Ward's Anti-Suffragist league. From the tone with which she writes, one might think she had done it just to annoy Nelly. *'A guinea well spent...for heaven's sake don't tell Miss Erichsen not at all events till Pisa is out. You'd be amused at her corrections of proofs. If there is any letter not quite well printed she puts two huge red-ink marks like that // but in one page she left 'ajaculate'...and 'had' for 'has'... she talks of angels 'haling' spirits out of the graves and I said I thought it rather ugly, even if English but she did not reply'.* Janet never changed her mind about the suffrage movement. A few years later she wrote to her niece Lina *'But what on earth induced you to become a suffragist? I hoped you had more sense. A nice mess we shall be in if women ever do get the vote. I hope and trust they won't. Fancy [being] ruled by a set of Mrs Rates, Miss Erichsen (much as I like her) etc mercifully nearly all my women friends are dead against it.... Universal suffrage is bad enough but to be at the mercy of millions of silly women would be far worse'.* The manuscript letter in the British Institute in Florence has an asterisk by Nelly's name; and in another handwriting, probably Lina's, an embarrassed note has been added: 'A very clever and delightful Danish friend'.

Back in 1908, Janet's rather limited literary patience had apparently been exhausted and, while Nelly prevaricated, she withdrew her offer to collaborate on the second volume they had promised to Dent, on Lucca. Nelly had hinted that she felt too busy, or too unwell, to continue, so Janet asked her to return the books she had borrowed - but at that Nelly rallied. Janet wrote to Lindsay *'Miss E clutches Lucca and is very angry at my attempt to take it back. She writes that I positively said I could go to Lucca in Sept and October.'* Nelly seems to have changed her mind frequently on the subject - in October Lindsay wrote again to encourage her give the project up *'I know that it is hard to give up work one has planned and collected for: but I do agree with you that in this case it is certainly best. It is very good in you to think of writing out your notes for Mrs Ross, but that seems a great deal of work to undertake - would the notes themselves not suffice without re-writing?'* Around this time, worried about Nelly's financial position, he suggested to Janet that she should pay Nelly for the work she had done on Lucca, a suggestion which Janet ignored, although it preyed on her mind.

Nelly and he continued to exchange letters full of academic references and enquiries, as well as thoughts on current affairs. In November, Lindsay wrote *'I fear I cannot get up any admiration for the militant suffragettes, save that they afford you interest. Your question: are not the militant suffragettes darlings? suggests to me the [fond] American mother, who when her cub has pulled some of the dishes off the table, spilt hot coffee on your knees, plastered your coat with sticky marmalade from his fingers in boisterous endeavours to get on your lap, and 'raised Cain' generally exclaims, her eyes beaming with maternal fondness: Isn't he a darling! Such high spirits!'*

Meanwhile, Mrs Ross had fallen ill with symptoms that started as laryngitis and developed into shingles. Her letters become short, infrequent and almost illegible. She was taking morphine for the pain. Lindsay made frequent enquiries through his friends in Florence, and wrote daily hoping to keep her spirits up. He also stepped in to help complete the Pisa volume: Janet wrote *'Fancy you doing that beastly index. It was made so hard by the incessant repetitions of Miss E. Things named and described 5 times over in various places. It drove me mad. If I had only seen her part all together I'd have insisted on cutting out 50 or 60 pages.'*

But Nelly had also now been taken ill - a recurrence of the mysterious pains she had suffered that summer, and in late November 1908 she was facing exploratory surgery at St Thomas's Hospital in London, under the care of an eminent surgeon, Mr Clutton. Janet wrote to Lindsay: *'I've also had a letter yesterday from Miss Erichsen from the nursing home, but she says 'if I have time I'll write before the operation'. She is delighted because she lies in a hurricane, it blows her hair about as she lies in bed. The mere thought made me shiver. Also there seems to be no privacy. Everyone hears what the others say as there are no doors, only curtains which wave in the wind. She finds it amusing. De gustibus.'*

It seems likely that the operation was to look for a cancer when Lindsay wrote afterwards to Nelly, he said *"it must be a great relief to you to know that one source of continual anxiety has been removed: for tho' you were very brave and patient about it and gave no sign, in letters at least, of worry yet you must have felt the strain that uncertainty cannot fail to cause. May I rejoice with you to some extent, and congratulate you on the less anxious life that is before you?"* Nelly was certainly alarmed, whether at the possible outcome of the exploratory operation, or just fearing that she would not survive the anaesthetic, because the last thing she did before going under the knife was to make her will, witnessed by Therese Redl, a niece of Edgar Lucas who happened to be a nurse at St Thomas's hospital. She asked for her body to be cremated and the ashes scattered in the churchyard at Chipping Campden. This was not to be.

A week after Nelly's operation, on 10 December, Janet wrote to Lindsay: *'I have just opened a huge parcel which came while I was so ill from Miss E...all my Lucca books, and pages and pages of her notes. They seem to me very dull, but Lucca I abominate at present.'* Nelly was still in hospital over Christmas, and had recovered well, tucking with relish into a Christmas lunch of plum pudding and beer. Then she went to recuperate at Alice's house in Elm Park Gardens, Chelsea. Later in January she was well enough to return to Chipping Campden, and her letters are full once again of the difficulties of securing a reliable supply of hot water and dealing with the irritating domestic staff. All the jam she had made had gone mouldy in her absence, much to Lindsay's amusement *'My dear Miss Erichsen do you mean to tell me that your jam closet is set against an outside wall? Or do you mean to say that you southern house-keepers do not know an infallible recipe for preventing jam from going mouldy?'* Her letters to Janet were full of the same complaints: Janet wrote to Lindsay *'she evidently has perpetual trouble with her servants. All her swans turn into geese in a few weeks. She also tells me she suffers from cold!!! I am almost glad!"*

Lindsay sympathetically remarked that it was much harder to be a single woman than a single man. His experience was that the servants looked on a solitary man as someone to be humoured, indulged, mothered even, but not disturbed with trifles. On the other hand, the lone woman, is *'recognised to be a fully grown up person, quite as intelligent as themselves. She is therefore worthy of consultation every ten minutes about all sorts of trifles and ought not to think that disturbance.'*

In February the printed copies of 'The Story of Pisa' arrived in Glasgow at Lindsay's house, together with news that Nelly was sufficiently recovered to start portrait painting again. The reviews were good, *'It is in fact exactly the book to guide the visitor by day and amuse him during idle evenings, and it is written throughout with intelligence and enthusiasm.'* (The Academy, 27 February 1909). Amusingly, the reviewer thought that Janet's section was *'rather fatiguing to the mind, for it contains too many facts crowded into a small space.'* He also thought she was a little confused in some of her facts. There are no such criticisms of Nelly's writings, only that her drawings have been reproduced too small within the text. One can imagine how that went down at Poggio Gherardo.

Nelly was beginning to feel happily settled in Chipping Campden - a letter to Ashbee in that same month from his secretary Phoebe Pook records that she had had tea with Nelly who was very proud of the work she had done to make The Martins comfortable. Nelly was also in a position to ask George Macmillan to return to her the original drawings she had made for the Derbyshire Highways and Byways book *'I have been too much of a wanderer to claim them before, but am now trying to gather my possessions around me.'*

In March 1909 Nelly wrote to Lindsay setting out the plan she had for her book on Roman villas, which delighted him. She was nervous that the market was saturated with Italian travel books, but he assured her that hers would be something special, and he implored her not to take up a suggestion of Dent's, that she collaborate with an Italian author. *'Let the book be your book. You will worry enough over it without gratuitously borrowing more...The very completeness of your scheme raises your work high above the usual class of books about Italy which are as numberless as they are unsatisfactory. If you carry it out as I believe you can, your book is likely to take a place of permanence and be a standard one.' What a lovely compliment.*

Meanwhile Janet had clearly been worrying away at Lindsay's dig about Nelly's financial difficulties: she wrote to him: *'I do hope Miss Erichsen will succeed with her Roman villas. It is sold to Dent. By the way, I always, for months, intended to say to you in answer to yr suggestion that I might give her something for her notes on Lucca (of which I can't make head or tail) that I paid for all the carriages at Lucca and Pisa. I gave her 400 frs in all. I told her she ought not and must not walk, and at each place I gave her 200 frs.'* This makes me laugh so much, and I think the lovely Lindsay would have chuckled as well. Clearly he had pricked Janet's conscience, but her pennypinching ways had won out!

Since his wife had died, Lindsay had lived with his one unmarried daughter Susie. At this point she had just returned from a prolonged stay in Oxford. Her return gave Lindsay a welcome respite from the cares of running a household and supervising the maids. But, as he told Nelly, he had found eating alone very monotonous. His solution gives us an insight into his genuine enthusiasm, as an attractive and intelligent widower, for female company: *'I appealed to five ladies, widows or spinsters over 45 (I do not care for the chatter of chits) to dine with me one by one. These dinners a deux take place twice a week. Out of real compassion, mingled with a slight curiosity I suspect to find out how I was getting on, & partly bribed by the prospect of onions a la Villa Passerini, each of the five accepted: promised to come back again if each was the only guest: did come back and therefore I think fairly enjoyed themselves. Indeed Mrs James MacLehose offered herself as a guest; was informed of the limitation to widows and spinsters: thought that she might rank as a widow when James was driving out by himself; and did figure once as a widow pro tempore. So long as Susie was away I thought a great deal of these delightful little dinners and was sincerely grateful to my guests.'*

(Nelly was 46 in 1908, although Lindsay may not have known this. But the reference to 45 year olds as the age at which women become interesting to him seems quite a nice coincidence. I wonder if Nelly wished she lived a little closer to Glasgow when she read this letter.)

In early May Nelly fell ill again, possibly, she thought, with mumps, although the pains she had described to Lindsay were not in the neck, so he felt her self-diagnosis may have been wrong. But he still enjoyed her letters: *'Even in calamity you seem to be inventive and original to a commonplace person like myself.'* She had teased him about his claim to do his own sewing and mending; she had asked him if he could kill garden snails, and he claimed great skill and perseverance. She was still hoping that he would visit Chipping Campden, but although he made it to London and Oxford earlier that spring, despite his being badly afflicted by asthma, Nelly had been in quarantine for possible mumps so they had not met.

In June 1909 Lindsay travelled to Florence to stay with Janet, only to receive news that Susie wished to be married in haste before her fiancé, Frederick Powicke, departed to take up a professorial position in Belfast and he had to rush home. Janet travelled back with him as far as Glasgow, but again the weather was very poor and spoiled her stay. Meanwhile Nelly was in England, staying with friends at Hambledon Hurst, near Godalming. It seems likely that her hosts were Edith Sichel and Emily Ritchie, a little known philanthropic and literary couple living an unconventional life together as lovers. She was keen to use her Macmillan connection and the promise made by the firm of more work when her health recovered, to pitch an idea for a book, to be written jointly with Edward Hutton, whom she knew through Janet Ross in Tuscany.

'Mr Hutton has asked me to collaborate with him in a book dealing with some Italian subject….Another piece of work I am doing has led to my being much in the Campagna of the Roman Hills, and as year by year one has seen the disappearance of this or that feature of their matchless charm, the slow insidious growth of a ring of factory chimneys without the city walls, the partial destruction of the walls themselves, the electric trams ploughing their way through tomb and villa, aqueduct and tower, & the petty suburbs that clothe the classic slopes of the hills, one becomes possessed by a vivid desire to record once more some of this fading beauty before it is too late.'

The idea being proposed was a Highways and Byways of the Campagna and Roman Hills, to be written by Hutton and illustrated by Nelly. If that failed, their next suggestion would be a larger book about Sicily, or Apulia and Calabria, which they felt was untrodden ground. For whatever reason, the eventual compromise reached with Macmillan was the 'Highways and Byways of Somersetshire', to be written by Hutton and illustrated by Nelly. She was again to receive £150 for not less than 50 drawings, which she was happy to accept, and the deal was agreed at the beginning of September 1909. But the project took off very slowly.

Edward Hutton was a prolific travel writer, particularly dedicated to Italy and Tuscany in particular, but also penning works for Macmillan on the English counties of Somerset, Wiltshire and Gloucestershire. His most significant achievement was the foundation of the British Institute in Florence in 1917, which flourishes today, and is the repository of Janet Ross's archives, among others. Hutton was younger than Nelly, born in London in 1875 and educated in Tiverton, Devon. He chose not to go to university but to make a career in publishing, and in the 1890s secured a position at The Bodley Head working for John Lane. In 1896 he came into an inheritance which allowed him to travel to Italy, and for the rest of his life he spent a significant portion of his time there, renting a small house close to Janet Ross and the Berensons.

In October 1909 Lindsay wrote to say that he was glad that Nelly was well and had returned with energy to her work on the Roman villas. But meanwhile Nelly had locked horns with Dent, and was trying to persuade him to send her an advance so that she could travel to Italy to complete the book she wanted to write and which Dent had agreed to publish. Somerset had to wait. All of this commercial activity shows that she was clearly in financial difficulties again. She was getting older, her parents were both gone, and she must have constantly had to deal with the worry of how she would support herself in her old age. Her sister Dora, now widowed, had found refuge with Alice and Edgar Lucas, but Nelly had been too independent for too long to want to admit defeat. As far as this negotiation is concerned, we only have the Dent side of the story, but it is pretty easy to imagine the firm line that Nelly was taking in her correspondence. She needed the money.

15 September 1909

Miss N Erichsen
The Martins
Campden, Glos

Dear Miss Erichsen

I really am so busy that I cannot get at the agreement. Mr Macrae is here from America and I shall not be free until about Wednesday or Thursday of next week. I hope that by then I shall be able to get your agreement drawn up.

Yours sincerely
JM DENT

24 September

Miss N Erichsen
The Martins
Chipping Campden, Glos

Dear Miss Erichsen

I am trying to send you particulars of the agreement as we made it. I am not quite sure what we decided about the coloured drawings, but I have left the agreement as it stood between us with the exception that I am net to pay you £100 on account of royalties on delivery of the

MS. I have also given you two years in which to prepare the [pack]. Any modification of this we must make between us, and if there is any point in it which you disagree with be kind enough to write to me at once. I am sorry that I have not been able to do this before but I have been exceedingly pressed.

Yours sincerely
JM DENT

27 September 1909

Miss N Erichsen
81 Elm Park Gardens, SW

Dear Miss Erichsen
I have received your letter and the agreement. You say that you have accepted it but have not signed it: until this is done of course nothing can be arranged.

I am somewhat astonished at the request for £30, to start the work with: I quite understood from you that you might only need this money at a much later date, when the book was very largely in progress. It is not convenient for me to send you £30 now, nor do I think it is quite in the spirit of our agreement. I am sorry that I cannot do this for you: it would have given me pleasure if I could have done so

Yours sincerely
JM DENT

29 September 1909

Miss N Erichsen
81 Elm Park Gardens, SW

Dear Miss Erichsen
I send you herewith the counterpart of the agreement, but I must confess that I do not like your letter at all. It suggests that I have in some way broken my promises, and I have in no way done this, as you must be fully and completely aware. You did say that, if you found yourself hampered [?] for money towards the end of the work, would I advance you £30, and I said that I would: now you write to say that you want £30, to go away with, and that is quite a different matter. It is sprung upon me entirely unexpectedly, at a time when I have no money free, and that is the reason why I did not send it. I work upon my own capital entirely, and

never have any money loose, and I have a perfect legal right to say that it is inconvenient to advance this money at this particular time.

As I have expressed to you, I fear this venture altogether, and did I not entirely from my own business standpoint I should not have[signed] ....this agreement at all, and I do not think it is kind to have written me a note such as you have written

Yours sincerely

It would seem that Nelly failed to get her advance, but she did set off for Italy that autumn, as we know that she was in Tuscany in time to see the grape harvest. She and Dent seem to have fallen out quite badly and she did not complete any further work for his firm. She never completed the work on Roman Villas or Roman Gardens.

The last paragraph of a letter from Lindsay in October 1909 tells us a little about her appearance at that time: *'I fancy, from your postcard, that the artistic is predominating over the matter of fact in your character at present. When I headed my letters 'Under the camphor tree' it was a simple fact: but will you say [the same] of your heading, 'Under the Ipomea Rubens Caerulea'? Come now! You are a tall and stately daughter of Denmark and do you mean to say that you can sit under a convolvulus, however 'enchantingly lively sky-blue'? I know the flower. It might serve to shelter a tiny fairy but scarcely for a Norse-woman. Your title is too artistic too Jack-&-the-beanstalky'! It sounds ill for 'Roman Villas'.*

That winter was a poor one for Lindsay, suffering badly now with asthma and without Susie living with him to look after him. In March 1910 he apologised that he had been too lazy to write, leaving Nelly's letters unanswered. He seems to have been mostly occupied, apart from his academic responsibilities, in answering a string of fashion-related questions posed by Lady Duff-Gordon who as 'Lucille' was now opening a boutique in New York and contributing weekly articles to the New York fashion press. In the summer of 1910, while Lindsay was staying with Janet, they received a telegram out of the blue from Lord and Lady Duff-Gordon asking to stay for a couple of days. *'Their visit was a great pleasure to me and I think a still greater satisfaction to Mrs Ross. At all events she has learned to know her cousin which she really never did. The two are in many mental characteristics extremely like each other: yet they get on capitally and talked family history and Italian agriculture from morning til night.'*

There is a suggestion in a letter written by Lindsay that autumn that Nelly, who was travelling in England preparing illustrations for one of the Macmillan Highways and Byways books at the time, felt herself the victim of 'black dog' depression and had been enquiring whether he felt himself a fellow sufferer. One gets a glimpse of his wonderful humour and also his fondness for Nelly in the reply: *'I do not think that "Black Dog" visits me much. If I understand the nature of the beast his visits make one discontented with oneself.... I fear I'm not nearly so good nor so humble minded as you are. Have I ever told you that I divide all mankind and womankind also, into Nehemiahs and Ezras? The Ezras, when they are put out, blame themselves and tear their own hair (Ezra ix.3): the Nehemiahs, in the same case, tear the hairs of other people (Neh. Xiii.25). I acknowledge that Ezra was the better man: but it is often more comfortable to be Nehemiah. Still I ought not to tempt you by such a suggestion.'*

In November 1910 Nelly was again planning a trip to Italy, although as Lindsay wrote, her 'old enemy' was back again, brought on, he believed, by overwork *'I feared for you when I heard about your exuberant work with all its luxe de detail of which you are so fond. Do restrain yourself. I know that it is better to wear out than rust out. Still...'* But she did not heed his advice, in December she wrote to say that she had been ill again, and he begged her to visit the baths at Mannheim on her way to Tuscany, as he felt they had been very beneficial to his heart condition.

In January 1911 Nelly declared herself recovered and well enough to work again, her 'mischief' as she called it could be controlled by periods of rest. Lindsay described her as *'an active, in-energy-abounding, strong-willed (that's better than 'self-willed', is it not?) creature...with a strong belief in the sacred right of insurrection.'* Nelly leaps from the pages when I read these letters, and Lindsay confirms everything I have ever guessed about her character and her interests, her independence of spirit and her liberal political views.

She had instructed him to visit Roger Fry's 'Post-impressionist' exhibition at the Grafton Gallery and his letter was mostly taken up with his reaction and to the paintings. He had not much liked the Gauguin, an artist he may have known she had a connection with, but '*The man who impressed me most, and as a rule with pure admiration, was Van Gough [sic]*'.

'You gave me an opening in your last letter but one, which I hasten to avail myself of. Friends pester you with good-meaning advice about your behaviour! I'm going to do the same. It concerns your 'walk', not your 'conversation'. It is this: do not walk uphill while your heart-trouble is still apt to manifest itself. I have not the slightest doubt that you have been

so badly brought [up] as to consider a 'constitutional' a necessary thing: in my tolerance for human weakness I'll further admit that the bad habit may, thro' long indulgence, have become a necessary evil. But DO NOT WALK UP HILL.'

In March 1911, Janet let Lindsay into a great secret: Nelly's wealthy unmarried cousin, Miss Ida Suhr, who had been staying with Nelly in Florence, had given Nelly a present of £40 on account as part of an annual allowance of £60 she would give her from the following year. Janet thought it would *'just make the whole difference to her.'* But it did not lead to Nelly being any less active in searching for new publishing commissions. That very same month, while staying in Tuscany, she pitched another idea to George Macmillan, commenting that there was a further delay anyway to the Somerset book caused by Hutton's lack of urgency, and glad that this would give her time to revisit some of the sites in Somerset such as Bath she had hurried through the previous autumn.

Her new idea was inspired by a manuscript she had found while working in the Seminary Library at Frascati the previous year *'A Journal of His Majesty King James the Third's journey from Commercy to St Malo, from that to Cap [Fiend] by sea and thence to DunKerque accompany'd only by Mr O'Flannagan &St Paul His Majesty's Valet de Chambre'.* This is clearly a personal hobbyhorse for Nelly, she writes that she will refer to James as The Chevalier of St George, not as The Old Pretender, his more usual title in British history. Nelly felt that the journal, being 'very simple and sincere in style' would appeal to the public if published, or at least to that section of the public that still has a warm spot in its heart for the Stuarts. Nelly proposed preparing it for publication with illustrations and a short introduction. Another project that never got off the ground. This manuscript did finally see the light of day in a Scottish History Journal, but it was in the 1920s, several years after Nelly's death.

Lindsay visited Mrs Ross in the early summer, where the highlight of the trip was a visit to Florence by Elinor Glyn, whom Lindsay was amused to introduce to Mrs Ross. But the rest of his summer back in Scotland was dominated by increasingly fierce asthma attacks which severely limited his ability to work or to travel. Nelly had travelled over the summer, subletting her house, but was now back at The Martins. Lindsay wrote *'I presume...that you are now in your own home and that its late occupiers are no longer ex officio enemies but again dear and pleasant friends. That must comfort you, who I think, are more inclined to friendship than enmity.'* He always found something positive and warm to say to Nelly *'your last was a specially delightful letter, and one bit of it, more than half a page was writing which Thackeray himself could hardly excel. I was so enchanted with those few lines descriptive of Bath, that I felt I must share them. So forgive me I typed them and sent them to Isabel MacDougall who enjoyed them as much as I did. So much so that she suggested a most nefarious scheme for Satan can appear in the guise of an angel that I ought to get you to describe to me in familiar letters all the places in which you happen to sojourn, collect your pen-pictures, make them into a small book and publish them with your name attached. I replied in politer language 'get thee behind me Satan!'. It was a real temptation, but conquered, pray observe!'*

In December 1911 Nelly was in very good spirits, Lindsay said that every line of her letter seemed *'to ring with the notes of health and contentment. It gave one the idea that the writer was enjoying quietly everything: that it was pleasant for her just to be alive.'* The change in her financial position may have alleviated many of her previous worries and concerns. Nelly had noticed that Lindsay had had no guests to stay that autumn and had offered to come. But if she had been hoping for a rapid response, she would have been disappointed: *'It is very good of you to offer a visit. I'll put you down. October is the best month for a healing visit from one who cannot come in November longest and most tedious of months for me.'*

However, the visit was definitely in prospect for some point in the New Year: the last of the letters preserved in Nelly's bundle, written on 22 December 1911, consisted for the first two pages of a meditation on the delicious toasted cheese that Lindsay was going to prepare for her late one evening over his electric fire. Flirtatious intimacy or harmless teasing? We will never know, nor indeed whether she ever made the trip to Glasgow. Nelly was taking the waters, or at least the air, at Bagni di Lucca, and writing her chapters of the Lucca book, according to Mrs Ross *'who does not know if you are to climb or be carried up the hill of the Gherardi.'*

In the spring she set off for home, via some Mediterranean island hopping, and in July 1912, while back in England collecting her things together for a more prolonged departure to Italy, she tried once again to interest Macmillan in a collaboration between her and Hutton on the Roman Campagna. But as Hutton had still not completed the text of the Somerset volume, one can imagine that Macmillan's frustration made him unenthusiastic about a new project. The Martins had been sold, she wrote, *'in a somewhat high handed fashion while I was in Malta. I am therefore homeless for the moment & am resolving to take a flat in Rome this winter, which makes this a particularly apposite moment for me to do these*

Campagna drawings.'

In October 1912, Nelly wrote again to George Macmillan regarding the Somerset proofs. *'I am sorry to find that owing to the fact that [Hutton] could only give me a general idea of his itinerary, the drawings are rather scanty in places. I think however that by using some of the Wells sketches as head and tail-pieces I can make the gaps less evident.'* She also offered to prepare more drawings of Bath. I can imagine George's face when he read this, more than three years after he had commissioned the work. However, he gritted his teeth and furthermore, arranged a small exhibition of her illustrations to be held at the Pump Room in Bath in February 1913. Nelly claimed that she had also been approached by a London Gallery with the same idea, but thought she would be more likely to make sales in Bath. The asking prices were to be three guineas for the larger drawings, and two guineas for the smaller. She was writing from rooms she had taken in Rome, and had been ill with pneumonia. But she was now recovered, and due to take lunch that very day with Lady Macmillan, Sir Frederick's wife.

A few months later, Nelly started work on her last set of drawings for publication - working again with Hutton on a volume covering Wiltshire. In early summer of 1913 she toured Wiltshire, cadging hospitality where she could, including at the Duckworth family home of Orchardleigh near Frome, but then the physical strain of her work caught up with her again and she wrote to Sir Frederick *'At a moment when I have not the means available my Doctors command me a rest abroad. It is a question of stopping soon for a short time, or later for a long one.'* She was short of money again, begging for an advance of £50 as she had completed one third of the work. With the cheque in her hand, she and her sister Alice set off for Switzerland, with a promise to send the drawings as she completed them.

Thomas Lindsay also suffered increasing ill-health, although he never gave up teaching his students, and he died in December 1914. Janet Ross subsequently published an edited collection of his letters to her. Her Preface began *'These letters do not need a long introduction: they tell their own story and depict the learned, witty, broad-minded and kindly man far better than any words of mine could ever do.'* I can only imagine how sadly Nelly must have missed his humour, affection and encouragement over the next difficult years. He was a man who treated women as his equals in intellect and in their capacity for professional endeavour, at a time when that was rarely true of men. He never patronised Nelly or Janet, even though he was an academic where they were in many ways enthusiastic amateurs. His wife must have truly taught him to appreciate the gift of female companionship.

His legacy lived on in his children's success Susie had married Maurice Cowicke, a distinguished historian, later Sir Maurice Cowicke. And his son Sandy, better known as AD Lindsay, became well-known as Master of Balliol College, Oxford in the 1930s, standing as the anti-Appeasement candidate in the 1938 Oxford by-election, and was later honoured as Lord Lindsay, the first Rector of Keele University, where the family papers are now kept. Finding this archive, and discovering literally hundreds of pages of letters between Lindsay, Janet and Nelly, was a welcome tonic after the disappointment of the Suhr archive. The bulk of the papers were in Lindsay's hand, but finding and handling letters that Nelly had written to someone she cared so deeply about was very satisfying. It was the closest we ever got to hearing her voice, and the truly delightful thing about it was how warm and funny she sounded. Even when she was complaining about Janet or her troubles with her house in Chipping Campden, her wit and her intelligence shone through. To me it is certain that she and Lindsay were more than just correspondents, more indeed than just friends. There was a spark there of love.

Don Carlos.

Our neighbour & his dog. Just a line to tell you that Summer is come, hot & lovely & we are both well. N E. Love

Evangeline Whipple

Rose Cleveland

Chapter Eleven: Eve and Libby

By 1912 Nelly's visits to Italy were becoming more and more frequent and prolonged. The climate probably suited her health more than smoggy London and at rural Chipping Campden her landlord had given her notice to quit and was selling The Martins. There was good literary work to be had around Florence - the British reading public's desire to dream of foreign climes was undimmed. It was in many ways easier to live as an unmarried professional woman in Tuscany than in claustrophobic Edwardian England, where family was everything and the spinster's lot was often to be pitied or, worse, exploited as unpaid domestic labour. Importantly, there were souls sympathetic to Nelly's artistic and literary interests in Italy. Nelly remained close to her old friend Janet Ross and to Janet's Florentine neighbours and family - but after more than ten years she felt that she had outlived her usefulness to this demanding widow, perhaps she was tired of playing mediator in the endless, bitter family squabbles. Her relationship with Janet had not been improved by the experience of literary collaboration, and everyone who knew them seemed to think that they were a bad influence on each other. And with help from her cousin Ida, her finances were a little more secure.

But where to stay? Hotels in Florence or Rome were either expensive, or damp and seedy, or both, and Nelly's budget was still constrained. She had enjoyed the experience of making a home in Chipping Campden, could she find a sympathetic landlord in Tuscany? Then in May 1912, a serendipitous meeting solved the problem. Janet had been watching with interest as a villa very nearby in Maiano was renovated and prepared for new owners. The story was that it had been bought by a couple of wealthy Bostonians, Mr and Mrs Kingsmill Marrs, who were planning to live there permanently after some years of continental travel, as the husband was now unwell. But then, within days of moving in, Kingsmill Marrs died. Janet paid a call, as a good neighbour, to offer sympathy, and was introduced by his widow, Laura, to her sister-in-law Evangeline Whipple, known as Eve, and to her good friend, and lover, Rose Cleveland.

Eve, who turned out to be an extremely wealthy widow, had recently bought a large property in the centre of Bagni di Lucca, and she and Rose admitted that it was probably too big for just the two of them, particularly as it boasted an annex with a separate entrance that would just suit someone living alone. Janet thought of Nelly, who jumped at the opportunity to settle somewhere, anywhere that wasn't Janet's house. And Bagni di Lucca held many advantages for Nelly, who already knew it well.

1912 was the year that *'The Story of Lucca'* was finally published. This volume seems to have been one of the most successful in the Dent series, running to eight editions and staying in print until 1970. Janet Ross had written the first five chapters covering the history of Lucca from Roman times until its incorporation into a united Italy in 1860. The remaining seven chapters by Nelly made up a very detailed yet practical travel guide a walking tour of the town, with two chapters on the Duomo outside and in, a chapter on the City's other churches, walls and towers, a chapter on 'Pictures, Palaces and Books', a chapter on nearby towns and palazzos, and finally *'You must come with us up the lovely valley of the Lima to that happy vale in which lies hidden one of the sweetest places in the world, the Bagni di Lucca.'*

Bagni di Lucca is a grouping of small riverside communities making up a town, mostly known for the natural hot springs that are believed to have healing properties. Nelly explained to her readers that its waters had been discovered in the tenth century and that the baths were first constructed by the citizens of Lucca around 1291. In the early 19th century its fame was established when it was visited by Napoleon's sister Elise, at that time the ruler of Tuscany. Thereafter its fame grew as it was visited by Shelley, by Byron, by the Brownings and Tennyson. As the Italian Gazette described it *'The climate is constant and temperate, and cool in summer...the ex-Grand Ducal Palace is now converted into the Grand Hotel des Thermes, and patronized largely in summer by numbers of American and English families resident in Italy, as well as the visitors returning to and from the Riviera or en route to Rome and Florence. The season is from May 1st to September 30th during which time the two Casinos and the municipal band provide the social distractions, while the mountains and surrounding neighbourhood supply lovers of Nature with constant occupation. There are numerous furnished villas and apartments to be let for the season and the cost of living in these as well as the hotels is extremely moderate.... There is a nice tennis club, a circulating library and the river provides good trout fishing.'* And of course there were the thermal baths claiming to cure an extraordinary collection of ailments from kidney stones to locomotor ataxy!

Bagni is situated in the hills north of Lucca, some 60 miles from Florence. By the time of Nelly's arrival, it was accessible by rail, but the drive up from Lucca was still the most picturesque way to visit. The road initially follows the River Serchio up into the hills, sticking closely to the eastern bank, while the railway hugs the west bank. Halfway there, at Borgo a Mozzano, visitors can stop to admire the thirteenth century Ponte Maddalena, also known as the Devil's Bridge, with its extraordinary arch, constructed as part of a pilgrim's way from France to Rome.

Janet Ross certainly knew Bagni well, she had been there more than once to take the cure, including seven weeks of bed rest after the death of her husband Henry in 1901. She had probably recommended a trip to the baths to Nelly during one of her invalid spells. Her motives may have been mixed: we know she had little patience with Nelly's complaints and may have wanted her out of her hair. But it is clear from the language in The Story of Lucca that Nelly felt particularly proprietorial towards the little town, and by the end of 1912 she had taken up residence as a lodger and companion with Eve and Rose. When, some years later, Madge Vaughan wrote about her visit to Bagni in October 1912 she called it Nelly's home.

Eve and Rose had met in Paola, central Florida, in December 1889, when they were both staying at a newly fashionable resort hotel, the Pine Crest Lodge, with a party of other snowbirds, residents of the northern states seeking some sun. After the terrible interruption of the Civil War, the delights of Florida as a winter destination were just becoming known among wealthier circles. On 30 December 1889, The Boston Evening Transcript carried a report from its special correspondent in Florida, H. Burton Milliken, setting the scene for his readers shivering back home in Boston, *'the verandas of the principal hotels have waked from their summer sleep and are all alive. ... Groups of loungers drink in the June-like air, toying with fans, perchance, as they idly rock in the dreamy sunshine. Parties of equestrians gallop off down the long archways of green that make forest-like vistas of the city's streets. Elegant equipages of all kinds bowl up to the St James Piazza, and fashion's favorites*

- young, beautiful and caressed of fortune - the delicate health-seeker and the rotund form of opulence take their daily airings side by side, without wraps or overcoats.'

A month later, Tampa's newspaper, the West Coast Department, edited by Lucie Vannevar, featured the doings of the party staying in Paola: *'Here at Pine Crest Inn are travellers. Egypt, Syria, Algiers as described by Prof and Mrs Charlier are more real to me today than they are to some who have been there, leaving their eyes at home. But to examine Mme Charlier's gems, her curios, are an education. Rings from India, swordpins of Damascus, crosses from Malta, tiger claw necklaces from the jungles, one cannot look at them without seeing pictures of far lands. There is here too another family who have seen the world, and all the glories of it, and who wear antiques as calmly as we would deck ourselves with pebbles and stones. I never see Mrs Simpson the daughter without being possessed with a frantic desire to demand her bracelets or well not exactly her life but her necklace. Mr Mars [sic] her brother kindly showed me glasses once the property of King Louis of Bavaria and a bit of the True Cross, also his. How some of you catholics will envy me when I tell you I held it in my hand. It is probably genuine as the Pope presented it to the poor mad king.*

'The circle at Pine Crest Inn has grown much larger since my former visit but it is still a very pleasant one. Miss Mollie Hastings, niece of Miss Rose Elizabeth Cleveland, is here for a brief stay. She is a very attractive young woman resembling her aunt in many respects. There are indeed many pretty girls here. Editor Gore of Orlando, who is spending Sunday at Pine Crest with his charming little daughter sighed woefully this morning because forsooth he was not a young man. But his loss is probably someone else's gain, whether the young ladies or the young men of the house, I must leave the public to imagine. The press is well represented. I am here (and please put as large a capital I as you can find), Brother Gore is here, and Mr Cummings who was of the Zanesville Ohio Times-Recorder. Accompanying Mr Cummings is a younger[brother] also of the fold of decidedly bright young men.

'I am no less enchanted with Pine Crest Inn than I was on my former visit. The weather is perfect. I find old friends, among them Mrs McMonagle. My mother's son-in-law is with me and we are the guests of Dr and Mrs Turner, a charming host and hostess. Yesterday we drove to the shell mound at Monroe, on the bank of the St Johns, and had a day of days. To those of us unaccustomed to the hummocks, it was quite a revelation of beauty. The shell mound was chiefly noticeable for its absence, as the vandals had been at work, and Sanford feet probably tread on the relics of long ago. Still probably quite as curious as would have been the mound were the trees standing with exposed roots where excavations have been made. Mr Wilson Barker, a travelled young Englishman, had with him his camera and we were photographed. I shall hope to receive a copy for, aside from reminiscences of the day, it will be

valuable. Miss Cleveland and her niece are central figures. Mrs Mars,[sic] Mrs Simpson, Dr and Mrs Turner, Mr Mars and my 'guidemen' are in it.'

The Mrs Simpson with the antique bracelets and necklaces was a wealthy widow, born Evangeline Marrs, and this was the first time she and Rose had met. Photos show Eve to have been a very pretty woman in her youth, and Rose was entranced: soon the passion became overwhelming. On paper, Rose Cleveland appeared to live a highly conventional life as a bluestocking spinster, sufficiently respectable in the public's eyes that when her batchelor brother Grover was elected President of the United States in 1884, she was asked to take on the role of First Lady. Grover was the one known to have skeletons in his cupboard during the election campaign he had been accused not only of fathering a child out of wedlock, but of sexual assault, and of masterminding a conspiracy to cover up the scandal involving coercion and kidnapping. One can only ask how bad the Republican candidate must have been for Grover still to triumph. But now, tempted by Evangeline, she flung herself headlong into an affair that would have shocked and scandalised American society had it become known - she was playing with fire.

Until the second half of the nineteenth century, romantic friendships between women were not unusual or frowned upon, as women were not considered to be particularly sexual creatures. But nor were same sex pairings particularly common, as for most women marriage was an economic necessity. The advent in the 1880s and 1890s of the New Woman, with opportunities for participating in further education away from the family environment and hence, an independent life, led to a change. Some middle-class women, for whom the traditional route of marriage was either not available or simply did not appeal, chose to form what was known as 'the Boston marriage'. This did not necessarily imply a sexual relationship but was certainly a convenient way to pool resources and companionship in a more equal relationship than heterosexual marriage. Frances Willard wrote 'The loves of women for each other grow more numerous each day.' However, the more common the phenomenon became, and the more frequently it developed into a romantic and then a sexual relationship, the more threatening it began to be to society, and such behavior came to be classed as deviant. Lesbianism, a word first used in this way in the 1870s, was seen as abnormal and immoral. Women who had formed these partnerships, even for economic reasons, started to feel the need to deny their sexuality and to conform to heterosexual norms.

Rose Elizabeth Cleveland, or Libbie as she was known to her brothers and sisters, was born on 14 June 1846, the youngest of nine children. She could not have come from more respectable, middle class stock. Her father Richard Cleveland was a Presbyterian pastor, educated at Yale and Princeton, and came from generations of Presbyterian ministers. When Libbie was born the Clevelands were living at Fayetteville, New York State. Her father's calling meant frequent house moves for the family - before she was seven, they had moved some 40 miles to Clinton and then in 1853 they moved again, just twenty miles north-east to Holland Patent, near Utica, where her father took charge of the Presbyterian church. They had no sooner arrived, however, when Richard died of complications from a gastric ulcer and the family fell on hard times.

The eldest Cleveland boy William had followed his father into the church, and one older sister, Anna, was working as a missionary in Ceylon, but this change of fortune was particularly tough for Stephen Grover Cleveland, the fifth child. He had harboured ambitions to become a lawyer but now at the age of 16, with his two youngest sisters Susan and Rose still in education, he was required to abandon his plans and look for work to support them and his mother.

At first he found employment as a dormitory supervisor at a school for the blind in New York, but in 1855 he traveled upstate to join an uncle in business in Buffalo, eventually becoming a clerk in a local law firm. He obviously knew how to work hard and make an impression, for by 1859, he had recovered lost time and was admitted to the Bar. Cleveland remained in Buffalo for more than twenty years building a legal practice, at the same time becoming increasingly involved in local politics. Two of his brothers, Cecil and Fred, fought for the Union in the Civil War but Grover, although he was drafted, did the same as many middle class professionals, and paid a Polish immigrant $150 to fight for him.

In 1863 he had his first taste of political life as Assistant District Attorney, but he failed to win the senior office of DA the following year and reverted to his bachelor life. He was by now a successful lawyer, known in Buffalo for hard graft and a raucous social circle. In 1871 he was elected Sheriff of the prosperous industrial Erie County, and the next two years were the financial making of him as he coined a (legitimate) fortune, estimated at $60,000, in legal fees and revenues. But in 1872, at the height of this success, the family suffered a double tragedy when his brothers Cecil and Fred, both of whom had survived the Civil War unscathed, were drowned in a steamship accident on their way to the Bahamas to open a hotel they had bought. Not surprisingly their mother Anne was desolate, having to take what consolation she could from reports from survivors that the brothers were heroes: they had last been seen helping others into the lifeboats, rather than saving themselves.

Meanwhile Grover's ambitions grew and he rose from Mayor of Buffalo (1882), to Governor of New York State (1883), to President of the United States (1885), in a mere three and a half years. Perhaps no-one was more surprised than he by this meteoric rise - it was certainly not his previously expressed ambition or intention. There just didn't seem to be any other sensible Democrat candidates. However, even as his Presidential nomination was being finalised at the Democratic Convention in Chicago, the scandal broke that threatened to derail him completely. Letters were sent to all the Chicago newspapers by a Buffalo-based cleric, the Reverend George Ball, accusing Cleveland not just of fathering a child out of wedlock, but of coercing and imprisoning the child's mother, incarcerating her in a lunatic asylum, and kidnapping the child. His letter concluded 'This I know to be true, for I have it confirmed by…Mr Whitney, her attorney, and by Mrs Wm Baker, where the woman boarded.'

According to several affidavits sworn and deposited in 1884, Cleveland had met and seduced Maria Halpin, a widowed shop assistant, while he was serving as Sheriff of Erie County in December 1873. The outcome of this liaison was a baby boy, who the press were now trying to find but who had disappeared from view, as the doctor who had attended the birth had subsequently adopted him. He was to be known for the rest of his life as James King. But his given name at birth was Oscar Folsom Cleveland. Worse still, Maria Halpin claimed that Cleveland had forced himself on her.

Maria said that when she discovered she was pregnant she had written to Grover and that he had at first promised marriage. At the confinement he had arranged for a Dr James King to attend as obstetrician, and had placed the baby with foster parents, related to King by marriage. After a year the baby was returned to Maria, who was constantly threatening Cleveland with exposure, still trying to force him to marry her - but in 1876 she was persuaded to place the boy in an orphanage, with a promise that Grover would pay $5 a week for his keep. Just six weeks later she stole the little boy away. Her story, supported by witnesses, was that an infuriated Grover then tracked her down, and sent men to take the child by force. Maria was committed to a lunatic asylum with a diagnosis of monomania and symptoms of alcohol poisoning. Eventually a happier settlement was reached Maria left Buffalo with a cheque for $500, and Oscar was adopted by Dr King and re-named. According to the biographer Lachman, baby James eventually qualified as a doctor and practised in Buffalo, dying in 1947 with the secret of his parentage never revealed.

The explosion of this story into the press in 1884 was massively embarrassing to Cleveland on two levels. Not only was he running for President, he had other more personal fish to fry - he was finally planning, at the age of 47, to embark on marriage and to a girl he had known since she was a baby, who was nearly 30 years his junior. Frances Folsom, born in 1864, was the only daughter of one of Grover Cleveland's closest friends, Oscar Folsom, a lawyer in Buffalo who had been killed in a carriage accident in 1872. It was this same Oscar Folsom for whom Maria Halpin had named her baby, which was to further complicate the murky rumours swirling around Cleveland as presidential candidate. On Folsom's early death, Grover Cleveland became executor of his will, and although he was not made Frances's guardian, as her mother was still alive, he took a keen interest in the girl's education.

In 1882, when Grover was running for office as Mayor of Buffalo, Frances was admitted to Wells College, Aurora, New York, one of the first Liberal Arts Colleges for women in America. Throughout her successful student career Cleveland wrote to her, visited when he could, and regularly sent flowers. Frances shared a room with Katherine ('Pussy') Willard, the niece of Frances Willard, a leading light in the linked causes of the temperance and Women's Suffrage movements. As Grover was resolutely opposed to both these campaigns, Frances must have found herself in some difficult situations.

When the story of the Halpin baby broke, on 21 July 1884, Frances and her widowed mother Emma were staying with Grover Cleveland and his two sisters Mary and Rose in the Governor's House in Albany. By coincidence, this was Frances' 20th birthday. Grover retreated from public view while the newspapers seethed with excitement - but eventually the Democratic party machine got its act together and promoted the story that Cleveland had indeed had a youthful indiscretion with Mrs Halpin, if a man in his thirties can be described as youthful, but that he had not been her only lover. Nowadays we would call this slut-shaming. The story they spun was that when Maria announced her pregnancy, Grover, as the only bachelor in his social circle, decided to do the honourable thing, or at least to make an effort to support the woman and thus shield one or two of his married friends from scandal. The hinted suggestion was that the child may have actually been fathered by Folsom he was after all no longer around to defend himself. It is hard to imagine how poor Mrs Folsom and her daughter would have felt about this, committed as they were by this time to the Cleveland camp.

Eventually the press tracked down Maria Halpin and, furious at the way she was being portrayed, she swore two separate affidavits naming Cleveland as the father, claiming that 'he accomplished [my] ruin by the use of force and violence and without my consent' - a pretty clear accusation of rape. Some of this testimony was published and widely promoted in the Republican press. Republican supporters haunted Cleveland's rallies with placards reading 'Ma, Ma, Where's my Pa?'. But by then the Democrat campaign was on a roll and the accusations were dismissed by Cleveland's staff as forgeries, with mud being flung in all directions, particularly at poor Maria. Interestingly, Cleveland never actually denied the tale himself. But it is not surprising that with this scandal lapping at his feet, Cleveland would want to look highly respectable when he came into possession of the White House. With no wife to turn to, he chose the most upright and respectable available relation - his youngest sister Rose. On 17 January 1885, with the presidency secured, he announced that Rose would occupy the position of First Lady.

Rose had been only seven when her father died, and times were hard, but luckily for her, the Cleveland family believed in education for girls and, according to a sketch published in 1888, the youngest Cleveland daughter was sent to Houghton Seminary, in Clinton, New York State *'where she proved a brilliant pupil, graduating with the highest honors. "Original People" was the theme of her graduating essay, which was declared to be a most happy effort.'* Houghton Seminary seems to have been founded not long before Rose arrived. It was a 'girls only' school, with a strong Christian ethic. An advertisement published in 1900 claims that 'Houghton Seminary has been known for 40 years as one of the most earnest, helpful and thorough-going schools in the land. Its policy has been to offer, on moderate terms, the best of educational facilities.'

On graduation, probably around 1864, Rose became a teacher in the Houghton Seminary, and then after two years, showing great independence of spirit and ambition, she travelled some 700 miles to Lafayette, Indiana, to take a position as Principal of the Collegiate Institute in that town. It was clear that she was determined on a life of academia. She taught in Muncy, Pennsylvania for a short time at a private school; it was here that she seems to have developed a strongly independent personality, preferring to read and study alone.

After a few years' teaching, Rose decided to become a freelance writer and educationalist. '.. *she conceived the idea of lecturing before classes, and proposed to the Principal of Houghton Seminary to make a beginning there. The Principal of the Seminary entering heartily into the arrangement, Rose Cleveland wrote a course of historical lectures which she delivered that season.' One of the lectures she gave was on the subject of 'Altruistic Faith': "We cannot touch humanity at large, except as we touch humanity in the individual. We make the world a better place through our concrete relationships, not through our vague, general good will. We must each find a true partner, someone who understands and appreciates us, someone whose faith in us brings out our best efforts. Our deepest craving is for recognition - to be known by another human being for what we truly are."*

The decision to return home in the early 1870s, after some ten years as an independent professional woman, was probably taken because as the youngest and unmarried daughter it fell to her to care for her now elderly mother. She found it harder to escape this responsibility in 1870s upstate New York than Nelly did in London some twenty years later. But she kept herself intellectually busy, developing her skills as a literary critic and writer, and becoming a well-known lecturer on historical topics. She continued to practise the Christian faith, and became a strong supporter of the temperance movement, which was led by Frances Willard in the United States. Rose made her home with her mother, who had continued to live rent-free at 'The Weeds', the parsonage in Holland Patent, since the death of her husband. Her mother passed away in the summer of 1882, when Rose was 36.

'After this sad event her brothers and sisters naturally expected that she would make her home with one of them, but being of an independent nature and self-reliant, she preferred to remain in the old home, where she continued to live when not away lecturing, until she assumed the position of mistress of the White House.'

Grover and Rose moved into the White House on inauguration on 4 March 1885 and the press immediately began to focus on this rather unconventional

First Lady. The New York Times was in modified raptures as she hosted her second evening reception at the White House. The paper reported that Miss Cleveland wore a dress of black satin, with an entire overdress of Spanish lace. The satin bodice was cut low and sleeveless, and the transparent lace revealed the shoulders and arms. *'In person, Miss Cleveland is of medium stature and build, with a shapely and highly intellectual face - good-looking but not pretty.'*

It soon became clear that Rose Cleveland did not fit easily into Washington high society during her tenure as First Lady. It was generally felt that she was a bluestocking, more interested in pursuing scholarly endeavors than in entertaining Cabinet members' wives and foreign dignitaries. Rumour had it that she amused herself by mentally conjugating Greek verbs during White House receptions. In some ways the public exposure was to be good for promoting Rose's new career as a writer, but she did not enjoy the constant duties of a political hostess. The attention from the Press must have been tiresome - as a schoolmistress and bluestocking from out of town, it would have been an unlooked-for burden. Rose tried to stay true to her own interests and political beliefs. One of her causes was the Temperance Movement - she had written an article for a temperance magazine in 1882 - *'it is only a strong man who can keep his wine glass upside down'* - and had taken the Pledge herself. She hosted a delegation from Frances Willard's Women's Christian Temperance Union for tea at the White House, despite the fact that the Prohibition Party had fielded a candidate against her brother in the Election - and Grover was certainly not a teetotaler. By standing firm to the beliefs and causes she had espoused before chance took her to the White House, most of which were more progressive and radical than the policies pursued by her brother the President, Rose can be seen as a new model for a First Lady, a more modern and intellectual role which would challenge the expectations of the press and public and allow future First Ladies to have their own sphere of political influence.

Meanwhile, as they tried to come to terms with the concept of a First Lady who had her own personality and agenda, the Press also began to notice that she kept different company from her predecessors. For example, she stirred up some controversy by visiting the theatre in Washington 'with a lady friend and without a male escort.' It would have been unthinkable for the President's sister to be challenged in the press as a lesbian, and yet I can see discreet questions being raised about her behaviour and her preferences even in the politest of the

American quality journals. After just six weeks the strain began to tell and on 29 April, having cancelled all White House receptions for the rest of the social season, Rose left on a short trip to New York.

Rose did return to Washington, but it turned out to be a short-lived arrangement, as by August 1885 Grover was secretly engaged to the young and beautiful Frances Folsom. Once the engagement was arranged but unannounced, Frances was whisked away to Europe by her mother but by the time the two women returned the following year, the various rumours around Grover's marital intentions were running wild. Grover decided to pre-empt the speculation and scandal by marrying Frances as soon as possible upon her return. But first he had to endure, or perhaps enjoy, being teased a little. Frances stayed in New York before the wedding, where the President had to visit to attend Decoration Day ceremonies. As the Presidential cavalcade passed the hotel where Frances was staying, and watching from a balcony, the band struck up 'For he's going to marry YumYum' from Gilbert & Sullivan's The Mikado, which had just finished a triumphant run on Broadway. Cleveland tipped his hat, Frances waved her handkerchief, and the crowd went wild.

The wedding was held in The White House on 2 June 1886, organised at short notice by Rose. The ceremony was held at 6pm, and although hundreds gathered outside, the wedding party itself numbered just 30. Rose had arranged for flowers everywhere, and a wedding march was played by The Marine Band conducted by John Philip Sousa, the prolific composer of marches. Grover Cleveland was described by the British Ambassador, Cecil Spring-Rice (author of "I vow to thee my country"), as 5 foot high and 4 foot wide, but he admitted that Frances was a real beauty. A strange union.

The very day after the wedding, Rose moved out, returning to Holland Patent. The New York Times reported that she had always planned to resume her literary career, and to be self-supporting. There is a suggestion that she turned down her brother's offer of a salary. But her life whenever she was in the United States would henceforward be prone to press interest, and increasingly, to escape this attention, she travelled abroad. She had now more financial independence to do this: *'Her career as first lady of the land was a social success, and her literary ability has earned her considerable money and a fair reputation as a writer. The book of "Studies" by which she became known as an author, was succeeded by other works.'* [12]

She had published two books while living in the White House. Her first

---

[12] *Prominent Men and Women of the Day by Thos. W. Herringshaw. 1888 A. B. Gehman & Co.*

successful publication was a volume of her lectures and essays under the title *George Eliot's Poetry, and other Studies* (New York, 1885), shortly followed by her only published novel, *The Long Run* (1886) - a love story. It is likely that she had started writing the novel well before her brother's election but her celebrity no doubt made it easier to find a publisher. The essays, which she now dedicated *'respectfully and affectionately'* to her fellow countrywomen, had been prepared as lectures earlier in her career. Her correspondence with Dr Hayes Ward, clergyman and editor of the New York Independent, a Congregationalist journal, bears this out - that as she would no longer be in a position to deliver her essays as lectures, as she had done before the move to the White House, her friends prevailed upon her to get them published. Her writings seem to have a very clear social purpose, whether they are essays, criticism or fiction, and that is to lead her female readership into an acceptance that a new dawn was coming for women in which they would be able to live fuller, freer lives. And there are many clues within her work as to the types of freedom she craved for herself and other women.

These books certainly paid well. Studies sold over 25,000 copies. Rose went on to write several essays on self-improvement, such as the introductions to three volumes: *"You and I: Or Moral, Intellectual and Social Culture", "How to Win: A Book for Girls"* (1887) and *"Social Mirror: A Complete Treatise on the Laws, Rules and Usages that Govern our Most Refined Homes and Social Circles".* For just a few months, in 1886, she was appointed as editor to the Chicago-based magazine Literary Life, quite an achievement in the male-dominated publishing industry, and announced that her editorial policy was to speak to her countrywomen and *'make my talk very simple and earnest and sincere'*, but within a few months she fell out with the proprietor, Mr Elder, who had got himself into financial difficulties.

In May 1887, Rose took a post teaching American history at Mrs Sylvanus Reed's School for Girls in Manhattan. But if this was intended to be a quiet haven, free from stress, Rose had yet again chosen badly. Within a year her wages were unpaid and Mrs Reed was trying to sell the school. Rose wrote an increasingly desperate series of letters to Henry Stetson, a partner in the same law firm in New York as Grover Cleveland, *'If you can come to my rooms any time today or this evening I shall be grateful. Of course I am distressed but I hope to hold out: I thank God for my friends. All this comes so suddenly and I am so near ill, that I must ask you to forgive incoherence.'* Was money the only trouble? It may have been while working at the school that she first met Clara Fuller, later headmistress of Ossining *'Miss Fuller is the lady who came with me. She has won all hearts this year by her courtesy, kindness and good service. Of course, as my friend and confidante, she is feared by Mrs Reed and you see by the note that Mrs R desires her to leave. I shall keep her as my guest until I leave. She knows all that has taken place between Mrs Reed and myself - please talk to her.'*

By June 1888 Rose was desperate to leave for Europe, but needed to reach a financial settlement with Mrs Reed before she left. In January 1889 she was back at Holland Patent, turning her attention to a campaign to get women admitted to Columbia University via the Annex Movement, but planning to leave for Florida *'where I expect to spend several months, returning North in March or April.'* She was still worrying again about how to claim the balance remaining to her from Mrs Reed. Her companion at this time was a Miss van Vechten. In February 1889 she was staying in Naples, and much enamoured of the Florida climate. She wrote to Stetson *'This place - location rather, for it is hardly a place yet, is cheering beyond anything I ever knew. When you get your yacht built you must sail down here with Mrs Stetson and see it for yourself.'*

Rose seems to have felt politically liberated after she left the White House, and became increasingly vocal on the subject of women's rights, particularly the right to vote. Lippincott's Monthly Magazine published a long satirical poem by Rose entitled *'The Dilemma of the Nineteenth Century'* about a young girl called Judith who falls ill at the age of 21. The doctors cannot agree on the cause of her ill-health– could it be her lack of a husband? Over-education? Too little outdoor exercise? The female doctors claim that she will be cured if she is given the vote but, says Rose the poet, there is a risk that she will never be cured unless she can become a man. Pretty heady stuff for a President's sister to be publishing.

In an essay published the same month Rose wrote of the need women have for financial independence –and argued that married women should be seen as equal home owners with their husbands - *'There can be no mature development where there is no conscious responsibility; there can be no responsibility without independence.'* If these writings seem mostly to be concerned with women's rights, her next work would pose even more challenging questions. The following January, *Godey's Lady's Book* published a very strange two-part story by Rose called *'Robin Adair'*. The love story revolves around a young female singer who falls for a young man because of his strong resemblance to a woman the singer has previously loved. The narrator asks his wife if she does not find this passion of a women for another woman 'queer', to which his wife replies 'No queerer than anything else!' This story has been described by Rose's biographer as *'a radical, empowering, lesbian story that implicitly transgressed the constructed assertions of acceptable, if not also respectable, womanly behaviour.'* It is as if Rose, in her writing, is prepared to court speculation about her own unmarried status and preferences.

The Cleveland family took care of Rose Elizabeth, trying to shield her from the press, but it must have been increasingly difficult for them to cope with the turn her life was to take after she left the White House. The Collected Letters of Grover Cleveland 1850-1908, edited by Allan Nevins, were published in 1933, and by this time Rose had almost vanished from the official records. She is referred to only briefly in family letters as 'Libbie', and if the President received any letters from Libbie, they did not make it into the published collection.

However, Nevins' introduction says *'It was characteristic of Cleveland that he wrote many letters about public business, few about his personal affairs or personal feelings....It is significant that I have not found it necessary to omit a single letter because it expressed too intimate a view of his private life (for some parts of every man's life are essentially sacred to himself and his family), or too frank an opinion of others ....Of his correspondence much has been lost. It was not his habit to keep copies...many must have been destroyed by the recipients.'*

Earlier in the 1880s Libbie had a close friend, Miss Nelson, who travelled with her and was a guest at her brother's White House wedding. She was also closely linked with Frances Willard, known to prefer the company of women to that of men. In the late 1880s her regular companions included Clara Fuller and Miss van Vechten. But this careful life of outward respectability and discreet relationships with other single women would be thrown into the air when she met the much more unconventional Mrs Eve Simpson.

Tracking down Evangeline has been a lot of fun. According to her sworn passport declaration in Italy dated June 1915, Evangeline Elizabeth Thurston Marrs had been born in Massachusetts in January 1862, (the same year as Nelly), and her father Dana, or Daniel, was a native citizen of the United States. In fact her parents may well have been Irish-born folk who had emigrated to Boston in 1846, at the time of the Potato Famine. Certainly the first public record of their presence in the United States that I can find is Dana's marriage to Jane Knaggs, recorded in Canton, Massachusetts on 29 October 1846, and the 1860 census lists them both as being Irish born. At the time of Evangeline's first marriage, to Michael Simpson, in 1882, her father was described as a prosperous farmer, but in the 1870 census he was listed as a machinist, and there is no reference to their Irish origin. Very confusingly, the 1880 census says that both he and his wife's parents were born in England. Later in Evangeline's life, her parents were referred to, for instance in the Biographical Dictionary of America, as Dr Francis Marrs and his wife Jane Van Poelien Marrs, of distinguished English and Dutch ancestry. It is not clear where the title of doctor, or Evangeline's mother's middle name, had come from. Dana and Jane had come a long way from Canton, and even further from Ireland. I wonder if Evangeline's very name is evidence of a romantic streak in the Marrs family: Evangeline is the eponymous heroine of Longfellow's hugely successful epic poem, published in 1847, just a few years before the Marrs had their baby girl. And Evangeline herself, in the poem, is a tragic heroine expelled from her native land by the brutal English invaders. If the Marrs had indeed been forced to leave Ireland by the Famine, the story may have struck a chord.

There is also an intriguing mystery about Eva's age. She is listed in the 1860 census as being 7 years old, which would have meant that she was born in 1853. This may just have been a slip of the pen, except that again in the 1870 census her age is noted at 17, which would match the 1853 birthday. By the 1880 census however, she had miraculously aged only 6 years, listing her age as 23, giving a birth date of 1857. As an unmarried woman of 27, it might have looked to the outside world that she had been left on the shelf - so was the alteration deliberate, or just an administrative error?

Eve had just one sibling, an older brother, William, born in November 1847, the year after his parents wed. In the census of 1870 he was working as a shop assistant, a humble yet respectable profession. He applied for his first passport in 1872, under the name of William D Kingsmill Marrs. The name Kingsmill does not appear on any previous records. It is as if the family has a predisposition to re-invent themselves, glossing over awkward facts, embellishing where required. The difficulty in pinning down Eve's age continues - in 1899 when she travelled with her second husband, she is listed on the ship's manifest as 38, when she was probably well into her 40s. When she lived in Italy during the First World War, her annual typed passport applications all say that she was born on 15th January 1862, despite all the evidence that she was some nine years older than this. One inconsistency could be put down to administrative error, but constant incidents suggest that Evangeline enjoyed throwing sand over her trail. It is particularly amusing that she still felt the need to conceal her true age when she was over 60 and no longer chasing husbands. Did Rose know the truth, I wonder?

Eve's first husband was an elderly and very wealthy widower, Michael Hodge Simpson, who owned a large textile mill complex in the Saxonville section of Framingham (20 miles west of Boston, Massachusettes). Michael was a local boy made good - his father had been a prosperous ship's captain and trader, who set Michael and his brother up to trade in hides, horn and wool - but the story goes that in 1835, when the market collapsed, Michael was left with a million tons of wool on his hands. Rather than dump his goods, he established his own woollen mill and patented a new type of burr-cutting machine. Within very few years he managed to sell the patent for the machine to an English company for £10,000, and invested his capital in a carpet yarn business in Saxonville.

Around this time he married Elizabeth Davies Kilham and they had four children who survived to adulthood - Helen, Grace, Michael Henry (known as Harry) and Frank. Harry died in Florence at the age of 19. He had been sent to Europe to tour manufacturing facilities, presumably with a view to joining the family business, but died of Roman fever, as malaria was known then. Michael continued to expand his business and develop patents. He was an earnest Republican and a philanthropic Methodist, he and his wife took an interest in female education, and were both trustees on the Board of Wellesley College, near Boston Massachusetts. When Elizabeth died in 1878, Michael endowed Simpson Hall at Wellesley in her honour.

On 1 June 1882, four years after his wife's death, and at the very respectable age of 72, Simpson married his young neighbour Evangeline Marrs. According to the local press reports, Evangeline was 27 at the time, although by my reckoning she was 29. The marriage entry in the local register cited her as Evangeline ET Marrs - elsewhere the name Thurston begins to appear. Like Kingsmill, it is not clear where this name comes from. Anyway, her husband set out to build her a splendid new house on Dudley Pond - *'a 50 by 200-foot Victorian eye-popper made of brick, wood and stone that cost $150,000 to build,'* according to local historians. It was close to Simpson's mills but also near Evangeline's family home. Work on the house progressed while the newlyweds honeymooned in Europe. A local historian, Hoyt, estimates construction took around one year to complete with 30 workers building the house, stables, servants' quarters and a windmill. But there was a great deal of local gossip about the marriage which made Michael very unhappy - in the Saxonville parade, fun was poked at them when characters arrived dressed as 'May and November'. Simpson died in Boston in December 1884, possibly before the house was even completed. They had been married for less than three years.

After Michael's death, his now very wealthy young widow seems to have disappeared from view. The year after his death the Marrs family sailed to Europe on Cunard's SS Cephalonia, arriving at Queenstown, Cork. The passenger list includes Francis Marrs, by then a gentleman of 60, his wife Jane, now 52, William Kingsmill, aged 32, and right next to them on the passenger list, a Marion Simpson, a matron of 25. Was this Evangeline? Or just a coincidence? If it is her, the given age is certainly wrong. And were the family visiting Europe for the first time on a Grand Tour, or returning to see their native land of Ireland and catch up with relatives? The record of the family's return to America eighteen months later is clear - the Scythia sailed from Liverpool via Queenstown on 16 July 1887, and on board are Daniel Marrs, his wife Jane, his son Kingsmill, and Evangeline EJ Simpson, a matron of 31. There is a portrait painted of the wealthy widow Evangeline in 1887: *'..a striking beauty. The artist portrays her as almost Latin, dark and sensuous. Her hair is cut short, an unusual style for the nineteenth century. She impresses the viewer as accustomed to wealth, self-assured and possessing a certain willfulness.'* [13] This is the Eva, flashing her elaborate necklaces and bracelets, that Rose fell in love with just three years later.

For almost a century, their passionate love affair remained a secret, the evidence lying hidden among the Whipple family papers in Faribault, Minnesota. In her will, Evangeline had requested that the papers be sealed for 50 years after her death. They were discovered and actually revealed to the public in 1978 by Paula Petrik, a historian working at George Mason University, Fairfax, Virginia, working on a tip-off from a 'mole' in the Minnesota Historical Society that there were actually ten boxes of Evangeline's letters, but only nine listed in the catalogue. Petrik's article explains that although only Rose's letters were preserved in the Whipple archives, the course of their passionate love affair

---

[13] *Into the Open: P Petrik 1978*

was easy to trace. After the 1889/90 season ended in Florida the two went their separate ways, both with social engagements to fulfil, but Rose's desperate letters, kept safely by Evangeline, make it clear that theirs was a physical relationship which required some planning and secrecy if they were to be able to spend time alone together.

Rose wrote *'Ah how I love you, it paralyzes me, it makes me heavy with emotion…I tremble at the thought of you….Sweet, Sweet, I dare not think of your arms…you are mine by every sign in Earth and Heaven - by every sign in soul and spirit and body.'* They saw each other for a week in New York in May, and then Rose returned to The Weeds to await a visit from Eve in the autumn. Evangeline was to spend the summer months in Europe. But clearly Rose could not bear the separation *'I tried to feel your hand but it is of no use, Eve. I am sure of you, but I do not see your delightful face or feel your enfolding arms and lose all else in the shelter and happiness of that haven.'*. We know that Victorian women wrote extremely passionate letters to their most platonic friends, but there can be little doubt that this was a physical relationship: *'her sweet life-breath and her warm enfolding arms appease my hunger and quiet my breast, and carry us both in one to the summit of joy, the end of search, the goal of love.'* In early August Rose wrote to her lawyer saying that she was rushing to tie up some loose ends *'so that I may have the opportunity to join some friends in England by September 1st, leaving from New York on the 23rd'*. We know that she did indeed arrive in Southampton on 31 August. Petrik assumes from the lack of any correspondence between October 1890 and April 1892, that after this trip, Eve came to share Rose's house in Holland Patent for eighteen months.

By the end of April 1892, the relationship was changing, Evangeline seems to have chosen to withdraw from a situation fraught with difficulty, especially for the sister of a once and future President. Dana Francis Marrs had just died while staying at San Remo in Italy. Perhaps when it became clear that Grover was planning to run again for President, and fearful of further press scrutiny, Evangeline decided she wished to pursue a more private and orthodox life. Rose wrote 'I do not think you need me now…*If after all, there is but this way for you, if you will do this thing, then I will not stand in the way….[I will] take myself out of your way for a while, at least and to reappear only when I can act gracefully and well in my new role.'* And she left for Europe, not returning until May 1893 on the steamship Etruria, as confirmed by the New York press. The assumption of course is that Evangeline stayed in the United States, but scrutiny of the handwritten

Evangeline and Bishop Whipple

passenger list of the Etruria shows that as well as 'Rachel Cleveland', there were two other familiar names on the ship: a Marion Simpson, right next to Cleveland on the list, and further down the list appears Kingsmill Marrs. What a coincidence!

Rose continued to write to Evangeline, but the letters became pleading, wistful, and there seemed to be no way back to their previous intimate relationship. Eve had decided to re-enter respectable society with a blue chip marriage. As early as August 1895 Rose was writing to Eve's suitor, congratulating him on his successful wooing. Again Eve had chosen an older man, and a widower - this time it was Henry Whipple, Episcopal Bishop of Minnesota. He was 74, she was 43, (but may have claimed publicly to be younger) and the marriage certainly set tongues wagging.

Bishop Henry Whipple was a celebrity of the religious establishment, known for his work among the Sioux. He had been appointed the first Bishop of Minnesota in 1859, and established his house and church at Faribault, the chief trading post in the state. The native peoples liked him, calling him 'Straight Tongue' according to the New York Times. At the time of the Civil War, during the Sioux uprisings, the Bishop travelled to Washington on their behalf to plead with Lincoln for clemency, and in 1865 he was appointed one of three Commissioners in an investigation into the people's needs. In Faribault he worked to improve educational facilities, building schools that would be attended by white children mixing with children from the Dakota and Ojibway tribes. He also founded a school for girls. In 1876 he was instrumental in securing the Sioux Treaty by which the Black Hills of Dakota were opened for settlement. Two years later his youngest son John Hall Whipple was murdered, at the age of 21, his body found floating in the Ohio River, and an anonymous note was sent to the Bishop claiming that this was a revenge killing. However, as the young man was described as 'errant' and 'reckless', the circumstances of his death remain a mystery.

Evangeline had met Whipple at the same place she had met Rose in Florida, but possibly a few years earlier, while his first wife was still alive. Henry had first bought land in the relatively undeveloped Maitland area of Florida in 1877, and in 1881 founded a church there. He and his wife Cornelia regularly wintered there, for the sake of Henry's health, and it was the injuries suffered by Cornelia in a train crash on the way to Florida in 1889 that led to her death.

On 24 October 1896, The New York Times reported Henry and Eve's wedding, which had taken place a few days earlier at St Bartholomew's Church in Manhattan, adding that the wedding had come as a surprise to the Bishop's friends in New York, who had thought his visit to the City to be on account of the session of the House of Episcopal Bishops, which he had been attending. The wedding was very small, attended by only a few of the Bishop's closest friends. The Times, presumably trying to minimize any scandalous implications, pointed out that 'The Bishop is in vigorous health and looks much younger than he really is' and also claimed that Eve was an 'intimate friend of the Bishop's first wife', confirming that the relationship did indeed date back to holidays in Florida before 1889. Henry and Eve honeymooned at the Buckingham Hotel in New York before returning to Minneapolis, and then departed for a year-long tour of Europe. In 1898 Henry received an Honorary Doctorate at Oxford

University and his ceremonial robes are still preserved in Minnesota.

I suspect that the people of Faribault did not know what to make of Eve, with her progressive lifestyle and dramatic tastes. But she seems to have been truly devoted to the Bishop and his causes, in the few years they were together in Minnesota. From her new home in Faribault, she travelled with him to the Native missions and worked with the young women living there. It would have been a courageous move for Eve, going to live in what was still frontier territory. But there are many photos and diary entries from the period suggesting that she took it all in her stride, made friends with some of the native leaders and worked to improve their conditions. She was particularly attached to the lacemaking school which her husband had founded to provide work for the women. She was also very generous, donating money to the missions and extending the Whipple home next door to the Cathedral. The extensions included a library, and space to exhibit items collected by the Bishop over his many years of travel. In her will she left a significant trust fund to St Mary's Girls School which boarded and educated native American girls. This generosity would be reciprocated in part over 100 years later.

Evangeline also brought a sophisticated collection of art objects into their home, reportedly including some of the items from the estate of "Mad" King Ludwig II of Germany. On 23 May 1899 the New York Times reported that Bishop and Mrs Whipple had arrived home from Europe on the Umbria. In 1901, Henry came down with a cold, which rapidly developed into heart problems. For a few weeks, Evangeline, Mary Mills Whipple and two of Henry's other daughters tried to nurse him back to health. But at dawn on 16 September 1901, Henry Whipple died. Neither of Eve's marriages were long-lived, but both left her wealthy.

The Bishop's funeral on 20 September 1901 was one of the largest gatherings ever held in Faribault. All the stores, schools and businesses closed for the day and a train brought over 300 people from St. Paul. Native Americans came from Birch Coulee and White Earth. For over two hours, people queued to see his coffin and to pay their respects before the funeral. Henry was buried beneath the High Altar in his Cathedral. After the funeral, Evangeline received condolence letters from all over the world. She remained in Faribault, finishing business there. She donated money for the construction of a bell tower on the Cathedral in Henry's memory - the bells were first played in 1902.

During Evangeline's married life, Rose spent many months abroad. In December 1896, within a few weeks of the wedding, she left the United States for an extended tour of Europe, travelling on to Greece and Turkey. By 1899 she was back in Utica, living with a new partner, Evelyn Ames, daughter of a former Governor of Massachusetts. In 1902 the two women were living together on Seven Hundred Acre Island off the coast of Maine, where Rose had purchased some land in the 1880s, and they spoke publicly about their intention to found a colony of like-minded people, an ambiguous term in the circumstances. While she was there she set about developing a farming business, and was happy to publicise the success she was having, in a news item which seems to have been syndicated across the international press. I even found a paragraph in the British press, the Walsall Advertiser of October 1903, which sang her praises, explaining that she employed numerous men on the estate but took full control herself and was producing high quality cows and chickens, butter, vegetables, cheese, fruit and cream 'and her small colony flourishes exceedingly.' But by 1905 Rose was selling off the land, and at a great profit. The Washington Post reported that she had originally acquired the acreage for $4,500, and had just sold part of it for $200,000. That would have made her very wealthy.

As a former First Lady, the gossip columns tried to keep up with her travels. There are various mentions in the Society columns of The New York Times: For instance, in December 1905 it reported that the 'Divine' Miss Sarah Bernhardt was to purchase a play written exclusively for her by Miss Cleveland, set during the French Revolution. The report said that Miss Cleveland 'has made her home in Paris for many years', although there is no other evidence for this. She certainly did return to the United States from time to time - Grover died in June 1908 and Rose attended his funeral in Princeton, New Jersey and a memorial service for him in Carnegie Hall the following spring. She continued with her literary works, publishing a translation of the Soliloquys of St Augustine in 1910.

Meanwhile, the Marrs family continued their extraordinary upward rise through Massachusetts' society. In November 1896 at the age of 48, Kingsmill, who only 25 years earlier had been working as a shop assistant, had finally married, his bride being the 52 year old Laura Norcross, whose father Otis had been Mayor of Boston in 1867. This was within a few weeks of his sister's marriage to Bishop Whipple in New York. Laura came from true Boston Brahmin aristocracy - her family tree can be traced from pilgrim settlers in Salem, Massachusetts in 1638 through noted political leaders and soldiers in the War of Independence. Her distant cousins included the painter Winslow Homer and the poet Emily Dickinson. Laura appears regularly in the Society pages of the Boston press until the winter of 1896, but may also have wintered in Florida. It seems unlikely, even if Kingsmill was not born of immigrant Irish parents, that his family would have been in the same Boston circles as the Norcross family - but he and Laura seem to have had many intellectual interests in common and were of an age where they could suit themselves. Nevertheless, the match would have been a shock to the Norcross family circle - the Brahmins were highly selective in their socialising and their breeding: this is the circle described in the "Boston Toast" by Harvard alumnus John Collins Bossidy:

"And this is good old Boston,
The home of the bean and the cod,
Where the Lowells talk only to Cabots,
And the Cabots talk only to God."

From 1896 to 1905, Mr and Mrs Kingsmill Marrs lived at South Park, the Marrs' family home in Wayland, Massachusetts. But in the winter they regularly travelled south to their other home, Maitland Cottage, in Maitland, Florida, where they became active in the Florida Audubon Society, established in 1900. The first President of the Society was that other snowbird, Bishop Henry Whipple, by then their brother-in-law. Laura Norcross Marrs served as an executive committee member for the Society during the early 1900s and was instrumental in creating a National Association of Audubon Societies. For many years, Kingsmill Marrs wrote the Florida Audubon Society's annual reports for Bird-Lore, the first official magazine of the National Audubon Society. He was also a keen amateur photographer, and the Massachusetts Historical Society now holds his collections. They include several studio portraits of Rose Cleveland, and a delightful photograph of a lady, with a striking resemblance to Rose, riding a bicycle.

After 1905, the Marrs went abroad to Europe and Egypt, where they devoted their time to travel and the collection of books and European prints and artwork. Laura was a friend of Howard Carter, later to be the discoverer of the tomb of Tutenkhamen, and owned half a dozen of his paintings. They were often accompanied in the United States and on their travels by Evangeline and her mother, as well as their English friend, the photographer William Wilson Barker. Eve's correspondence with Rose became far more regular over this period. In 1907 Mrs Marrs died and Eve must have felt finally free to do what she wanted with her life. Rose was also free as her relationship with Evelyn Ames had ended. Their romance began again. After all, Eve had never destroyed the incriminating love letters that Rose had written some fifteen years earlier.

But by 1910 Kingsmill's health was a cause for concern and in July Evangeline closed up the Whipple mansion and left for Italy, accompanied by Rose on the Lusitania, and sharing a cabin. She never did return to Faribault. Once she and Rose had made their home in Bagni di Lucca, it seemed to be too hard to return home, even after Rose's death.

Evangeline had first visited Bagni di Lucca in 1910, taking residence at the Continental Hotel, perhaps with her brother and sister-in-law visiting the spa and hoping for a cure. She and Rose obviously fell in love with the little town, and looked for a property to acquire. The house Eve found was Casa Bernardini at Bagno alla Villa, which she bought from the Burlamacchi family, as well as the adjoining small house, "Casa Piccola" (now called Villa San Francesco). The small house had its own separate access with a stone drive which leads down to the Piazza del Bagno and its thermal baths. This was where Nelly made her home from 1912.

How much of these stories of Eve and Rose did Nelly know or guess? We know that she was not scared of unconventionality, she and her family had many friends who lived beyond the bounds of normal Victorian and Edwardian sexual respectability, including Edward Carpenter and the Misses Sichel and Ritchie. The relationship between Bertha Newcombe and Shaw was hardly conventional. Over the next six years, as they worked and suffered together, Nelly would certainly have learned both Rose and Eva's life stories, including many of the secrets they had been forced to hide in their native land.

Around 2009, as I waved Hattie off to University and began to find some time for myself in between work and family commitments, I began to squirrel away the odd hour to turn all the Nelly Erichsen internet searches and archive extracts into a narrative, a story. And it is a great story, if only because the punchline of the elevator pitch is so good 'and then she ended up living with two famous American gay lovers, one of whom had been the First Lady and the other was a Bishop's widow'. That always made people sit up and listen. But Nelly's story deserved to be taken seriously: the professional life that I enjoyed with very little discrimination to overcome, and the life I want for my daughters, has been hard won over many generations by women who did not have it easy at all. Nelly's life seemed to be an exemplar of how great changes can be made in incremental stages.

Gradually my jottings took shape and I had a skeleton of a book and a few chapters were written. This, I thought, would be the perfect project for my retirement. When we had time, which wasn't often, Peter and I did try to create space for self-indulgent research trips, the best being a few days on our own, off-season in Florence, staying in a glamorous hotel on the banks of the Arno near the Ponte Vecchio and spending time in the library of the British Institute of Florence with the enthusiastic and helpful Alyson Price, reading the letters of Janet Ross and Lina Duff-Gordon. This was the same Institute that Lina had helped to establish and run with Edward Hutton in 1917, still providing a library and holding cultural events to promote Anglo-Italian understanding and friendship after nearly 100 years. Alyson told us that there were one or two books being written about Janet Ross, but was very encouraging about our project, as she loved Nelly's illustrations and felt that she deserved to be better known. That was in 2010, and life rolled slowly on for two years until out of the blue Alyson forwarded me an email from an American academic who was planning to publish her work on Nelly. That put the cat among the pigeons!

My initial instinct was panic and suspicion. Here was someone far more qualified than I to research and write biography, and furthermore someone who could do it full time for a living. But luckily curiosity got the better of me, and in no time at all I was swapping emails with Etta Madden, someone who became a friend and who gave me huge encouragement to keep going with my project. And through whom I met other female academics who could throw light on the next characters in the story: Rose Cleveland and Evangeline Whipple. The book project began to take shape and urgency.

I need not have been so worried by the email from the Institute in Florence: Etta Madden, the professor from Missouri, was not, as it turned out, planning a rival book about Nelly. In fact she was working with two fellow academics to prepare very specific papers to be delivered at an event to be held in Bagni di Lucca. The three consecutive papers were to deal with Rose, Evangeline and Nelly, and the weekend conference, the seventh annual such event organized by the Michel de Montaigne Foundation in collaboration with the University of

Pisa to promote Anglo-Italian scholarship, was entitled 'English-Italian cultural relations in nineteenth century Tuscany'. Previous conferences had focused on literary subjects including the Brownings and Ouida.

Sirpa Salenius, a Finnish author and editor living in Florence was researching Rose, her paper was entitled 'The passion and fire of Rose Cleveland', which certainly implied that she had read the letters written to Eve. Tilly Laskey is an ethnographer whose day job was Curator of the Ethnology Science Museum of Minnesota in St Paul, Minnesota. The coincidence that had brought an ethnographer to Tuscany was the Whipple/Marrs collection of native American artifacts, some of which had been acquired after Evangeline's death by the Science Museum in St Paul, while some closely linked items had found their way to the Natural History Museum in Florence through Kingsmill and Laura Marrs. Tilly had been trying to discover what had taken these items to Italy, and had become as fascinated by Evangeline, as I was by Nelly. Sirpa was later to publish the only biography of Rose Cleveland I have ever seen. And Etta had an interest in the relationship between writers and publishing houses, and was planning a talk entitled 'Nelly Erichsen: Writing and Sketching for the House of Dent'.

Between March and September 2012 Etta and I swapped many emails, notes and ideas, and in September Peter and I headed back to Bagna to sit in the back of the English Church in Via Evangeline Whipple, listen to the presentations and be treated as special guests. Not something we had ever expected. It was a truly Anglo-Italian event, with academics from Pisa and Florence, Sheffield and Ulster, Michigan and Missouri. One of the grand old ladies in the audience was apparently the granddaughter of Puccini - she insisted in talking to her neighbour throughout the lectures, presumably no-one in Tuscany would dare to reprimand a relation of the great composer. The whole weekend was very special - the people of Bagna di Lucca made us all so welcome, there were meals in the Foreigners Club, or Circolo de Forestieri, and an evening trip into the hills to see a remote chapel by candlelight. The best surprise was on the Saturday morning when we all walked over the bridge to visit the English churchyard, and discovered that a major restoration project was underway. The three gravestones of Nelly, Rose and Evangeline were glistening white again. The only disappointment was that somehow we missed joining the others in the party on a private tour of Villa San Francesco, Eve's house.

The following year the papers from the conference were published and Etta ensured that I was named as the joint author of her paper, so I made it into print in an academic journal. Nelly had taken me on another journey, one that would have delighted her, considering her academic efforts on behalf of the Society of Hellenic Studies, the British School at Rome and the Institute in Florence. She had not only got me into print, but as part of an initiative designed to improve Anglo-Italian relations.

Cafaggiolo

Chapter Twelve: The Outbreak Of War

'And now when half my life is spent, as I wait on Beacon Hill in these September evenings for the sunset to transfigure the vast, low, empty moors and to discover to me the sea, I ask myself what it means to me, this my home, now that between it and me there shines all the gold of Italy. And it seems to me that I think of it as perhaps the last stronghold of English life, of English poetry and legend. It keeps alive for me and in me the ideal England of my heart. It actually embodies a life that never perhaps really existed, but is the only true life nevertheless. And the noble architecture both of manor and cottage, village church and cathedral, set as it is in natural surroundings often of rare beauty and always of great peace, seems to me the expression of something that is perhaps no longer to be found in the world, or is there in no satisfying quantity.

'Indeed, what remains in my mind most deeply, coming home as it were, as I have done, after a long absence, is a curiously solemn sense of having witnessed the passing of the old order, the crumbling of the old system, feudal still and with much that we shall regret.

'And I ask myself as I wait on Beacon Hill, the old Roman road dim in the twilight before me, what is to take the place of all that I have known and loved and thought good? And I ask myself, what is about to befall my home?'

Edward Hutton, 'Highways and Byways of Somerset', 1912

When the First World War broke out in August 1914, Nelly was happily ensconced in her new home in Bagni di Lucca and content to stay in Italy to see how the situation developed. It does not seem likely that once hostilities began she was able to leave Italy, and the three woman grew closer together. By 1918 she was to write of her companions in Bagni *'We three are in a sense jetsam of the war'*.

The previous few months before the war she had been rushing around Italy and England. In February 1914, after a *'good quiet winter of work and enchanting country sights and sounds'* in Bagni she had paid only a brief visit to Janet Ross, 60 miles away at Poggio Gherardo, preferring her new home with Rose and Eve. Janet was unwell and tired, but Nelly thought that twelve days of what she called *'organpipe rain which ceases not day nor night'* was enough to make anyone 'white and weary'. This was in a letter she wrote to Edward Hutton, who was preparing the text for the Wiltshire volume of Highways and Byways, enquiring into his progress, as she did not want to set off for England until the weather had improved. Her illustrations of the Somerset edition had been very well received. *'Miss Nelly Erichsen's drawings are delightful. She excels in architectural subjects, but with few exceptions, the drawings in this volume are among the very best that have adorned the Highways and Byways series.'* (The Antiquary, March 1913).

By June 1914 she was hard at work in England, preparing the next set of drawings, staying with various friends in Wiltshire (firstly with her friend Miss Davies at Parnella House School in Devizes, in June 1914, and then with the Noyes sisters in Sutton Veny) and must have returned to Italy shortly after the assassination of the Archduke, before the troops started to mobilise. She wrote to Hutton from Devizes: *'I wish I were at home in Italy there, even this icy year, the sun shines sometimes. Here it hails, it freezes, it sleets, and blows a perpetual north-westerly gale But I am bent on getting thro' with this county, which I hope to have done in 3 or 4 weeks from now &then I fly back to the Bagni di Lucca to finish up my drawings. This Devizes is an excellent centre & I've been beating the country all round. On Saturday I go on to Marlborough Highworth Malmesbury as centres which will finish the northern part. Then I hark south again, for I still have the Stonehenge region and some of the river valley to do. If you have any pet places you would like drawn please let me know and also when you think you are likely to be ready with your MS. Please address to 81 Elm Park Gardens SW as my moving camp gives no certainty of getting letters.'*

It is possible that Nelly had learnt to drive when in Italy, perhaps borrowing Evangeline's car, (a photograph of which is preserved in the library in Bagni), as her letters to Hutton suggest that she was driving herself around Wiltshire that last summer.

[The Outbreak of War]

c/o Miss Noyes
Sutton Veny
Wilts
July 13 1914

Dear Mr Hutton
Where are you? I'm here, after flying about in a motor all over N. Wilts & S. Wilts & hope you will be able to come over and see this pretty place. My kind hostesses the 3 Miss Noyes ask me to say they will be very pleased to see you next Saturday 19th for lunch. Do come, for it will be my last chance of seeing you before starting for Italy. There now only remains a small corner of SE Wilts for me to do, which I hope to cover before the 23rd when I return to town.
'The Devil was sick' etc. That's my history too. I'm all right again since I saw you last, & the mercury has gone up again. I hope yours is high.' For Nelly, work always seemed to bring on poor health, whether physical or mental, but here she was determined to conquer it one final time. Sadly her next major physical exertion would be her last.

Before the war started, Italy was in a loose alliance with the Austro-Hungarian Empire, but when war broke out it was not obligated to fight with the central powers, and took time to ponder its options. There were areas such as the Alto Adige and Trentino in the north of the country which were still in Austrian hands but had a large ethnically Italian population, and it occurred to the Italian Government that the war might present an opportunity to annex these areas. But things moved slowly, and in 1915 a secret treaty was signed with the Western Powers. When this became known, there was bitter discontent in some quarters opposed to war, and violence spilled on to the Italian streets, with the pro-war interventionists led by a young activist called Benito Mussolini. With civil war threatened, the anti-war faction caved in and in May 1915 Italy declared war on Austria, on the side of the Allies. Until then life in Tuscany for the Anglo-American community probably went on very quietly. In particular, Nelly had less to worry about than most, as her family were mostly not of military age. Nelly's brothers were too old to fight and her only nephew Frank was playing his part as Principal Private Secretary to Sir Austen Chamberlain, Secretary of State for India.

Janet Ross was now in her 70s but going strong, and still inclined to form enthusiastic new relationships with young men. Her current attachment was to a young artist called Frank Crisp, who had first visited Poggio Gherardo in 1908 while travelling on a scholarship from the Royal Academy. Crisp painted Janet's portrait, and she seems to have developed quite a crush on him. Unfortunately, Frank enlisted in the British Army and was an early casualty, killed in January 1915. His death, coming so soon after that of Lindsay just the month before, sent Janet into a terrible emotional and physical decline: Nelly was staying with her when the news broke and stayed on until March to look after her, but as Mary Berenson reported in a letter to her sister Alys, it was never a good idea for Janet and Nelly to spend time together, especially when aggravated by stress : 'They have thoroughly got on each other's nerves.' Nelly felt the house to be a 'prison' and 'full of spiritual dry rot' and Janet complained that she had never had such a fussy and inconsiderate guest who had upset all the servants and contradicted everything Janet said. They were clearly missing Lindsay's gentle peacemaking skills. Mary said that she would find either of them impossible to live with for any length of time, but also noted that Nelly was 'really ill', but with no other explanation.

There was some family comfort to be had: at least Janet and her niece Lina were now partially reconciled, and when Aubrey enlisted and went away to fight, Lina brought her two youngest children to stay with Janet for the duration of the war. Meanwhile, Nelly returned to her new friends in Bagni di Lucca.

By spring 1917, there was felt to be a need to boost pro-Allied morale in Italy. Mass conscription had brought terrible hardship to the Italian people, and the war was at a stalemate with the Italians and Austrians at a standoff in the Alps. The Italian Socialist party blamed the British, and extremely ugly anti-British propaganda began to be heard. Edward Hutton visited Lina Waterfield and Janet Ross at Poggio Gherardo with a proposal to improve Anglo-Italian cultural links. He had been approached by the British Government, which was finally, thanks to the efforts of Lloyd George and his ally Lord Beaverbrook, beginning to get its international propaganda machine into gear. They were to establish a cultural centre in Florence. Lina wrote: *'We both agreed that the library should be entirely English and under English management. Mr H, who was staying at Poggio Gherardo, has come to Florence on a semi-official visit. He asked me to find suitable premises and I was fortunate to obtain the lease of the Loggia Rucellai ...Fortunately there were many people to help in laying the foundations of the embryo British Institute... Walter Ashburner, the Greek Scholar, ...many friends gave money and books: among these were*

Bernard Berenson, Lady Sybil Lubbock, Mr Arthur Acton.... and Aunt Janet.'

Meanwhile, in May 1917, Nelly was helping a young American woman called Klyda Richardson Steege to negotiate a publishing contract with Dent. The book she had written was called 'We of Italy', and was dedicated to *'The brave defenders of Italy on land or sea; to the soldiers and sailors who are offering their lives and their all; to the memory of those who have fallen, and to the conquerors who are to come.'* In the acknowledgment she wrote, after thanking a former prime minister of Italy for allowing her to include two letters from a soldier, *'My especial thanks are due to my friend Miss Nelly Erichsen, whose advice and encouragement have been of inestimable value to me, and whose revision of the book has done so much for it. If it meets with any success I shall consider that it is largely because of her assistance.'* This does suggest a very considerable amount of editing and re-writing by the experienced Nelly. Klyda also thanked Lina Waterfield, Evangeline and Rose - they were obviously all part of the same busy and concerned circle of women, doing their bit for the war effort.

In September 1917 shocking news reached Nelly that her younger brother Frederick had died suddenly, aged only 47, while travelling on business in Buenos Aires. Frederick had been educated at Rugby School but had been keen to follow his father's interests, specialising in maths and science and taking a pupillage at an engineering firm in Grosvenor Road, Pimlico. He worked in the Drawing Office for many years, and in 1900, having been promoted to head of the 'Outdoor Department', he became a fellow of the Institute of Mechanical Engineers. He had married Sara in 1904, a widow with two young daughters, and after many years in Tooting had recently moved to live near his sister Alice in The Vale, Chelsea. Nelly had now lost both her younger brothers abroad in sudden and difficult circumstances. She must have felt very isolated from the grieving family in London. But she did not have long to dwell on her loss as events closer to home were about to sweep her along, and within a month the physical impact of the war would have reached Bagni.

In October 1917, the Austrians, reinforced by the Germans, broke through the Italian lines at Caporetto, on the North-eastern border. The fear of an imminent German-Austrian invasion drove thousands of refugees south and Florence became a clearing post. When Edward Hutton left for a new post in London, Lina was put in charge of the work of 'British-Italian good relations for Tuscany' by John Buchan, the author and diplomat, at that point acting as

Director of Information in London. In spite of the tragic events in the autumn of 1917 and the continual influx of refugees, the work of the Institute went on without interruption. Buchan arranged for the Library to be taken over financially by the British Government 'until it can support itself'. Mr Francis Spender, uncle of the poet Stephen Spender, became the first Honorary Director in the spring of 1918 when the Institute moved into larger premises at 18 Via dei Conti, and the Loggia Rucellai became Lina's propaganda office. Nelly had already taken on significant responsibilities in Bagni, but offered help and assistance to Lina as well.

In the summer of 1918, Edward Hutton's new publication, The Anglo-Italian Review, published a lengthy article by Nelly entitled 'Debris of the War', which chronicled her experiences with the refugees.

'My acquaintance with the refugees began on the last day of October. Business took me to Lucca, and all unsuspicious of trouble at the front, I rattled down the fifteen miles of valley in a shaky scappavia. We pulled up with the usual jerk at the old Hotel Campana, where Montaigne lodged in 1581, and the friend I had come to meet, who had just arrived from Florence, ran hurriedly out to greet me.

"Have you seen the papers?" he asked, holding out the Nuovo Giornale.

And then he read me the first news of Caporetto.

"It's bad," he said. "They're beginning to come. The train was full of them."

They were the refugees from Gorizia, and the invaded Veneto. From that day on they had never ceased coming.'

The article may have been meant as a plea for financial assistance from readers in Britain, but if it was, the plea is not articulated. Instead Nelly writes with affection and clarity about the humanitarian work she and her friends had been able to promote in their little village. After all, as she explained, the population of Bagni was no more than two thousand, mostly desperately poor, and now they were being asked to cope with a thousand refugees with only a few days' notice. There was a difficulty which needed to be resolved about who was going to be in charge, after all the three women at Casa Bernardini were incomers, aliens, forestieri as they were called in the village. The initial proposal had been that the refugees would sleep on straw in the town hall, but then it became clear that they could more easily be housed in the vacant hotels and pensiones around the villages. And, as Nelly writes *'When once they had roughly shaken down, and one began to know them by sight, they ceased to be mere wreckage of the war and suddenly became intensely interesting human beings who were in bitter need of more things than it was possible for the overburdened government to provide. This fact gave us our opportunity.'*

Rose, Nelly and Eve divided the problem between them, with the Americans taking responsibility for the women and girls, leaving Nelly to fend for the men and boys. In no time at all the women were organised into workrooms turning out clothes and bedding for the hospital in Lucca as well as more pressing local needs. Nelly had to find some way of keeping the males warm and occupied. She took charge of a large dining room in a local hotel, requisitioned an enormous open-fronted terra cotta stove from Lucca, and then, when she had *'hunted up many chairs and tables and stocked the latter well with newspapers, books, writing materials and games, had laid in a regiment of coffee cups, good stores of biscuits and cigarettes, nothing remained but to hang up the portrait of King Victor Emmanuel, flanked by the flags of Italy and England, and to stick little banners of the Allies round the walls, with war posters below them, telling forcibly why Italy is at war, why Germany must be beaten, how the invader has desecrated the sacred soil of Italy, and many other useful things.'* Maybe this all reminded her of the struggles of the Danish against the Prussians in the 1860s and her mother's committee work in Newcastle raising money for those war victims. But Nelly felt called upon to do far more practical work than just sitting on a committee or organising a cake sale.

At the time of her article, this men's club, open in the afternoons, had a membership of some 200. They could buy strong black coffee, biscuits and cigarettes, and if they did not have the money Paolo the servant had instructions to hand them out anyway. *'The air is thick with cigarette smoke, and there is, for Italians, a wonderfully subdued murmur of conversation. The refugee psychology comes in there, no doubt, the strangeness and uncertainty of life leading to low tones, but besides this, quite half the men are not Italian, but Austrians and Slovenes, and speak Italian haltingly. They would prefer to talk German, but it is a forbidden tongue here.'* There were games for the boys, and a letter reading and writing service, often used to petition the authorities to trace missing wives and husbands. *'These separations of families are frequent, and perhaps not surprising in such panic days...Fortunately, our letters sometimes find the strayed sheep and the men rush to the club to tell us all about it.'*

They found they were dealing with not just a mixture of races and tongues, but ages, backgrounds and education. *'Shoemakers and carpenters abound…we have set them up in business and they are doing well, the war having claimed most of our village craftsmen...almost everyone who wants work has found it.'* The only troublemakers were the boys. *'At the outset we fixed sixteen as the minimum age for members, and at first when entering names we were greatly struck by the smallness of stature of refugee boys. We were astonished, too, that every boy gave his age as sixteen. Finally it dawned on us that if we wished to prevent an epidemic of mendacity the age limit must be withdrawn.'*

When it became clear that these boys' apparently innocent card games were actually encouraging gambling, Nelly started evening classes as a distraction for them - an instant success. Among the refugees they found a qualified schoolmaster from the Veneto. The classes had to be relocated to larger premises and became a properly equipped day school with 85 pupils. However, grouping that many boys together in one place made it clear that a trip to the bathhouse and clean linen was required, which again Nelly organised. Each was given a parcel of linen and soap and the mothers had to pledge to send them to school every Monday in a clean shirt. 'Our little lads are still a ragged regiment as far as their outer clothes go, but the red band they wear on the arm, with the name of the school, proclaims them a unity.

'The Venetians are gentle, with ox-like eyes and great refinement of feature, but the master says that the blonde street arabs of Gorizia are the more intelligent. He is ambitious to make good Italians of the last as well as the first, and has taught them to sing EVVIVA L'"ITALIA! with a fine fervour, and to sing the patriotic songs of Italy like little thrushes.'

And thus her article ends, but it seems to me to be brimming with enthusiasm, humour and real love for her refugee band. She also wrote about it in a letter to Dent dated 14 February 1918, as follows: *'As I helped Mrs Steege in her negotiations with you, which ended so happily with the publication of 'We of Italy', I think it is still my part to continue the correspondence for her. I heard from Mrs Steege today. Owing to the non-arrival of remittances from America (and how many people are not in the same position thanks to the submarines!) she tells me she is put to great temporary inconvenience. And her position is indeed a hard one, with her eager family of 3 daughters and a son who are all being educated in Siena, entirely dependent as she is on the small income that comes to her from America, & which is now very much overdue.*

'She hopes, & I hope with all my heart, that as her book has now been out for some months, even if the day of settlement has not yet come, you will be kind enough to advance her £20 on royalties due to her, which is for the moment the only source of income she has in Europe. My remembrances of your many kindnesses makes me very hopeful that you will do one more for her.

'I am over head and ears in work among the refugees. We have in this small village 600,

& on behalf of the English Propaganda for which I work, I have opened a club for men with 150 members, a co-operative carpenters' business, & a boys' school of 70 at present but always increasing. Also thanks to lovers of Italy at home who have been good enough to send me funds I've been able to do a good deal of clothing relief, providing milk for infants etc etc so there is no time to think of anything else - I hope you are well.

With very kind regards
I am yours truly
Nelly Erichsen

'Did you happen to see my drawings for Mr Hutton's Wilts in Highways and Byways? For Mrs Steege's sake I shall hope for an immediate answer from you.'

The reply was indeed swift, considering the difficulties of getting post right across Europe. On 22 February 1918 Dent replied:

Miss N Erichsen
Casa Bernardini
Bagni di Lucca (villa), Italy

Dear Miss Erichsen

I have your letter dated Feb 14th, asking me to advance Mrs Steege £20 on account of the royalties of her book. I am very sorry to tell you that I cannot do so. I enclose herewith a list of the sales and the royalties due upon them - if they were sold, that is to say. Mrs Steege has had 134 copies herself, which if she has sold them will produce something like...[text missing]......I believe, and that is owing to us, of course. The enclosed slip shows you the absolute sales of the book, and I want you to understand it clearly. The sales in England have been only 160 copies. We were fortunate enough to persuade our American agents to buy 365 copies, but that does not mean they have been sold to the public, but only that they are in their stock. Miss Steege's books were sent to her on sale or return and we also sent Miss Wilson 20 copies on sale or return, of which we cannot know the results for some time to come. I am still, therefore, on a serious loss on the book, and I cannot add to that loss another £20 in royalties. If Mrs Steege has actually sold her copies she can take £10 out of that. That is the amount the royalties would come to on the whole of the books, if her copies and Mrs Wilson's are sold; but there is due to me from her something like £30 if the books are sold.

This is the best I can do. I am very sorry for her loss, but the loss, however, is greater to me, for we have done all the work and have lost into the bargain also. I did hope that this book would have sold, and I cannot understand why it has not, at any rate sufficiently to have made a small profit for us both. We still keep it forward among the booksellers as much as we can; but evidently it has not caught on and none of the papers have reviewed it to any extent. There seems to be a lack of interest in Italian affairs which I cannot comprehend at all, but that is the truth.

I would so much like to help you in your work, but everyone wants help now and we are perplexed to know how to divide up our small charities. I am sure you will give me credit when I say I would have been only to glad to send Mrs Steege money, if there had been any likelihood of royalties accruing to that extent.

I am
Yours sincerely

Nelly replied on 27 February:

'My dear Mr Dent

I thank you for your letter of 22nd February, but am sorry to see how poorly We of Italy has sold in England. In America on the other hand Mrs Steege has just heard that every copy Dutton had was sold, & that he is very anxious to have more. And I may also tell you in confidence that Miss Cleveland has kindly consented to do what she can to make the book known in America where owing to the great number of Italian Immigrants there is a lively interest in Italy.

'I very much hope therefore that you will kindly send more copies as quickly as possible to America where I hope the book may yet have a good sale.

'I will send your letter to Mrs Steege with your kind arrangements to allow her to take £10 out of the proceeds of the sale of the copies she has with her - I do not know exactly how her sales stand, but will ask her to let you know.

'I very greatly hope that you can still make a profit instead of a loss out of the book. In my world in England there is the greatest interest in Italy. I have just sent a copy of the book to an English officer serving here in Italy in the hope of interesting, through him, our other officers here. Do please keep it forward as much as you can. How I wish we could get one good review of it.

Yours sincerely
Nelly Erichsen

There really doesn't seem to be any need to reply to this letter, but Dent clearly felt he was being attacked. He replied

6th March 1918

Miss N Erichsen
Casa Bernardini
Bagni di Lucca (villa)
Italy

My dear Miss Erichsen

It was really painful for me to write and refuse to send the £20 which I know Mrs Steege wants - but I have done all I could for this book, for old acquaintance sake for one thing, and for my love of Italy for another, and I cannot seem to get people to take any interest in Italy at all. I have a wonderful book by Vivian of Italy in War Time and people will not take an interest in it. I cannot tell why. Everybody loves Italy in England, and it bothers me to explain it.

I have written to America about the book, I think our agents there had 250 copies. They never applied to us for any more, and, of course, we cannot send them without their order; but I have written at once to my friend there and begged them to do all they can to make it sell. There is, of course, an Italian colony in America which is tremendous. I know it very well, as I have frequently gone to the Italian settlements there, and I am surprised, after all, that the sale has not been larger - but perhaps you will remember that Italian people who go to America are not the well to do, but the working folk, who are saving up all their dollars to get back to the Fatherland. However, that is the fact, and I am doing all I can. I assure you I will do my best to get the book sold. We are even now advertising it whenever we can get space at all.

I hope you are well. Please give my kind regards to Mrs Steege, whose postcard I have. I am so sorry the people are not being able to get her book in America. The Italian cause, somehow, is not understood in England or in America either. They want some propaganda, among the various things to do which the government cannot manage.

I am glad to say I am better and able to get to business again.

Sincerely yours

The impact of World War I was devastating to Dent. Business was slow, but his personal experience of the war had been particularly bitter - he lost one son, Paxton, in 1915 in the trenches at Neuve Chapelle, and a second son Austen was killed at Gallipoli just three months later. *'We have tried to bear our great sorrow as gallantly as they gave up everything.'* In August 1915 he wrote to his friend Vida Scudder in America *'I have a letter from a friend in Italy this morning in which she says, "Oh, the shame of it if Italy had stood out!" She is realising as she never did before that everything for which life is worth living would be gone if the Germans won.'* Perhaps this friend was Janet, perhaps it was Nelly. In October he wrote *'I am at times absolutely in the depths of despair; but generally speaking I am sane, and have some optimism left even yet; still the times are very hard to bear.'*

By the autumn of 1917 all able-bodied Italian men had left for the front. The galleries and libraries of Florence were deserted, fuel and food were rationed and the restaurants were serving cat. In September 1918, Janet wrote of the changes to her life from the absence of Italian menfolk on the estate and generally in Florence....even the postman's job was now done by a woman. Janet had *"only wood enough for 2 months. I've no men to cut down any of my trees. I can mend my road and hoe my turnips but I can't cut down a tree."*

By the following month, however, her main concern was the spread of the influenza epidemic. Slowly but surely the horror of the Spanish flu, which had first been recorded at a military camp in Kansas in March 1918, had been making its way across the Atlantic, carried on the troop ships full of American soldiers, and spreading down through the military lines until by June it had reached Italy. The first wave of the disease, in the spring of 1918, was highly infectious but mild, and by the end of July and early August appeared to be dying out. But in fact the virus had been gathering strength and mutating into something far more deadly. In Europe, where food and fuel shortages combined to make the population weak, and where refugees huddled together spreading disease, the result was catastrophic. The speed of infection and the rapidity with which victims succumbed were terrifying. Many died of the accompanying pneumonia, but the physical manifestation of the illness was horrific. It began with dark spots on the skin over the cheekbones, then changed the colour of the skin to dark purple, known as heliotrope cyanosis. Finally a black pigmentation spread up from the fingers and toes, and death followed swiftly, often within 24 hours of the first symptom. Corpses deteriorated very rapidly, with swollen chests. The illness had a smell like musty straw, and was accompanied by hair loss, dizziness, blurred vision and delirium. The fit and strong, male and female, in their twenties and thirties, seemed to suffer the most. There was no cure - we now know that the disease was caused by a virus but in 1918 microscopes did not have the power to detect something so small. Aspirin was prescribed in large quantities, but probably did more to damage the lungs than it helped. As the wise knew, the only chance of survival was to be isolationist and utterly selfish.

Janet's letters shows how little understanding there was of the nature of the illness even among the educated English.There were many theories about what "the malady" was and why it was claiming so many victims. *"I don't believe this disease to be due to any poison gas. It is pure and simple influenza, just what we had here in 1890 or was it 91? How is the gas to get to Africa where the malady is raging… We have been very lucky. But I allowed none of the poor people who came for help to come into the house. I went out to them having put essence of eucalyptus on my handkerchief first"*

"At Settignano the malady is ceasing a little and I hope it will leave. Four funerals a day is rather lugubrious. The young men are dying of influenza at the front and the young women here. Hardly any young children or old. The sad thing is when the mothers die and leave children all alone in the world. I have four cases and don't know what to do. One woman has left six, all under 10 and yesterday came the news her husband was dead on Monte Grappa."

We know more of the last year of Nelly and Rose's life in Bagni di Lucca than we do of most of the rest of their time there, as after their death, Evangeline wrote detailed notes in letters which went to a New York clergyman, the Reverend Charles Lewis Slattery, and he used them in a sermon given to commemorate Rose's life, in January 1919. Slattery wrote that when the war broke out, the three women *'threw themselves into work, first for England and Belgium, and then, when Italy entered the war, for Italy. It was like them not to go to Rome and Florence, to which multitudes flocked to give aid; they stayed in the little town of Bagna di Lucca….The people knew them, and these American ladies were instinctively aware that they could help the more because they were known and trusted.'* Evangeline also wrote a long letter after Rose had died to a Mrs Miller, a friend in Philadelphia, and the letter was reproduced in full in The Utica Daily Press in January 1919. In this she wrote: *'the third member of our household was a beautiful English friend who had been doing splendid propaganda work in this province under the auspices of the Italo-British Mission.'*

It is worth remembering that at the beginning of the war, Italy had been allied to Austria, although it did not declare war, and thus the Anglo-American colony found itself in potentially hostile territory. Slattery wrote *'In the early days of the war, when many people in the Italian villages were of doubtful loyalty to the Allies, Miss Cleveland, though seventy years old, went about among the people far and near, making eloquent speeches which explained the meaning of the war, and then aroused her hearers to go out to the help of the Lord against the mighty.'* To us today, it seems wrong to bring religion into a discussion of the Great War, which we tend to view as an inglorious series of campaigns and wasted lives. But to Rose, who was deeply religious, the daughter of a minister, God must be on the side of the righteous. And so she spoke out.

Then came the defeat at Caporetto and the flood of refugees down into Tuscany, placing enormous economic and social burdens on a population already under stress. Rose remembered words she had written some thirty years earlier, in an essay on Joan of Arc : *'For each of us there waits an Orleans…we need to see our visions, to hear our voices, as Joan did hers; those visions which open to us from the summits of our holiest resolve, our highest endeavor, our most painful abnegation; those voices which lay on us most strenuous commands and whisper to us, in secret chambers of our beleaguered soul, words of conviction, of courage and of cheer.'* The crisis in Tuscany was Rose's Battle of Orleans.

Slattery says that initially Rose and her friends sought to bolster morale by more talks and lectures, some of which were reproduced in the local Italian press. Slattery says: *'An Italian paper with one of these speeches was sent to me, and I can bear testimony to its ringing appeal. Not only the Italians' language had become hers, but their fire, their emotion. It seemed almost impossible to me that this quiet reserved American woman could have freed herself in such Latin ecstasy as I was reading……Meanwhile, ceaseless work went on for children and older people in Bagni di Lucca. A hospital, a workroom for refugees, schools for refugee children, all were started and continued: in all these Miss Cleveland did her generous share.'*

Rose and Evangeline were also obliged to appeal to their friends in the United States for funds to help the refugees. Evangeline funded from her own resources a boarding school which took in some 100 refugee children, run by the Stimmatine nuns.

But then Spanish influenza blew into town, carrying terrible suffering and death in its wake. Slattery's sermon takes up the tale *'One night Miss Cleveland awoke from a sound sleep: there was absolute silence; then she heard distinctly a voice saying;*

"You must act for these people. Open the church if there is nothing better. Send for trained nurses. Begin work at once.'" Evangeline, Rose and Nelly set to work raising funds from friends in America, organising nurses to come from Florence and Livorno, setting up isolation wards and workrooms for women to make bandages. Lina Waterfield despatched Miss Turton,a well-known nurse whose sister Maud was to die of the disease herself, to help Nelly. Evangeline described a horrific journey she had made up into the mountains behind Bagni to discover the state of the villagers in these remote spots, and had written to Slattery appalled by what she had seen *'In every house the inmates lay sick, dying, and dead.'* When we visited Bagni di Lucca with the Montaigne Foundation five years ago, we were taken up one evening to a chapel on the hilltop, with no houses anywhere around. This must have been one of the villages that Evangeline visited - the influenza must have played its part in depopulating the area.

It is from Slattery's sermon that we hear the tale of Nelly and Rose's death. Nelly succumbed to the disease first 'after heroic service to the refugees'. She fell ill on the first Sunday in November 1918: by the Friday, just four days after Armistice Day, she was dead. Eve and Rose saw her buried in the English cemetery, but Rose, who had nursed her friend through her last days, was dead exactly one week later. The Report of the Death of an American Citizen,

The graveyard at Bagni di Lucca, showing the tombstones of Nelly and Rose

produced by the American Consular Service, gave the cause of death as Septicaemia. Bagni turned out in force to honour Rose: Evangeline said *'The funeral was the most impressive sight I have ever seen. She was wrapped in the American flag....By order of the Mayor all shops and business places were closed. From every house was a flag at half-mast, tied with black....After two carriages for the household, there followed a long, long procession on foot the citizens, the schools of the Commune, the two schools of the refugees, bearing flags at half mast, and then the great procession of the refugees themselves, bearing wreaths. Not a sound was heard in the streets as the silent procession moved on to the little English cemetery on the banks of the Lima. At the grave the American flag was lowered by the Consul and then all the people threw in each a flower, and the sun turned the snow-clad mountain into a dazzling scene and I came back!'*

Slattery's sermon finishes *'Let them that love thee, O Lord, be as the sun when he goeth forth in his might.'* Rose would have approved of the sentiment.

It seems hard that yet again Nelly has been eclipsed, we hear of her death in passing, as an adjunct to the story of someone apparently more important. There is only Eve's passing mention of her funeral, nor any suggestion that her family or other Florentine friends were able to accompany her to her grave. Rose was already ill, there was no time to mourn at Casa Bernardini. Janet Ross does not mention attending the funeral; she hardly mentions Nelly's death at all in her correspondence. But there was recognition of her life and sacrifice in the British press: an obituary appeared in The Times, possibly written by Hutton. Nelly would have been pleased that it began by stressing her professional success:

'Miss Nelly Erichsen, who died from influenza at Bagni di Lucca on November 15, was well-known in England, Italy and America for her admirable drawings in black-and-white. She illustrated many of the best-known English books on Italian travel, as well as several volumes of Messrs. Macmillan's 'Highways and Byways' Series, notably the volumes on Somerset, Wiltshire and Derbyshire. Some of her most ambitious work was done for Mrs Janet Ross's book, "Florentine Villas' which Messrs Dent published.

'During the last three years Miss Erichsen has been working for the English propaganda in the Province of Lucca, and with a success all her own. In October 1917, after Caporetto, when the refugees poured down into Central Italy from the invaded districts, Miss Erichsen organised the relief in Bagni do Lucca, and helped to

establish schools for the refugee children. An account of her work from her own pen appeared in the June number of the Anglo-Italian Review, under the title of "Debris of the War.'

'When the influenza epidemic descended upon Italy this autumn, she eagerly threw herself into the work of organising relief and nursing, the need for which, owing to the dearth of nurses and doctors, was acute. Her devotion led her into the infection from which she died, in the service of those she knew and loved, the Italian peasantry of the Lucchese. She will be mourned by a very large circle of friends and all who cared for her conscientious and truthful work.'

There is no mention in this obituary of her paintings, or her work as a writer or translator. It does not say that she had exhibited at the Royal Academy. But it is very clear that, in the writer's eyes, she stood alone as an independent and extremely talented professional woman, worthy of notice in her own right and not as someone's wife or daughter. That may have given her some satisfaction.

Nelly left very little money: her estate, valued at £474 15 shillings and 2d, was to be administered by her niece Rosamund Rootham and her brother Herman. There is an interesting letter in the Dent archives from Ella Noyes written on 31 December 1918, thanking him for sending them Christmas wishes and a drawing by Blake: *'a lovely expression of the great feelings which this annus mirabilis has brought to us.'* After some discussion of the Armistice and the general election, it goes on *'Of course you have seen the notice of Nelly Erichsen's death - it was a great blow to us - I think you had not seen her for some years - we all - her old friends - felt that she had grown so much sweeter of late years. There was a very nice little notice of her in The Times, mentioning the Florentine Villas as her chief work, published by you. It was when she was doing that book, that we first met you, through her introduction, at Miss Godkin's in Florence. How long ago those happy days seem!'*

After the war, the political unrest of Italy began to touch upon Janet Ross's life: her initial tendency to favour fascism was reversed when blackshirts intruded into her house, demanding money. After several years of deteriorating health, she died at her home on 23 August 1927, leaving Poggio Gherardo to Lina and her son John. Janet's own son, Alick Ross, disputed the legacy, and legal costs and high taxes eventually forced Lina to sell it in 1946.

Evangeline lived on in Bagni di Lucca until 1930, tending the graves of her two friends, continuing her charitable work among the villagers, looking after her whippets, studying and writing. Her book 'A Famous Corner of Tuscany' was published by Jarrolds in 1928 *'Dedicated to the memory of my beloved friend of many years Rose Elizabeth Cleveland who first encouraged me to write this book.'* It was indeed a book she had started to write before the war broke out she writes *'This book, begun years ago, would have come to light in the Great War period, had not the call to join the multitudes of relief workers made its more urgent appeal.'*

In the Preface she refers to 'My beloved friend Nelly Erichsen', reminding her readers that Nelly had written a whole chapter on Bagna in the Medieval Towns book on Lucca. Evangeline's book is long, well-illustrated, including many photos that she had taken herself. The text is more gossipy and light-hearted than some of Nelly and Janet's efforts, although Evangeline, like Janet and Nelly, had also toiled in Italian archives and consulted Italian scholars. Her survey of the history of the town is meant to appeal to Anglo-American readers, with many mentions of the well-known literary celebrities, Browning, Montaigne, Leigh Hunt. Rose and Evangeline were never forgotten in Bagna. They had been decorated by the King of Italy for their philanthropy and the citizens of the town named a street after Evangeline, which leads up from the main road past the English chapel to Casa Bernardini.

Evangeline died in 1930 in London on her way home to Minnesota, accompanied by Rose's niece Carrie Lawrence. She was staying at the Burlington Hotel, in Cork Street. In her will, she directed her executors to bury her alongside Rose in Bagni, or if she died in a place that made that difficult *'I direct my executors to place any Lot under which I am buried under perpetual care and authorise them to pay for a stone - a Latin cross like the one marking the said grave of Rose Elizabeth Cleveland…In addition to the Memorial Cross, a duplicate erected for me on said Lot at Bagni di Lucca.'* In fact her body was embalmed in London and sent back by ship to be buried alongside her beloved Rose in Tuscany.

After Evangeline's death, the many artefacts in her collection at the Whipple home in Minnesota were sold to the public, but some can still be seen in the Faribault Cathedral. In 1934, the Whipple home, which had remained untouched after Henry's death under Evangeline's ownership, was torn down. However in her will she left a very substantial endowment to fund St Mary's Girls School in Minnesota for the education of native American women, and many other generous gifts and legacies to the causes close to her heart.

Evangeline left a second will in Italy, which makes it very clear just how closely she was linked to the Cleveland and also the Erichsen families. Some items were left to the British Institute, some to Miss Florence Hancock, her companion in later life. She gave her whippet dogs to her coachman. Several of Rose's nephews and nieces received mementoes of Rose. But all the remaining property in Bagni di Lucca, including the three houses, was left equally to Rose's niece Carrie Lawrence, to the local Anglican priest, and to Cecil Veronica Lucas, Nelly's niece, one of the younger, unmarried daughters of Edgar and Alice Lucas. When Cecil died in 1939, her estate was valued at over £13,000, quite a tidy sum. Cecil had never married, and was still dependent on her parents, possibly because she had some unidentified mental incapacity. It was kind of Evangeline to make provision in her will for Cecil's future needs, and shows how close she had become to Nelly's family.

Descendants of Edgar and Alice have told me that the Lucas family kept a house of their own in Bagni, which Alice continued to visit even after her husband's death until the outbreak of the Second World War. I believe this must have been Casa Bernardini, left to Cecil. In 1932, so the family legend goes, Edgar said to Alice 'If you make me go to Bagni this year, you will kill me.' And indeed the journey was too much for a man of 87 and he died there. He is buried in the churchyard just a few yards from Nelly. I had taken a photograph of his grave on our first visit there in 2003, without knowing anything of the Lucas family connection, it was just a nearby, very English-looking tombstone. Leafing through the folder of our photographs some years later was a real shock - there he was, Nelly's much-loved brother-in-law, and I did not then known who he was. The inscription on his tomb says *'Well done thou good and faithful servant'* and round the grave are stones commemorating those of his children who had predeceased him: *'In carissimam memoriam Estelle Dagmar mortua infans' ; Francis Lucas filius noster 'Frank' April 13 1920;* and also to *Helga Dorothea Filia Carissima in Pace requiesca morta a Londra 17 October 1934.'* The latter inscription at least must have been commissioned by her mother Alice, who was to live another ten years, and died in England in 1944, nearly 90 years old. She was still remembered in Bagni as late as 1960, according to a grandson who visited and met the former sexton. Signor Gusmano remembered burying Edgar, soon after he had arrived that summer, and said that Alice 'Fu molto gentile con me' - 'had always been kind to me'. She continued to visit every year until war broke out again - to be with her beloved sister and husband.

Drawings from Nelly's sketchbook Circa 1880

Epilogue

At some point after our first visit to Bagni di Lucca, the marvellous Michel de Montaigne Foundation, part of the Istituto Storico Lucchese, began work on a complete restoration of the English Graveyard at Bagni di Lucca. Sponsors were found to pay for repairs to the graves and tend to the surroundings, and the cemetery now has regular daily opening hours and a very informative website. Descendants of Evangeline's old friends at the cathedral in Faribault, Minnesota, returned her generosity from a hundred years earlier by paying for the three friends' graves to be repaired and cleaned. The transformation is remarkable. The graveyard has been carefully planted with box and cypress trees and the grass is neat and tidy. Nelly's tomb is gleaming white, simple and dignified.

The piecing together of Nelly's biography has involved a great deal of sleuthing, and some extraordinary, serendipitous discoveries. It has taken us through the streets of Tooting to the galleries of Whitby, from the archives of Keele University and the warehouses of Copenhagen, to the street markets of Lucca, the heart of the Cotswolds and the secondhand bookshops of Amsterdam. We have exchanged emails with complete strangers across the Atlantic, attended an academic conference in Italy, and visited private homes in Yorkshire, Warwickshire and Dorset, where we have met with enormous kindness, mingled with surprise. Nelly may have been dead for nearly a century but her name has been remembered by her family, and some of her letters preserved in archives, down the generations.

One hundred years after their death, Nelly, Rose and Evangeline had all but disappeared from view. The deterioration of their gravestones was just a symptom of this process. The three women left no children of their own to preserve their memories, and only a couple of nieces, the beneficiaries of their wills, their grateful servants and dependents, would have had any reason to venerate their names or pass their stories down to the next generation. Yet all three women deserve more recognition than this for what they achieved as individuals: their parents had little to offer them Rose and Evangeline both came from humble stock, and Nelly was borne to immigrants in a country which spoke a different tongue. Despite these handicaps, all three worked hard to fashion a life that they could enjoy, at a time when being a woman, and a woman living with no male protection, was to live as a second-class citizen. I would argue that Eve and Rose had some assistance: Eve through two careful, financially advantageous, marriages, and Rose through her brother's public profile. But Nelly did it completely alone.

I believe that their last few years in Bagni may have been more peaceful and fulfilling for all three of them than anything they had experienced before, and that they came to feel that they finally mattered in their own right. For Rose and Evangeline were now in a loving relationship, out of the public eye, and were well-provided for. Nelly, though still struggling financially, was living with friends who respected her talents and who had a passion for the literary and artistic work that supported her. This peace gave them the confidence and the strength, when called upon, to sacrifice themselves for the good of others.

Nelly has been almost forgotten, just a name mentioned with affection by family members, a portrait on a wall, a collection of dusty pictures kept in an attic, some old books on library shelves. However, I have loved her, not just for her extraordinary talent, but for the bravery of her determination to keep struggling on, preserving her independence as best she could, and ultimately risking and giving everything for her fellow men and women. She is my Dorothea Brooke:

'But the effect of her being on those around her was incalculably diffusive: for the growing good of the world is partly dependent on unhistoric acts; and that things are not so ill with you and me as they might have been is half owing to the number who live faithfully a hidden life, and rest in unvisited tombs.'

George Eliot, Middlemarch

Acknowledgements

It has been nearly twenty years since Peter found the illustrations to Florentine Villas in a London saleroom, and fifteen years that we have been working on this project together. The book would never have been written without all Peter's belief in the project and the support, encouragement, suggestions and guidance he has given me. As well as two trips to Copenhagen and several trips to Italy, he has come with me to Dorset, Whitby and Keele, carrying maps and cameras, just like Lina Duff-Gordon and Nelly Erichsen. I am also enormously touched by the enthusiasm of my children Hattie, Max and Zoe who have been very patient with me and stopped me from giving up when things got tough.

Along the way we have met incredible kindness from strangers, firstly Dan Rootham, who is Alice Lucas's great grandson and who searched in attics and storerooms for photographs and drawings, and his sister Tutu in South Africa who sent me photographs of so many lovely works by Nelly from her own collection. Then Nicholas and Serge Zvegintsov, Dan's cousins, were persistent in their encouragement and in helping me eventually to get access to the Suhr Archives; I owe them a great deal. Other people have given generously of time and wisdom, including Alyson Price at the British Institute in Florence who is a fan of Nelly's art; Alysoun Saunders at the Macmillan Archives; the staff of the Library of the Royal Academy; Ingrid Maria Ericsson, who helped with some translation and Carol Jackson of the Chipping Campden Historical Society. I also need to thank the friends who we met through the Istituto Storico Lucchese: Tilly Laskey, guardian of Evangeline Whipple's treasures and secrets; Sirpa Salenius, the first biographer of Rose Cleveland; and especially Etta Madden at Missouri State University - who cared as much about Nelly and her works as we did. I would like to thank Veronica Millington for sharing her work on Fanny Johnson and the Johnson family, and Jane Lucas in Vancouver for pointing me at the family history she has documented. Brad and Anne Plimmer welcomed me into their lovely home in Welford-on-Avon and showed me the archives of the Welford and Weston Local History Society, including some wonderful photographs of Victorian artists at work in Welford, and walked with me to look for the cottage where Nelly may have stayed.

In Copenhagen and at the Suhr Archive at Bonderup we were greatly helped by Professor Charles Lock of the University of Copenhagen and particularly by our enthusiastic and cheerful translator and research assistant Peter Semstad Baerenholdt. Thanks also to Bo Jung, Land Agent for The Suhr Foundation, for his hospitality and assistance.

Victoria Roddam of Cornerstones Literary Consultancy gave me some much-needed advice and support on improving this manuscript. Nikki Coffey did a fantastic job of turning it into a beautiful book.

Finally, I would like to thank The Friends of the Wilson in Cheltenham for encouraging me to give a lecture on Nelly's life and works. I really hope that this is not the only time that people ask to hear and see more of this talented and sadly overlooked artist.

List of Illustrations and Credits:

All extracts from letters written by Janet Ross and Lina Waterfield are taken from the Waterfield Collection, Archives and Special Collections of the British Institute of Florence

Extracts from letters written by Nelly Erichsen to Macmillan & Co courtesy of University of Reading, Special Collections

Extract from the manuscript of Mrs Louis Dyer and portrait of Joseph Lucas by kind permission of Mrs Janet Stevens

Extracts from the Lindsay Papers courtesy of the Special Collections and Archives, Keele University Library

Permission has been granted by the Louis Round Wilson Special Collections Library to quote extracts from the archives of JM Dent and Sons held in the Rare Book Literary and Historical Papers, Wilson Library, The University of North Carolina at Chapel Hill